second edition

Dyslexia

Margaret J. Snowling

This book is dedicated to my parents, Jean and Walter, who taught me much about dyslexia.

second edition

Dyslexia

Margaret J. Snowling

First published 2000

2 4 6 8 10 9 7 5 3 1

Blackwell Publishers Ltd
108 Cowley Road
Oxford OX4 1JF
UK

Blackwell Publishers Inc.
350 Main Street
Malden, Massachusetts 02148
USA

British Library Cataloguing in Publication Data

A CIP catalogue record for this book is available from the British Library.

Library of Congress Cataloging-in-Publication Data

Snowling, Margaret J.
    Dyslexia / Margaret J. Snowling. – 2nd ed.
        p.   cm.
    Includes bibliographical references and index.
    ISBN 0-631-22144-1 (alk. paper) – ISBN 0-631-20574-8 (alk. paper)
    1. Dyslexia.   2. Cognition disorders in children.
RJ496.A5 S65   2000
618.92′8553 – dc21

00-029241

Typeset in 10½ on 13 pt Galliard
by Best-set Typesetter Ltd., Hong Kong
Printed in Great Britain by TJ International Ltd, Padstow, Cornwall

This book is printed on acid-free paper

Contents

List of Figures   vi

List of Tables   ix

Acknowledgements   x

Preface to the Second Edition   xiii

Chapter 1   What is Dyslexia?   1

Chapter 2   The Definition of Dyslexia   14

Chapter 3   The Phonological Representations
             Hypothesis   29

Chapter 4   Learning to Read And to Spell   62

Chapter 5   Dyslexia: A Written Language Disorder   87

Chapter 6   Individual Differences in Dyslexia   105

Chapter 7   The Severity Hypothesis   124

Chapter 8   Biological Bases of Dyslexia   138

Chapter 9   Dyslexia: A Sensory Impairment?   158

Chapter 10   Helping to Overcome Dyslexia   177

Chapter 11   Proficiency and Deficiency: The Role of
             Compensation   198

Chapter 12   Conclusions and Future Prospects   215

References   217

Index   249

List of Figures

Figure 1.1 Graph showing JM's performance across the
sub-tests of the WISC-R in scaled scores   3

Figure 1.2 Samples of JM's free writing at 8 and 12 years   5

Figure 1.3 Rey Osterreith Figure   6

Figure 1.4 Performance of JM when reading regular
and irregular words of high and low
frequency, at two points in time, compared
with RA-controls   10

Figure 1.5 Reaction time distribution for JM's reading
of high-frequency words, showing automaticity
when compared with controls   12

Figure 2.1 Graph showing the relationship between
IQ and reading skill in a sample of
6-year-old children   17

Figure 2.2 The progress over time of poor readers
who showed a very good response to tutoring,
a good response, limited response and very
limited response, compared with that of
normal readers of average and above average
ability   20

Figure 2.3 A causal modelling diagram applied to
dyslexia   27

Figure 3.1 Improvement in nonword reading over two
years by dyslexic and normal readers   33

Figure 3.2 The relationship between memory span
and speech rate for words and nonwords   38

Figure 3.3 Stimuli for (a) naming and (b) vocabulary
recognition for the item *microscope*   41

List of Figures

Figure 3.4   Numbers of errors made by dyslexic and
               normal readers when repeating high-frequency
               words, low-frequency words and nonwords   47

Figure 3.5   Typical speech identification function showing
               the classification of stimuli varying along the
               voice onset time (VOT) continuum   49

Figure 3.6   Speech identification functions for three
               dyslexic cases with low phonemic awareness,
               compared with CA- and RA-controls   51

Figure 3.7   Causal links among the different phonological
               processes and reading   59

Figure 4.1   Theories of literacy development: stages in
               the development of orthographic knowledge as
               viewed by Marsh, Friedman, Welch and Desberg
               (1980 and 1981), Frith (1985) and Ehri (1985)   64

Figure 4.2   Schematic representation of the 'dual
               foundation' model of reading development   67

Figure 4.3   Hierarchical structure of the monosyllable *trap*   70

Figure 4.4   The framework for single-word processing
               from Seidenberg and McClelland (1989)   83

Figure 5.1   Recognition of visually presented nonwords
               in the auditory modality by dyslexic and normal
               readers according to reading age   90

Figure 5.2   Spelling in free writing by three dyslexic
               children from the same family   96

Figure 5.3   Histogram showing the distribution of
               phonetically acceptable and unacceptable
               spelling errors made by dyslexic readers
               and RA-controls   98

Figure 6.1   Schematic representation of functional model
               of basic reading processes   112

Figure 6.2   Figure showing the response times of LT, a
               phonological dyslexic, and GS, a morphemic
               dyslexic, for words of high and low frequency
               and nonwords   113

Figure 6.3   Castles and Coltheart's (1993) method for
               classifying dyslexic readers   116–17

Figure 8.1   Extracts from tests of print exposure devised
               for a UK sample of 15- to 16-year-olds   143

List of Figures

Figure 8.2   (a) Figure showing the brain indicating the
              four lobes; (b) Figure showing the language
              areas of the brain and depicting the pathway
              used for reading aloud a printed word   150
Figure 8.3   Patterns of activation across the left hemisphere
              during (a) rhyme and (b) verbal short-term
              memory tasks by normal and dyslexic readers   154
Figure 9.1   Schematic diagram of the visual system
              showing some of the main neural pathways   161
Figure 9.2   Sine wave grating such as commonly used
              in vision research with spatial frequency
              channels   162
Figure 10.1   Example of a phonological training activity   188
Figure 11.1   Schematic representation of Plaut, McClelland,
              Seidenberg and Patterson's (1996) semantic
              and phonological pathways   204

List of Tables

Table 1.1 JM's spellings of a set of three-syllable words
at ages 8, 10 and 12 years   7

Table 5.1 High-frequency words varying in syllable length
with stress on either the first (Stress 1) or
second (Stress 2) syllable   99

Table 6.1 Examples of the spelling errors made by
dysphonetic dyslexics for words which they
can and cannot read   107

Table 6.2 Examples of the spelling errors made by
dyseidetic dyslexics for words which they
can and cannot read   108

Table 6.3 Performance of NW and CHD on cognitive
processing tasks   121

Table 7.1 Examples of the reading errors made by
dyslexic children of reading ages 6 and 7 years   125

Table 7.2 Examples of the spelling errors made by dyslexic
children of reading ages 6 and 7 years   126

Table 7.3 Examples of spelling errors made by three
children with developmental dyslexia   127

Table 7.4 Spellings of three-syllable words by MC, a
child with a phonological disorder   134

Table 8.1 Mean performance on literacy tests for identical
(MZ) and same-sex fraternal (DZ) twins in
which at least one twin is dyslexic   140

Table 8.2 The planum temporale in reading disorders   152

Table 9.1 Properties of the sustained and transient
visual systems   162

Acknowledgements

The author and publishers wish to thank the following for permission to reprint copyright material in this book:

Figure 2.3 is reproduced with permission, from Frith, U. 1997: Brain, mind and behaviour in dyslexia, in C. Hulme and M. J. Snowling (eds), *Dyslexia: Biology, Cognition and Intervention*, London, Whurr, p.2.

Figure 3.2 is adapted with permission, from Hulme, C., Maughan, S. and Brown, G. D. A. 1991: Memory for familiar and unfamiliar words: Evidence for a long-term memory contribution to short-term memory span, *Journal of Memory and Language*, 30, p. 690, figure 1.

Figure 3.4 and Tables 7.1, 7.2 and 7.3 are reproduced from Snowling, M. J., Stackhouse, J. and Rack, J. 1986: Phonological dyslexia and dysgraphia: A developmental analysis, *Cognitive Neuropsychology*, 3, 309–39, copyright 1986, reprinted by permission of Psychology Press Limited, Hove, UK.

Figure 3.6 is reproduced with permission, from Manis, F. R., McBride-Chang, C., Seidenberg, M. S., Keating, P., Doi, L. M., Munson, B. and Petersen, A. 1997: Are speech perception deficits associated with developmental dyslexia? *Journal of Experimental Child Psychology*, 66, p. 227.

Figure 4.2 is reproduced from Seymour, P. H. K. and Evans, H. M. 1994: Levels of phonological awareness and learning to read, *Reading and Writing*, 6, p. 244, figure 2, with kind permission from Kluwer Academic Publishers.

Acknowledgements

Figure 4.4 is adapted from Seidenberg, M. S. and McClelland, J. 1989: A distributed, developmental model of word recognition, *Psychological Review*, 96, p. 526, figure 1. Copyright © 1989 by the American Psychological Association. Adapted with permission.

Figure 5.3 is reproduced from Snowling, M. J. 1994: Towards a model of spelling acquisition: The development of some component skills, in G. D. A. Brown and N. C. Ellis (eds), *Handbook of Spelling: Theory, Process and Intervention*, Chichester: John Wiley & Sons, p. 123, figure 6.2. Copyright John Wiley & Sons Limited. Reproduced with permission.

Figure 6.1 is adapted with permission, from Seymour, P. H. K. 1986: *A Cognitive Analysis of Dyslexia*, London, Routledge, p. 14, figure 2.1.

Figure 6.3 is reprinted from *Cognition*, 47, Castles & Coltheart, M., Varieties of developmental dyslexia, pp. 149–180, (1993), with permission from Elsevier Science.

Figure 8.2 is reproduced from *Images of the Mind* by Posner and Raichle © 1994, 1997 by Scientific American Library. Used with permission by W. H. Freeman and Company.

Figure 8.3 is reproduced from Paulesu, E., Frith, U., Snowling, M., Gallagher, A., Morton, J., Frackowiak, F. S. J., & Frith, C. D. (1996). Is developmental dyslexia a disconnection syndrom? Evidence from PET scanning. *Brain*, 119, pp. 143–157. Reproduced by permission of Oxford University Press.

Figure 9.1 is adapted with permission, from Johnson, M. H. 1997: *Developmental Cognitive Neuroscience*, Oxford: Blackwell, p. 78, figure 3.4.

Figure 9.2 is reproduced with permission, from Goldstein, E. B. 1984: *Sensation and Perception*, 2nd edn, Belmont, CA: Wadsworth Publishing Co., p. 278, figure 10.17(b).

Figure 10.1 is reproduced with permission, from Hatcher, P. J. 1994: *Sound Linkage*, London: Whurr.

Acknowledgements

Tables 6.1 and 6.2 are drawn from Boder, E. 1973: Developmental dyslexia: A diagnostic approach based on three atypical reading-spelling patterns, *Developmental Medicine and Child Neurology*, 15, 663–87, with permission from MacKeith Press.

Table 8.2 is reproduced from Filipek, P. A. 1999: Neuroimaging in the developmental disorders: The state of the science, *Journal of Child Psychology and Psychiatry*, 40, p. 119, table 4, with permission from Cambridge University Press.

Table 9.1 is reproduced from Lovegrove, W. (1991). Spatial frequency processing in dyslexic and normal readers from *Vision and Visual Dyslexia*, Stein, J. F. (Ed.). Basingstoke: Macmillan Press Ltd. Reproduced by permission of Macmillan Press Ltd.

Every effort has been made to trace copyright holders but if any have been inadvertently overlooked the publishers will be pleased to make the necessary arrangements at the first opportunity. The publishers apologize for any errors or omissions in the above list and would be grateful to be notified of any corrections that should be incorporated in the reprint or next edition of this book.

Preface to the Second Edition

Since publication of the first edition of this book, *Dyslexia: A Cognitive Developmental Perspective*, in 1987, there has been an explosion of research on dyslexia. This burgeoning of research evidence has made it necessary to write a completely new book, rather than to update the first. The slight change in title reflects this: the review is, by necessity, much broader than that presented in the first edition, although I still draw primarily upon research stemming from the perspective of cognitive psychology.

The book begins with a case study illustrating that although the definition of dyslexia continues to be debated, it is a life-long, developmental disorder that primarily affects a person's ability to learn to read and spell. I go on to provide a synthesis of the very large body of research on the cognitive deficits of dyslexia within the framework of normal literacy development, and to argue that dyslexia is a consequence of a phonological (speech processing) deficit. In two chapters on individual differences in dyslexia, I show how phonological processing problems compromise the development of reading, and propose that variations in the pattern of reading deficit that are observed might be traced to differences in the severity of underlying phonological skills.

There are three completely new chapters in this book. The first reviews the growing body of knowledge concerning the biological bases of dyslexia, showing that it is an inherited condition associated with abnormalities of brain function, and documents exciting new findings on the precursors of dyslexia in the pre-school years from children at genetic risk of the disorder. I then proceed to discuss the intriguing speculation that sensory processing impairments are involved in the genesis of dyslexia, before going on to consider the now considerable body of research on how to help dyslexic children to overcome their problems with literacy. This book, like the first edition, closes by arguing that individual differences in dyslexia depend on the cognitive strengths that the child brings to the task of learning to read as well as the weaknesses. The behavioural outcome of dyslexia also depends upon the language in which the child is learning and the teaching they receive.

In writing this second edition, I have been very much aware of the important contribution to my thinking made possible by the many stimulating conversations that I have had with eminent researchers in the field. I note particularly amongst these: Dorothy Bishop, Brian Byrne, John Hogben, Bill Lovegrove, Ingvar Lundberg, Dick Olson, Bruce Pennington, Philip Seymour, Don Shankweiler, Keith Stanovich, Joe Torgesen and Heinz Wimmer. Closer to home, I have benefited from challenging discussions within our group in the Centre for Reading and Language at the University of York, and from my long-time collaborations with Uta Frith, Nata Goulandris and Joy Stackhouse.

I am grateful to many people who have helped me with the preparation of this book and I acknowledge the support of a Wellcome Trust grant 040195/Z/93/A. I thank Sara Bailey and Julia Carroll for the enormous amount of assistance they gave me with referencing, and Peter Hatcher and John Hogben for commenting on some of the chapters. I am particularly indebted to Kate Nation and Keith Stanovich, who read the manuscript and made insightful comments that have spurred me on at various stages. Finally, my heartfelt thanks are due to Charles Hulme, who not only supported me throughout the writing of the book, but also read many drafts and helped in the final stages of preparing the manuscript. None of this would have been possible without the insights I have gained from my clinical work with dyslexic children and their families; I thank them all, and especially JM.

Chapter 1

What is Dyslexia?

Reading is a skill that is highly valued by society and in most communities holds the key to education. In evolutionary terms, however, written language is a relatively new acquisition. Writing systems evolved as ways of representing spoken words in a more permanent form for the purposes of communication across time and place. The ways in which different writing systems do this varies. In this book, we will be solely concerned with alphabetic orthographies that represent speech in writing at the level of the single speech sound or phoneme (in fact we will focus primarily on English). Learning to read in these orthographies is a complex task requiring the translation of written symbols, or graphemes, into speech forms, or phonemes. This mapping process engages a number of different brain mechanisms that are specialized for other purposes. It is the smooth interaction of these systems that brings about fluent reading and spelling performance.

In spite of the complexities of written language, the majority of children who are given appropriate instruction learn to read with relative ease. However, a substantial minority of children have specific difficulty acquiring literacy skills, and these difficulties can be considered 'unexpected' because they occur in otherwise bright and able children who master other tasks well. These children are sometimes called dyslexic, and current estimates suggest that between 3 and 10 per cent of the population are so affected.

Terminology in the field of reading difficulties is often unclear and inconsistent. While there is no doubt that intelligent individuals with severe reading and spelling problems exist, they have been described in ways that vary widely. Terms such as reading disabled, reading impaired, reading disordered and retarded reader add confusion to what some would prefer to call plain 'poor reading'. Reading

1

disability carries the connotation of a persisting handicap, while reading impairment perhaps suggests a milder deficit. The term reading disorder implies that reading is developing not only slowly but in an atypical fashion, and retarded reader suggests the affected person is globally impaired. In fact, the plethora of terms listed here are all used loosely with little regard for the implicit meaning they carry. It is only the use of the term 'dyslexia' to describe these problems that has been controversial since its inception. The controversy centres around whether dyslexia can be differentiated from other forms of reading problem. Before discussing definitions of dyslexia, let us begin by examining the case of JM, a dyslexic child with a very clear profile of difficulties. Such children are typically of above average intelligence, with significantly delayed literacy development. In addition it is often the case that reading and spelling strategies are different from those of normally developing children. We first saw JM when he was 8 years and 5 months old (Snowling, Stackhouse and Rack, 1986) and we subsequently followed his progress into adulthood. His case provides an excellent illustration of how a specific cognitive deficit can constrain reading development and pose a life-long problem with literacy.

JM: Case History

JM's birth and early development had given no cause for concern. He was born into a supportive family in which there was a history of reading and language problems. JM was late in starting to talk and his motor milestones were also delayed. His first words appeared at around 2 years and, although he could make his wishes known, he was difficult to understand. Some of the time he used immature speech forms for his age, and at other times he used combinations of sounds that were unacceptable in English. He was referred for speech therapy at 3, when the therapist wrote that his speech (more formally, his phonological system) was characterized by 'both delay and disorder'. However, the therapist was in no doubt that his language comprehension was good and his vocabulary development was proceeding along normal lines.

JM responded well to speech therapy and was soon discharged to nine-monthly review. There were no further concerns about his

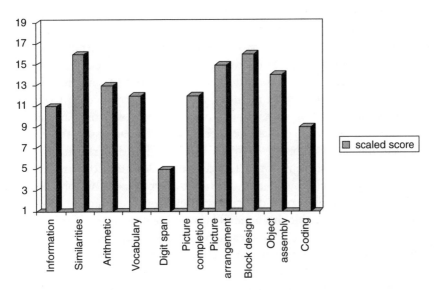

Figure 1.1 Graph showing JM's performance across the sub-tests of the WISC-R in scaled scores. In the normal population, sub-test scores have a mean of 10 ($SD = 3$)

development until, towards the end of infant school, it became apparent that he was not learning to read at the rate to be expected given his seeming intelligence. When he was 7 years old, he was seen by an educational psychologist, who found him to be of high IQ; but it was some time before his problems were properly acknowledged. His parents' concerns led them to seek a second professional opinion when he was just beginning his fourth year in school. Their worries were affirmed. He was indeed dyslexic, and he presented with a clear-cut profile of strengths and difficulties.

In order to ascertain the degree of discrepancy between JM's expected and actual reading skills, he was first administered a test of intelligence, the Wechsler Intelligence Scale for Children – Revised (Wechsler, 1974). On this test, he gained a full scale IQ of 123, placing him within the superior range of intelligence. His profile across the various sub-tests of the scale can be seen in figure 1.1. Sub-test scores can range from 1 to 19 and 10 is average; JM's performance was average or above on all but one sub-test. Indeed, he obtained superior scores on four tests; his excellent performance on Block

3

Design and Object Assembly, both constructional tasks, indicated well-developed spatial abilities. His verbal reasoning skills, as measured by his ability to sequence pictures to tell a story (Picture Arrangement), and his performance on Similarities, a test of tapping verbal concepts, were also excellent. In contrast, he showed a deficit on Digit Span, a test of verbal short-term memory, and his performance on Coding, a timed task involving copying, was poor relative to his own average.

Although JM displayed some specific verbal weaknesses, there was no significant discrepancy between his Verbal and Performance IQ (the Digit Span score is not included in the calculation of Verbal IQ). Vocabulary development and arithmetic were comfortably above average and, despite some difficulty retrieving names, such as those of cities or famous people, his general knowledge was average for his age. More of a problem had been learning common sequences such as the days of the week, months of the year and the alphabet sequence, none of which JM could yet recite.

JM's expected reading level for an 8-year-old with his IQ was around the 9-year level, and his expected spelling level was at least age appropriate. However, he only achieved a reading age of 7 years 5 months for single word reading, and of 7 years for reading accuracy when required to read text aloud. His spelling skills were even further behind at the 6½-year level.

The Development of Reading, Spelling and Phonological Skills

A more significant indication of JM's difficulties came from the strategies that he was using to read and spell. In reading, he relied exclusively upon a small sight vocabulary, and he made many visual errors, such as reading *saucer* as 'supper' and *thirsty* as 'twenty'. When he could not recognize a word he tried to sound it out, but without success. Indeed, he was unable to pronounce letter strings presented as 'nonwords' and even his knowledge of single letter-sounds was insecure. Some of his many confusions included thinking that *q* was [u], *d* was [t] and *b* was [p].

JM's prose reading strategy was ingenious. He relied heavily upon context, often substituting semantically acceptable words, for example, he read the word *Saturday* as 'Sunday' and the phrase *they shouted*

4

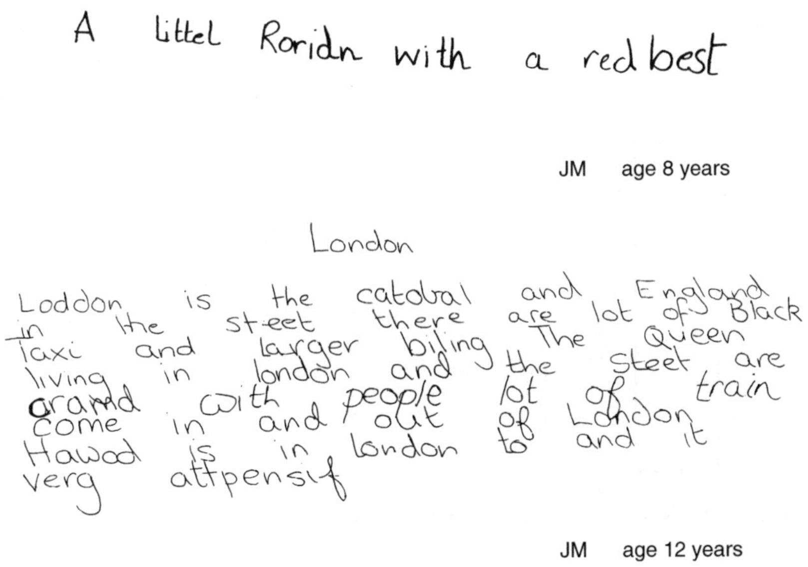

A littel Roridn with a red best

JM   age 8 years

London

Loddon is the catobal and lot Engloynd Black
in the street there are of the Queen
Taxi and larger bijing The steet are
living in londýn and the of train
aramd with people lot London
come in and out of and it
Hawod is in london to
verg attpensif

JM   age 12 years

Figure 1.2   Samples of JM's free writing at 8 and 12 years

with delight as 'there were shouts and screams.' Spelling was by far his weakest area. His spelling attempts seldom portrayed the sound sequence of the word correctly and therefore the majority of his attempts were difficult to decipher. He had considerable difficulty in segmenting the speech sounds of words he was asked to spell, and often assigned the letter of a phonetically similar segment: for example, he spelt *cut* as 'khad'; *dot* as 'tond'; *peg* as 'beg'. When asked to write a short story he produced a single sentence and said it was: *I saw a little robin with a red breast.* His sentence is reproduced in figure 1.2 together with some free writing he produced four years later at the age of 12 years.

What was the cause of JM's problems with literacy? Could it be that he had difficulty in retaining the visual images of words in memory so that each must be read anew and effortfully? This did not seem a likely explanation. For one thing it did not explain JM's small but effective sight-vocabulary or the striking dissociation he showed between his ability to read familiar words and his more or less complete inability to read nonwords. Furthermore, JM had excellent

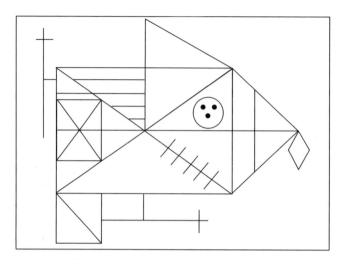

Figure 1.3 Rey Osterrieth Figure. JM could copy this from memory without difficulty

visual memory, as demonstrated by his ability to reproduce almost per-fectly the complex Rey Osterrieth Figure after a delay of 30 minutes (figure 1.3).

In contrast, JM had poor auditory skills. He performed below age norms when required to discriminate between pairs of phoneti-cally confusable words presented auditorily (for example *pin – bin*), and he also had difficulty with phonological tasks that required him to reflect on the sound sequence of words. Although he could segment words by syllable, he could not analyse them at the level of single speech sounds or phonemes, and he performed at chance level on a rime oddity task in which he had to decide which of four words sounded the odd one out, for example, *sun, bun, tin, run*. In addi-tion, subtle speech problems marred his performance on a test of sound blending where he synthesized *p-o-g* to make 'bog' and *g-l-e-b* to make 'cleb'.

Taken together, these phonological processing problems seemed a likely cause of JM's slow literacy development. Since learning to read in English requires children to associate the letters of printed words with the speech sounds of spoken words, a child like JM with a

Table 1.1 JM's spellings of a set of three-syllable words at ages 8, 10 and 12 years

Target	Age 8	Age 10	Age 12
umbrella	unenprl	unbrl	unberller
adventure	afveorl	addfch	venter
cigarette	sikeoleg	cigeragg	citterlit
membership	meaofe	membship	menbership
understand	unenstand	understant	unstand
instructed	inthder	intrmu	interdie
refreshment	refent	reafrestmint	refeashment

significant degree of difficulty with the analysis and organization of speech sounds was likely to have problems. In the face of these difficulties JM had tried to learn to read by different means, memorizing the pronunciations of sight words without an appreciation of the links between their sound segments and the spelling patterns they contained.

Soon after this assessment, JM transferred to a special school for dyslexic children. Here he was offered specialist teaching on an intensive basis in a small class. The teaching he received involved highly structured reading activities coupled with a multisensory approach to the development of spelling (looking, saying and writing words that are being taught). This school placement made a great difference to JM's morale and self-esteem, but even with the extra support his reading development was slow. When seen four years after his initial assessment, JM had progressed by roughly half the average rate in reading and somewhat less in spelling development (Snowling and Hulme, 1989). Moreover, the pattern of his reading and spelling impairment had changed little. At 8 years, JM had been unable to read aloud nonwords that he was shown. His ability to decode such novel words had improved by the time he was 12 years old, but only to the level expected of a 7-year-old. His spelling errors remained difficult to decipher, being primarily 'dysphonetic'. In particular, his spellings of multisyllabic words were often a long way from the sound structure of the target word (see table 1.1), and it was not uncommon for the phonological 'skeleton' of the word to be distorted by reducing a consonant cluster or dropping an entire syllable.

In addition to the problems that JM had on auditory and phonological tasks, he also had some subtle yet persisting speech difficulties. In particular, he had significant difficulty repeating multisyllabic words and nonwords. These repetition problems led us to believe that JM had a severe deficit in the way speech sounds and sequences were represented in his mind. Another way of stating this is that he had a problem at the level of 'phonological representation'. One consequence of this was his limited ability to store verbal information in short-term memory. Another was his failure to set up mappings between phonemes and letter sequences in words. JM also had word finding difficulties and it was not unusual for him to have difficulty recalling the names of words he used often. Among JM's naming errors on a picture naming task were 'terescope' for *microscope*, 'harmonicum' for *accordion* and multiple attempts for *aquarium*: 'fish tank, ack aren, fisharian, ackareen'.

The Development of Compensatory Strategies

One of the important questions that JM's case raises is how, in the face of poor phonological skills, dyslexic children learn to read. As will be argued later, there are likely to be different ways in which dyslexic children meet this challenge. Their strategies are likely to be related to the severity of their phonological deficit and their proficiency in other areas. JM had very severe phonological difficulties. In contrast, his memory for visual information was excellent and his good vocabulary indicated that his semantic skills were good. Could it be that he had learned to read by relying on a visual approach, making use of semantic skills to 'bootstrap' the process? JM's reading comprehension had always been better than his decoding skills suggested, so this was at least a plausible idea.

To investigate the reading strategies that JM had at his disposal, we asked him to decode sets of nonwords that we knew he would find difficult. We began by assessing his performance on nonwords that sounded like words, such as *breth, munth, burds* (so called pseudohomophones). Half of these nonwords were constructed to be visually similar to words by changing a single grapheme (*cake* → *caik*;

clown → *klown*); half were visually dissimilar to words in that they differed by two graphemes (*kaik*; *kloun*). This manipulation of visual similarity made little difference to the performance of a group of normally developing readers, who read similar numbers of visually similar and dissimilar nonwords correctly. In contrast, JM read more of the nonwords that were visually similar to words than those that were dissimilar. This finding suggested he was using a visual approach to reading (Hulme and Snowling, 1992).

We next provided a context in which to read these nonwords by presenting them after a semantic clue word or 'prime'. For example, the nonword *sawce* was presented after *tomato* and *snease* after the prime *cough*. JM's performance improved significantly when he was provided with a semantic prime. However, this manipulation had a much smaller effect on the reading of the younger controls. Indeed, placing the nonword in context brought JM's performance close to the ceiling of the test – he could have done no better. Thus, our hypothesis that JM had learned to read by building up a visual memory store of words, bootstrapped by semantic context, received some support from this demonstration. This idea is consistent with the view that learning to read is a highly interactive process to which a child will bring all of their spoken language skills, most particularly their phonological and semantic abilities.

Orthographic Development in Dyslexia

Another question that might reasonably be asked was what was the longer-term outcome of JM's dyslexia? To answer this question, we carried out a further assessment of his literacy skills when he was 15 years of age (Snowling, Hulme and Goulandris, 1994). We were interested in the nature of JM's reading system now that he was coming to the end of his specialist educational placement. In particular, we wished to assess the accuracy, consistency and speed of his word reading, and his ability to decode novel words.

We asked JM to read 112 words varying in frequency and spelling–sound regularity, each presented on a computer screen so that we could time his responses. He did this twice on two occasions, separated by a period of 12 months. We also asked him to read 25 computer-presented nonwords of one and two syllables (for example,

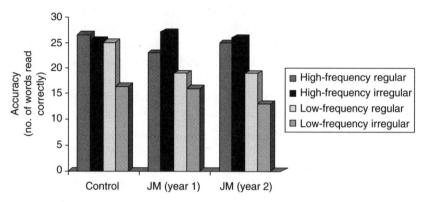

Figure 1.4 Performance of JM when reading regular and irregular words of high and low frequency, at two points in time, compared with RA-controls

ner, *resords*) and 12 more complex nonwords (for example, *balrid*, *etmung*). On all occasions, his performance was compared with that of normal readers who, like JM, were reading at the 10-year level.

JM's ability to read words was similar to that of younger children of similar reading age (RA-controls). In contrast, his ability to read nonwords was severely impaired on both occasions. He was able to read only nine of those he was shown and it took him between 4 and 14 seconds to decode each one. In contrast, all but one of the control children were at ceiling on this test and their response times were generally under 1 second.

Figure 1.4 shows his performance when asked to read high- and low-frequency words. For simplicity, we will focus here on the data from year 1. JM's ability to read familiar words (high frequency in their occurrence in English) did not differ from that of controls, confirming he was well matched to the control group. On low-frequency words, normal readers showed a regularity effect, reading regular words containing consistent sound–spelling correspondences (for example, *gap*, *mar*) more easily than irregular items (for example, *chasm*). Unlike them, JM did not show this advantage. He read both types of word equally well (or badly).

What does this absence of a regularity effect suggest? As will become clear later, it is unusual for a child not to find it easier to read regular than irregular words, even if they are dyslexic. The fact that JM could read regular words only as well as irregular words indicates that his reading was not sensitive to the consistencies of spelling–sound correspondences. It also lent credence to the idea that he had been learning to read by building up a vocabulary of word-specific associations between printed words and their pronunciations.

What about the consistency of his reading from one occasion to the next? We reasoned that if JM had been learning words on a word-by-word basis, then it was likely that his memory for these words would be more global than if they had been learned following the application of phonologically based decoding strategies. To our surprise, this was not the case. JM was just as consistent in his responding as were younger controls. It seemed that his memory for the visual forms of words he knew (orthographic representations) was sufficiently well specified to support the word recognition process.

Another way of testing the integrity of JM's orthographic skills was by assessing the speed and automaticity of his reading responses. It has sometimes been argued that dyslexic children fail to automate the reading skills they possess (Nicolson and Fawcett, 1990; Yap and van der Leij, 1994). Again we did not find this to be the case for JM, whose reading of high-frequency words was just as fast as that of controls. The distribution of his reaction times to words he could read correctly is shown in figure 1.5, where it can be seen that the majority of his responses were made within 1 second of the presentation of the word.

Our findings on both the consistency and the automaticity of JM's reading of familiar words forced us to conclude that, even though he had set up an orthographic system using atypical reading strategies, it was remarkably efficient in its operation and a noteworthy demonstration of the self-righting tendency of development. Even if JM had not been able to develop mappings between the phonemes of spoken words and the letter strings of printed words, it appeared that he had been able to establish connections between orthography and phonology at a somewhat coarser level, possibly involving word-specific links. Scrutiny of his reading errors provided some support for this hypothesis. Twelve of the words on the word reading test provoked a large number of errors among the normal readers. In each case, we were able to identify the most typical error response provided by the control group. For *chasm* this was [chasum]; for *bough* it was 'bow' and for *aisle* it was [ay-sl]. In marked contrast, JM's reading errors included

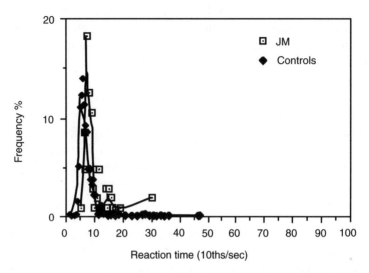

Figure 1.5 Reaction time distribution for JM's reading of high-frequency words, showing automaticity when compared with controls

chasm → 'charm', *bough* → 'brought' and *aisle* → 'alas'. Whilst his word recognition system served him well for high-frequency words and words in context, it was error prone and of course it was not conducive to spelling accuracy.

JM left school still with significant writing difficulties, and his written work in no way reflected his underlying ability. At least in part his persisting difficulties reflected the fact that it is harder to draw upon compensatory strategies for spelling than for reading. The only such tactic that we could discern in JM was a tendency to use syllabic segments as a way of analysing the spoken forms of words. For example, at 13 years, he spelled *uniform* → 'youofrom', *tomato* → 'tomanto' and *wilderness* → 'wilonest'.

It is fortunate, and a testament to JM's own efforts, that his literacy skills were sufficient to allow him to go on to higher education. At university he studied Psychology. This was no mean feat; in spite of his superior intelligence, he struggled with the demands of his degree course. JM graduated successfully three years later, and since then he has turned his attention to a vocation working with young people. By his own admission, he does not enjoy reading, he has problems with spelling and the pronunciations of certain words still trip him up. When we last saw him he was 24 years old and he had compensated for his reading problem; his reading was at the average level for the population (a standard score of 93). However, he remained unable to decode nonwords (he read only two out of 15 correctly on a graded test) and he had persisting difficulties with phonological awareness tasks. Like most adult dyslexics, his spelling was poor and although his mistakes were now more phonetic in their form, he still committed some that were difficult to decipher, for example, he spelled *biscuit* → 'bistic', *puncture* → 'pinshire' and *inspect* → 'insipate'. It is to his credit that none of these problems had prevented him from successfully negotiating the world of work.

In summary, JM has been presented here as a classic case of developmental dyslexia. He is a bright young man who has always understood spoken language well and is an excellent communicator who expresses his ideas clearly in oral language. However, he has experienced severe and persisting phonological processing deficits. These are seen as the cause of his problems in learning to read and spell. The reading and spelling skills he has developed seem to reflect an excessive reliance on memorizing words as wholes and using meaning and context whenever possible to compensate for his inability to decode. He could never (and still cannot) read nonwords and, even as an adult, the phonetic structure of his spellings is often inaccurate. With his case as backdrop to our discussion, we now turn to consider formal definitions of dyslexia.

Chapter 2

The Definition of Dyslexia

According to Tønnesen (1995), the definition of dyslexia should be a hypothesis that is clearly falsifiable and can be judged by objective criteria. The case of JM, discussed in the previous chapter, provides clear illustration that dyslexia is a developmental disorder extending across the life-span. It also shows that the cardinal symptoms of dyslexia, reading and spelling problems, plausibly stem from oral language difficulties. But how widespread are the difficulties experienced by JM among dyslexic people, and where should the line between dyslexia and other reading difficulties be drawn? We explore here the strengths and limitations of a number of different definitions of dyslexia before going on to propose a cognitive description of the disorder.

The Medical Model of Dyslexia

Developmental dyslexia was first described just over 100 years ago in the *British Medical Journal* (Pringle-Morgan, 1896). That case report described a 14-year-old boy named Percy who, in spite of being of normal intelligence, had been unable to learn to read. Pringle-Morgan, a general practitioner, and Hinshelwood, an ophthalmologist also writing at the turn of the century (Hinshelwood, 1917), speculated that such difficulties with reading and writing were most likely due to a form of 'congenital word-blindness'.

Following these early clinical reports, dyslexia remained the preserve of medical specialists until the 1960s, when research turned towards identifying systematic differences between 'dyslexic' and normal readers. It was clearly important at this stage to clarify the definition of dyslexia if further advances were to be made, both at a theoretical level and in terms of educational practice.

Thus, in 1968, a meeting of the World Federation of Neurology came to the following consensus (Critchley, 1970):

> [Dyslexia is] a disorder manifested by difficulty in learning to read despite conventional instruction, adequate intelligence and socio-cultural opportunity. It is dependent upon fundamental cognitive disabilities which are frequently of constitutional origin.

There are several problems with this definition. First, it contains a number of terms which are ill-defined. What for example is conventional instruction? How much intelligence is sufficient for learning to read? What is meant by socio-cultural opportunity? Perhaps a more serious weakness is that it is a *definition by exclusion*. The definition only states what a person with dyslexia should *not* be and does not include criteria for its positive diagnosis other than to state that it is a reading difficulty dependent on fundamental cognitive disabilities.

The World Federation of Neurology's definition carried with it the proposal of a set of diagnostic symptoms. These included associated speech and language difficulties, visual perceptual deficits and a host of common features of dyslexic reading and spelling, such as rotations and reversals of letters, bizarre inconsistent spelling errors and untidiness of penmanship (Critchley and Critchley, 1978; Miles, 1983). However, clinicians were hard-pressed in the absence of objective criteria to decide whether or not to 'diagnose' a person as dyslexic. The World Federation of Neurology's definition has fallen out of use.

Specific Reading Difficulties

Educationalists have never rested easy with the medical model of dyslexia. At the very least, the body of knowledge derived from studies of highly selected or referred samples of children is open to question. More specifically, many so-called 'dyslexic' signs, such as reversing *b* and *d*, are a normal feature of reading development. To get around the problem of sampling bias, it has been common to turn to the findings of studies of large representative samples of children, referred to as epidemiological studies. These studies are important because they are free of the biases inherent in studies of clinical groups.

Perhaps the most influential population study with regard to children's reading problems was the landmark Isle of Wight study (Rutter and Yule, 1975), which introduced the distinction between children who have specific reading difficulties (specific reading retardation) and children who have reading difficulties in the context of more general learning problems (reading backwardness). It is the former group, those with specific reading difficulties like JM, to whom the term 'dyslexia' is usually applied.

The classification of poor readers into those with specific and those with more general reading difficulties takes as its starting point the relationship between reading skill and intelligence in the normal population. For the most part, brighter children learn to read more easily than slower children, and this is reflected in the correlation between IQ and reading attainment. By taking account of this relationship in a particular age-group of children, it is possible to use a statistical approach, known as regression, to predict for any child in that population their expected reading age given their age and IQ. The next step involves a comparison of expected reading age with actual reading age. A child is deemed to have a specific problem with reading if their reading attainment is significantly below that predicted from their general cognitive ability, in other words, if they show a *discrepancy* between expected and actual attainment. By contrast, children whose reading age is significantly below their age-level but not out of line with expectation because their IQ is also relatively low, are classified as generally backward readers within this approach (these children are sometimes referred to as garden-variety poor readers, particularly in the US research literature).

The use of the regression approach can be illustrated with reference to figure 2.1, a graph that shows the relationship between reading attainment and cognitive ability. The substantial correlation between IQ and reading can be seen in that most cases cluster around the central diagonal (the regression line). The two outer diagonal lines show the area within which it can be stated with reasonable confidence that a child's reading is within normal limits. Children with specific reading difficulties have reading skills that fall below the lower diagonal. For comparison, the horizontal line shows the cut-off for poor

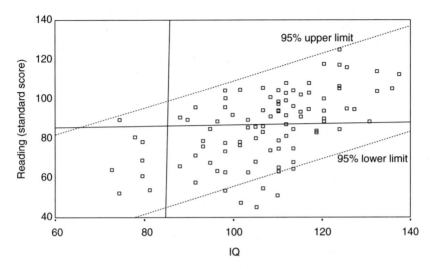

Figure 2.1 Graph showing the relationship between IQ and reading skill in a sample of 6-year-old children. The two diagonals show the 95 per cent confidence limits for the prediction of reading from IQ. Cases that fall below the lower diagonal have specific reading difficulties. Cases in the lower left quadrant have general reading difficulties

reading when this is defined as having a score that falls one standard deviation below the mean for the population, regardless of IQ. Cases that fall below this line and also to the left of the vertical line are children who have poor reading skills in line with low IQ – the so-called generally backward readers.

The prevalence of specific reading difficulties (dyslexia) in a given population depends critically upon the cut-off point taken as indicative of reading disability. This cut-off point is always to an extent arbitrary. Assuming a normal distribution of discrepancy scores which describe the difference between expected and actual levels of attainment, 2.28 per cent of children should score more than two standard errors of measurement below their expected attainment score. Using this cut-off, Yule, Rutter, Berger and Thompson (1974) reported a prevalence of specific reading retardation ranging from 3.1 per cent among 10-year-olds in the Isle of Wight to 6.3 per cent in London, based on the discrepancy between IQ and reading accuracy. When reading comprehension rather than reading accuracy was used to define expected and actual levels of attainment, the comparable figures were 3.6 per cent and 9.3 per cent. These figures illustrate clearly that the prevalence of specific reading retardation depends upon environmental factors; it was higher in an inner-city population. Prevalence figures also depend on the tests use to assess reading skill. A national survey in Britain using a reading test with better psychometric properties than that used by Rutter and Yule reported a lower prevalence of 2.29 per cent (Rodgers, 1983) and a similar study in New Zealand found only 1.2 per cent of 9-year-olds to have specific reading retardation (Silva, McGee and Williams, 1985).

The most recent epidemiological data, from a longitudinal study of 414 Connecticut children, used a less stringent cut-off of 1.5 standard errors of measurement below expectation, and reported prevalence rates of 5.6 per cent in first grade, 7 per cent in third grade and 5.4 per cent in fifth grade (Shaywitz, Escobar, Shaywitz, Fletcher and Makugh, 1992). These figures show that the diagnosis of dyslexia is not a stable entity, even when it is defined by the seemingly rigorous regression approach. Rather, there was year-to-year variability; only 7 out of 25 children (28 per cent) defined as dyslexic at the end of first grade were given the same diagnosis by third grade, and only 47 per cent of these fulfilled the criteria for specific reading retardation in fifth grade (cf. McGee, Williams, Share, Anderson and Silva, 1986). These figures alone should make us cautious about accepting an operational definition of dyslexia that focuses on the discrepancy between expected and actual attainment. Furthermore, the discrepancy definition may be over-inclusive. To take an absurd example, a child who does no reading is unlikely to have literacy levels in line with expectation, but the reason for the discrepancy should not be assumed to be dyslexia.

Vellutino et al. (1996) carried out an important study that highlights the issue of 'false diagnosis'. The study began with a cohort of 1,407 children enrolled in 17 schools in the Albany area of New York State. The children were first tested on a battery of pre-reading tests in kindergarten, and then in the middle of first grade the teachers of these children rated their reading skills. Those who were deemed to be poor readers were matched with a classmate who was a normal reader and each child was then given an extensive battery of tests. Altogether, 118 poor readers were identified as fulfilling the criteria for specific reading difficulty, some 9 per cent of the population. These children's reading skills fell below the 15th centile in word identification or word attack, and their IQ was at least 90. The poor readers defined in this way were assigned at random into tutored or non-tutored groups. The tutored children received 30 minutes of individualized help daily, according to their needs. The untutored children acted as controls and received school-based remediation of a variety of kinds.

After only half a school year of remediation, a large proportion of the poor readers had reading scores within the normal range. In round terms, this applied to 67 per cent of the tutored children and slightly fewer of the children given small group instruction in school. Thus, with a relatively small amount of early intervention for children who are failing to learn to read, there can be a substantial reduction in the prevalence of specific reading difficulties. In fact, only 1.5 per cent of the cohort now fell below the 15th centile in their reading skills, compared with the original figure of 9 per cent identified by the exclusionary criteria.

One might ask whether the children who had not responded, the 1.5 per cent, were the true dyslexics, and, if so, how did they differ from the children who were readily remediated? The first step in addressing this question was to band children into groups according to their rate of progress. For tutored children, this led to the differentiation of four groups: very good growth (VGG), good growth (GG), limited growth (LG) and very limited growth (VLG). The progress over time of the children in these groups compared with that of normal readers of average and above average ability is shown in figure 2.2. It is clear from this graph that the children in the VGG group showed a steep increase in reading skill as a response to remediation, which soon brought their performance into line with that of normal readers. In contrast, children in the limited and very limited growth groups continued to have difficulties over time. A further point of note is that the groups maintained their status over time, suggesting that initial response to intervention is a good indicator of prognosis.

Is it possible to tell from this study what differentiates the symptoms of dyslexia (VLG) from the skills of poor readers who are readily remediated (VGG)? In kindergarten, the children in these groups did not differ in IQ. However, there were differences in letter knowledge, sight word learning and number skills, all abilities that draw upon a

19

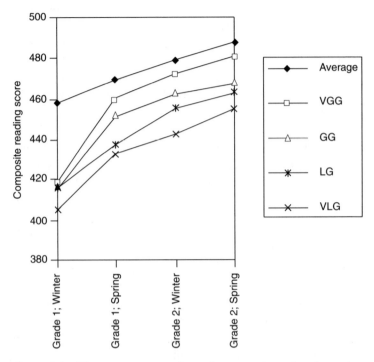

Figure 2.2 The progress over time of poor readers who showed a very good response to tutoring (VGG), a good response (GG), limited response (LG) and very limited response (VLG), compared with that of normal readers of average and above average ability

Source: adapted from Vellutino et al., 1996

facility to learn 'names'. In first grade, the 'dyslexic' children performed worse on tasks that tapped phonological skills. Difficulties encompassed poor verbal short-term memory, poor phonological awareness and rapid naming deficits. However, their performance was similar to that of the VGG group on tests of semantic processing, visual skills, attention and planning.

Putting these findings together with what we saw in the case of JM, there seem to be good grounds for supposing that dyslexia is characterized by a particular cognitive profile that places the child at risk of reading failure. Moreover, these sorts of finding highlight that it is not correct to assume that literacy problems are the only symptoms of dyslexia (Morton and Frith, 1995). Indeed, whether or not a child has a specific *reading* difficulty at a particular point in time depends upon several factors in addition to their cognitive disposition. The demands of reading in that phase of development are also critical, as are the teaching the child has received and the extent to which they have been able to compensate.

Differences between Generally Backward and Specifically Retarded Readers

We have seen that there is some evidence of cognitive differences between children with dyslexic difficulties and both normal readers and children who have a good response to intervention. One of the main objectives of epidemiological studies of reading has been to answer a slightly different question, namely, what characteristics outside of the literacy domain set apart children with specific reading difficulties from generally poor readers? Findings from a comparison of 86 children with specific reading retardation and 79 generally backward readers reported by Rutter and Yule (1975) revealed surprisingly few differences. However, the groups did differ in sex ratio; there were 3.3 males to every female with specific reading retardation, whereas equal numbers of boys and girls were classified as generally backward. Among generally poor readers there was also a higher incidence of neurological impairments (for example epilepsy) and more widespread neurological 'soft' signs, including movement disorders such as clumsiness. Finally, the two groups differed in prognosis; despite an IQ advantage, children with specific reading difficulties made less progress in reading and spelling during a 4–5 year period than generally backward readers. In contrast, they showed better progress in mathematics (Yule, 1973).

Regarding possible causes of reading problems, as opposed to differences in IQ, it is interesting to note that both groups showed a raised incidence of speech and language problems. Speech delay was three times more common among poor readers than it was in the general population, and a family history of difficulties with speech and reading was reported three times more frequently. In fact, the only language measure on which the specifically retarded and generally poor reader-groups differed was one of complexity of language usage; here the children with specific reading retardation were superior, consistent with their higher IQ.

An epidemiological study carried out in New Zealand by Share, McGee, McKenzie, Williams and Silva (1987) failed to confirm the poorer prognosis of the group with specific reading difficulties compared with those with more general reading problems. Furthermore, while the study confirmed the excess of boys among children with specific reading retardation, Share et al. argued that this was simply a consequence of the fact that, overall, reading scores were lower in boys than girls. This point is worth bearing in mind; reading tests tend to be standardized on whole-school samples in which males and females are not differentiated. It follows that, when an arbitrary cut-off point is used to define reading disability, it will always reveal more male than female poor readers (van der Wissel, 1981). In contrast, family studies that examine the number of relatives of a reading-disabled child (proband) who are themselves reading-disabled suggest a more even distribution of affected individuals between the sexes.

More recently, Shaywitz, Fletcher, Holahan and Shaywitz (1992) assessed the differences between children with specific and general reading difficulties in their Connecticut sample. Thirty-two children identified as having specific reading difficulties in second grade (at the age of 7 years) were compared with 38 generally poor readers and a control group of normal readers, both retrospectively in kindergarten and prospectively in fifth grade. In kindergarten, when the children were around 5½ years, there were no overall group differences either in motor development or dexterity, language skills, or visual perception. Groups were also similar on indices of neurological function. However, children with specific reading difficulties did better than generally low-achievers on three individual tests, namely finger agnosia (identifying which finger had been touched with the eyes closed), sentence memory and object naming, and they were poorer than normal readers on the latter two tests. The study also failed to find group differences in parental reports of health problems, pre- and peri-natal difficulties or speech and language problems, but generally poor readers were perceived as having more behaviour problems. In fifth grade, teachers' ratings of the academic work of specifically retarded and generally backward readers were similar, but those with specific difficulties were considered to have fewer maths problems.

Like Share et al. (1987), Shaywitz et al. (1992) did not find that children with discrepancy-defined reading difficulties had an especially poor prognosis. Rather, there was some evidence that children with specific reading difficulties progressed better in their reading between second and fifth grade than generally poor readers. However, this finding must be tempered by the fact that the children in the Connecticut study were younger than those followed by Rutter and Yule. Furthermore, group differences might reflect a statistical artefact, namely *regression to the mean*. Regression to the mean refers to the fact that, when groups are selected from the extremes of the population, there is a considerable likelihood that, on subsequent testing, their scores will be found to be closer to the average for the population. In this study, the specifically retarded readers, who were more extreme in terms of correlated IQ and reading scores, were more likely to show this pattern than the generally backward readers.

Finally, the Connecticut Longitudinal Study also addressed the critical issue of predictors of reading-group membership. Put simply, what is it that leads a child to be classified as having specific reading retardation as opposed to general reading backwardness? The only significant predictor was IQ, and this accounted for nearly all of the power to discriminate between the groups.

So where do these findings lead? If the only substantial difference between 'dyslexic' or specifically retarded readers and generally backward readers is in IQ (the very characteristic that defines the groups), and there is an imperfect correlation between IQ and reading skill in the normal population (Stanovich, 1986, reported that on average this was only 0.31), these findings call into question the usefulness of the distinction. The findings speak neither to the causes of reading difficulties nor to whether poor readers of different IQ require different forms of remediation. Thus, there are distinct limitations inherent in the approach that seeks to define dyslexia as a discrepancy between a child's reading attainment and that predicted from their IQ. Like the World Federation of Neurology's definition discussed earlier, the discrepancy definition fails to provide positive criteria that allow children who will learn to read normally to be distinguished from those who will encounter significant reading problems.

Did Discrepancy Definitions of Dyslexia 'Lead Us Astray'?

At the same time that evidence was accumulating on the similarities between discrepancy-defined and generally poor readers, the regression approach to dyslexia was beginning to fall from favour for an entirely different reason: its reliance on the global construct of IQ (Siegel, 1988). As Stanovich (1991) noted, the use of IQ in the definition of dyslexia conceals 'illogical assumptions about the concept of potential' (p. 7). IQ is a general measure of intelligence, comprising abilities in both verbal and non-verbal domains of functioning. Verbal IQ, which is assessed by performance on tests such as vocabulary and verbal concept attainment, is more strongly correlated with reading skill in the normal population than Performance IQ, as assessed by tasks tapping visuo-spatial skills and perceptual processing. It follows that in practice, fewer children show discrepancy-defined reading problems relative to Verbal than to Performance IQ (Bishop and Butterworth, 1980).

From a slightly different standpoint, Stanovich (1986) highlighted the problems surrounding the assessment of IQ in poor readers whose verbal skills may decline as a consequence of their limited reading experience. If low verbal IQ can itself be a consequence of reading disability, it could, ironically, mask the specificity of a child's reading problem. With no diagnostic criteria to fulfil other than statistical ones, the discrepancy approach runs the risk of missing the very real reading problems of dyslexic children who have relatively poor verbal skills. On the other hand, children who do not fulfil the criteria for specific reading retardation because they have learned to read despite their problems will also be left undiagnosed unless deficient spelling or other skills are included among the diagnostic criteria.

With these issues in mind, the Orton Dyslexia Society of the USA (now called the International Dyslexia Association) offered the following definition (1994):

> Dyslexia is one of several distinct learning disabilities. It is a specific language-based disorder of constitutional origin characterised by difficulties in single word decoding, usually reflecting insufficient phonological processing abilities. These difficulties in single-word decoding are often unexpected in relation to age or other cognitive abilities; they

are not the result of generalised developmental disability or sensory impairment. Dyslexia is manifested by a variable difficulty with different forms of language, including, in addition to a problem with reading, a conspicuous problem with acquiring proficiency in writing and spelling.

This definition contains a number of important points. First, it notes that dyslexia is one kind of learning difficulty; dyslexia often co-occurs with other disorders and it is important to consider these separately for both clinical and theoretical purposes. Second, as we saw in the case of JM, it acknowledges the importance of phonological processing difficulties in the etiology of dyslexia. The definition also stresses problems with word-decoding rather than reading comprehension skills. As we shall see later, this is a critical difference between children who have specific reading difficulties and those who have more global language impairments. Finally, it makes clear that dyslexia encompasses spelling and writing problems. Notwithstanding these advantages, the definition is vague. This makes it difficult to falsify.

Ironically, therefore, a major problem with the commonly used methods for defining specific reading difficulties is that they may miss some of the children whom they aim to identify. It is also noteworthy that these methods are silent with regard to the identification of children at risk of reading failure. For clinical utility, the discrepancy approach needs to be supplemented by positive diagnostic markers that will allow practitioners to identify children who show early or residual signs of dyslexia that require intervention, and do not depend solely on the extent of the child's reading problem. To an extent, the Orton Society's (1994) definition satisfies these criteria in pointing to *insufficient phonological processing abilities*. Just such insufficiency characterized the difficult-to-remediate poor readers described by Vellutino and his colleagues (1996). Focusing on outward manifestations of dyslexia in the school-age child, Stanovich (1991) suggested that a candidate behavioural marker might be the discrepancy between listening and reading comprehension. Theoretically it is reasonable to expect a child's ability to understand what they hear to be in line with what they understand from print, provided they can read. When reading comprehension falls short of listening skill it is reasonable to hypothesize that the child has a specific reading difficulty. We now turn to consider a way of differentiating these different hypotheses about what dyslexia is.

A Developmentally Contingent Model of Dyslexia

Some of the difficulties encountered in attempts to define dyslexia arise from an apparent confusion about whether they should explain or describe a particular kind of reading problem. Advocates of the medical model of dyslexia used the term 'dyslexia' to describe a syndrome, presumed to be of neurological origin, that explained a clustering of behavioural symptoms with deficits in reading and spelling. In their view, dyslexia had a biological basis and an associated symptomatology that included but was not restricted to literacy difficulties. In contrast, the discrepancy definition of dyslexia focuses solely on reading and IQ-test performance. Within this view, dyslexia is synonymous with specific reading difficulty.

One way out of this conundrum is to consider dyslexia as a disorder that carries with it different levels of description. Being a disorder of development, dyslexia can be expected to have behavioural features that will change with maturation and in response to environmental interactions (cf. Bishop, 1997). It may therefore be unrealistic to agree upon a simple and unchanging definition of dyslexia. As Frith (1997) argued, there are causal links from brain to mind to behaviour that must be considered when attempting to understand dyslexia. It is important to seek explanations at the three different levels in this causal chain, the biological, the cognitive and the behavioural, in order to develop a comprehensive theory of why some children fail 'unexpectedly' to learn to read (Morton and Frith, 1995). Moreover, it is important to show how environmental factors influence the causal pathway (see figure 2.3).

Dyslexia, according to Frith (1997), is a cultural phenomenon that has its main effect on literacy and therefore would not be observed in non-literate cultures. The literacy difficulties central to the definition of dyslexia are seen at the behavioural level, the lowest level of the framework. It is here too that other symptoms, including perhaps poor speech development, reside, and that the putative discrepancy between listening and reading comprehension will be observed. However, it is important to bear in mind that the pattern of behavioural signs and symptoms will vary according to the age of the child, their ability, motivation and experiences and, not least, the writing system in which they are learning. A primary aim of research on dyslexia is therefore

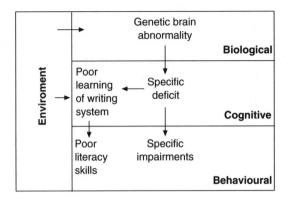

Figure 2.3 A causal modelling diagram applied to dyslexia
Source: Frith, 1997

to describe the pattern of difficulties observed in affected individuals and how these difficulties change with age.

A second aim of research on dyslexia is to understand its cognitive basis. According to Frith (1997) it is at the cognitive level (which is 'unseen') that a dysfunction can unite the varied symptoms of dyslexia and show that it is a distinct entity. In chapter 3 we will discuss the phonological deficit hypothesis of dyslexia. This is a causal hypothesis at the cognitive level of explanation. The cognitive dysfunction in dyslexia could be in a single mental component, or alternatively, it could be the outcome of developmental interactions between two or more cognitive deficits. Investigating changes in the nature of dyslexia through development is one way of assessing causal links between putative deficits in underlying cognitive mechanisms and behavioural manifestations.

The ultimate aim of a cognitive-developmental approach to dyslexia is to understand the biological basis of the disorder and how this brain-based disposition can lead to subtle impairments at the cognitive and behavioural levels. The advent of cognitive neuroscience has revolutionized the medical approach to the study of dyslexia and made it possible to study links between brain and behaviour in this specific developmental disorder.

Since the 1970s, there has been a huge increase in research on developmental dyslexia at all three levels of explanation. This book can at best cover some of this research. It begins with a review of the cognitive deficits in dyslexia and shows how these compromise the process of learning to read. We will then discuss ideas about the possible biological substrates of these deficits. Finally, we will consider how suitable teaching can help dyslexic children learn to read and to spell, and explore possible reasons for the wide variety of outcomes seen among dyslexic people.

Chapter 3

The Phonological Representations Hypothesis

The search for cognitive explanations of dyslexia was taken up by psychologists in the 1960s. This research continues today with the focus on the unfolding picture of dyslexia across the life-span and the exploration of causal links between cognitive skills and written language abilities. This chapter will be concerned with what might be described as 'the deficit approach' to dyslexia, an approach which has met with considerable success in pinpointing the cognitive difficulties that are putative causes of reading failure.

In order to investigate these issues, cognitive psychologists have remained neutral about use of the term 'dyslexia'. Most researchers have adopted an operational definition of the disorder by setting criteria for the degree of reading impairment and the level of intelligence a child must show to be regarded as having a specific reading difficulty. Although a strict regression approach has seldom been used to select children for experimental studies, some form of discrepancy definition is usually employed. Typically, dyslexic children in published studies are of at least average intelligence, the lower limit being an IQ score of 85 though more commonly children with IQs of 90 or above are included. The level of reading attainment regarded as impaired is less consistent. A reading lag of 18 months below expectation for age is usually the minimum. However, because of the psychometric properties of age-equivalent scores, the significance of the delay varies with the age of the child. Clearly it is worse for a 7-year-old to be two years behind than for a 14-year-old to show the same delay. To get around this, many studies set the criterion as scoring within the bottom 25 per cent of the population of individuals of the same age, that is, below the 25th centile on a standardized reading test.

It is perhaps worth dwelling for a moment on the rationale for this research strategy. If clear evidence for the distinction between discrepancy-defined and low-ability poor readers is lacking, why focus only on those with higher levels of intelligence? The reason is quite simple. The tasks that have been used to compare dyslexic and normal readers carry with them varying cognitive demands. Even if IQ does not account for reading failure, it could well affect levels of performance on related cognitive tasks. This would have the effect of blurring the distinction between deficits associated with reading difficulty and deficits associated with low intelligence. It follows that, a priori, it is better to compare good and poor readers who do not vary in intellectual ability. Extending this rationale, Vellutino (1979), who set the stage for the contemporary study of dyslexic deficits, considered that dyslexia was best studied in children who have 'average or above average intelligence, intact (or corrected) sensory acuity, no severe neurological damage or other debilitating physical disabilities and who have not been hampered by serious emotional or social problems, socio-economic disadvantage or opportunity for learning' (pp. 321–2). It is primarily such children who have been tested in the studies that will be reviewed. Variations in the extent and severity of the reading difficulties characterizing different samples need to be borne in mind when evaluating findings which at times might seem inconsistent.

The Issue of Comparison Groups

The study of dyslexia by experimental psychologists has involved comparing the performance of dyslexic readers with that of normally developing readers. The aim has been to uncover possible causes of reading impairment. There is no doubt that this approach has been successful and there is a large body of converging evidence regarding the deficits that characterize dyslexia. It is important to note, however, that this has only been possible because researchers have paid due attention to methodological issues and, in particular, have chosen comparison groups carefully.

Early approaches to the experimental study of dyslexia used a variant of the Mental-Age (MA) match design, borrowed from the study of developmental retardation (O'Connor and Hermelin, 1963). In the MA-match design, a control group of normally developing children is selected to be comparable (or matched) with the experimental group in terms of performance on a test of mental aptitude, such as an IQ test. This design brought with it many problems. Not least of these was matching the IQs of a control group with those of an experimental group of dyslexic readers who often varied in verbal and performance abilities. A more major problem was that MA-matching left reading skill free to vary and, in essence, these studies boiled down to comparing good and poor readers. One of the criticisms of the approach is that if a particular deficit is uncovered among dyslexic readers, it is impossible to decide whether it is a cause or a consequence of dyslexia. The problem is compounded if participants are asked to deal with printed materials.

A simple but ingenious experiment by Vellutino, Pruzek, Steger and Meshoulam (1973) highlighted the problem. In this experiment, dyslexic and normal readers aged between 10 and 13 years copied printed words of three, four or five letters from memory, following a short exposure. Not surprisingly, the dyslexics were worse on this task than their controls. It would be tempting to infer that they were subject to a visual memory deficit. However in another condition of the experiment, the children reproduced from memory words printed in Hebrew orthography, a writing system with which neither group was familiar. Dyslexics performed just as well as normal readers in this part of the experiment. So it would have been wrong to conclude that their problem was one of visual memory. Rather the difficulty the dyslexics showed here was a consequence of their difficulty either in decoding or in remembering the printed word that had been shown to them.

The Reading-age Match

An alternative research strategy which avoids some of the problems inherent in the MA-match design is one which involves groups of dyslexic and normal readers matched in terms of their level of reading skill. This approach, known as the reading-age (RA-match) or reading-level match design, is now frequently used. In matching groups for reading level, it is important to exercise care to ensure that performance on the reading test is not spurious; ideally, dyslexic and normal groups should perform at the same level in at least one other test than that used for matching purposes. The main advantage of this approach that by pre-selecting groups of good and poor readers who, at the time of testing, do not differ in reading ability, the argument cannot be levelled that a deficit in the dyslexics is a consequence of their poor reading.

The RA-match design is a highly conservative one that provides important information if group differences are found. Its disadvantage is that it will tend to yield null results, that is, a failure to find group differences. Null results are impossible to interpret. It could be that there are really no group differences on the target task or, alternatively, it could be that there might be a difference but the tests employed have not been sensitive enough to detect it (Snowling and Nation, 1997). The RA-match design is therefore not without its pitfalls (Backman, Mamen and Ferguson, 1984). The most obvious problem follows from the fact that when dyslexic and normal readers are chosen to be of the same reading level, by definition the dyslexic readers are older, often by up to four years and sometimes more.

With a developmental disorder like dyslexia, maturation itself can be one explanation for a null result. To take an example, if the cause of dyslexia is a cognitive deficit X at the age of 6 years, but X gradually improves in dyslexics to reach a normal level of function, an investigation of X which compared 10-year-old dyslexics with younger RA-controls would run the risk of missing the major effects of the deficit on learning to read. A related problem is that studies have sometimes used tasks that are relatively difficult for young normal readers but relatively easy for dyslexic children who may already have had the benefit of remedial teaching. In one of our own studies, we followed the progress of 9- to 10-year-old dyslexic children and that of younger RA-controls aged 6–7 years at the beginning of the study (Snowling, Goulandris and Defty, 1996). Since it is well established that dyslexic children have deficits in nonword reading, we were surprised to find that, at the first time of testing, the two groups performed at the same level on a test in which they had to decode novel letter strings, such as *smade, holtcom*. However, by the second time of testing, significant group differences had emerged (see figure 3.1). The

32

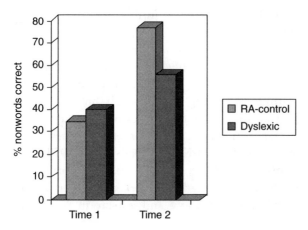

Figure 3.1 Improvement in nonword reading over two years by dyslexic and normal readers. The controls made better progress

most likely reason for the null result at Time 1 was that, at this stage in development, beginning readers were only just starting to develop decoding skill and therefore did not perform differently from the dyslexics who had already received several years of instruction in phonic reading skills.

Since both age- and reading-age matched designs have short-comings, the best studies are likely to employ both control groups. Comparison of the dyslexics with their age-matched peers will eluci-date the areas in which they are developmentally delayed, while comparison with younger RA-controls will highlight developmental deficits that are more likely to be the cause (rather than the conse-quence) of their reading problems. In practice, this is a costly way to do research and often practicalities preclude it. In what follows, dis-cussion will be primarily restricted to experiments that have employed satisfactory controls. Where relevant studies appear to have method-ological faults, we need to be cautious when evaluating their findings.

Dyslexia as a Verbal Deficit

Ever since Orton (1925) wrote about the difficulty that dyslexic readers have with printed symbols, especially reversible ones such as b/p, p/q, was/saw, there has been interest in the idea that dyslexia is the result of a visual perceptual problem. However, it is misleading to build a causal explanation of dyslexia on findings which may only reflect the relative inexperience of such children with the writing system. To the extent that most young children go through a stage of confusing letters with their mirror images, such findings serve only to highlight the fact that the children Orton worked with were at the beginning stages of literacy development. Furthermore, Liberman, Shankweiler, Orlando, Harris and Bell-Berti (1971) reported that reversal errors accounted for only a small proportion of the reading errors made by disabled readers. Other kinds of error, for example, confusing letter sounds such as *k* and *g*, were in fact more common.

In his seminal publication *Dyslexia: Research and Theory*, Vellutino (1979) presented a comprehensive evaluation of dyslexia research at the end of the 1970s. In this book, Vellutino concluded that the bulk of the existing findings suggesting a perceptual deficit in dyslexia were in fact entirely consistent with the view that dyslexic readers have verbal coding deficits. Converging evidence from epidemiological studies pointing to delays in speech and language development among poor readers bolstered this reinterpretation. Vellutino's verbal deficit hypothesis united the dyslexia field and provided a firm theoretical foundation for later research.

Arguably, however, the verbal deficit hypothesis was too general. Cases of highly articulate dyslexic individuals with specific reading difficulties did not rest easily within this framework. Moreover, an accumulation of evidence pointing to dyslexic deficits in some but not all verbal domains led gradually to a refinement of the view. It might be helpful here to think of the language system as made up of different sub-systems which interact during normal communication. Higher levels of language include the semantic system, specialized for processing meaning, and pragmatics, which is concerned with language use. The building-blocks of language are, however, within the syntactic system, which is concerned with grammar and sentence-level processing, and the phonological system, which maps speech sounds to units of meaning (Pinker, 1994). Dyslexic children appear to have a specific impairment of phonological processing while other language systems are relatively intact. Many dyslexic children can use language well for the purpose of communication but have subtle difficulties with speech processing which, it seems, interfere with the acquisition of a written language system.

Phonological Deficits in Dyslexia

Although the most obvious symptoms of dyslexia are reading and writing problems, there is abundant evidence that the difficulties of dyslexic people extend beyond the domain of written language and affect performance on a range of tasks that require phonological processing. It is for this reason that it has become widely accepted that in cognitive terms, dyslexia is the consequence of a phonological deficit. A more specific hypothesis that we will consider is that the deficit in dyslexia is in the way in which the brain codes or 'represents' the spoken attributes of words. In short, dyslexic readers have poorly specified phonological representations. We shall see here that this cognitive deficit has a number of consequences, not all directly related to the literacy problems that are key symptoms of dyslexia (Fowler, 1991; Snowling and Hulme, 1994). These include limitations of verbal short-term memory, naming difficulties and poor repetition ability. We begin by reviewing evidence for these deficits in dyslexia before turning to consider the implications of the phonological deficit for learning to read.

Verbal short-term memory deficits

Perhaps the most consistently reported area of difficulty for dyslexic people is in short-term memory; while dyslexic readers have normal memory span for visual information, they can remember fewer verbal items than expected for their age (Hulme, 1981; Shankweiler, Liberman, Mark, Fowler and Fischer, 1979). Indeed, JM could only remember 4 digits forwards despite his high IQ. In everyday life, verbal information is retained in short-term memory over a relatively short period. Hulme, Newton, Cowan, Stuart and Brown (1999) showed that spoken material could be held for only about 4 seconds whilst it was being output in a recall task. The duration for which items can be held by poor readers is even shorter and this can lead to problems, for example when trying to follow a list of instructions. It is also the case that, typically, dyslexics perform poorly when their memory is assessed using tests such as the Digit Span task, in which sequences of digits have to be recalled in forwards and backwards order. But how, theoretically, should their memory difficulties be explained?

It is generally accepted that verbal material is held in short-term memory in terms of a speech code. This view originated from the work of Conrad (1964), who showed that people find it more difficult to remember lists of items when their names sounded similar (for example, b, v, p, d, t) than when they sounded dissimilar (for example, b, x, s, w, f). This effect, known as the phonetic confusability effect, can be seen in young children as well as adults (Hulme, 1984).

Early research suggested that dyslexic readers were not susceptible to the phonetic confusability effect; their recall of rhyming lists was reported to be as good as that of non-rhyming lists (Liberman, Shankweiler, Liberman, Fowler and Fischer, 1977) and they also remembered similar numbers of confusable and non-confusable sentences (Mann, Liberman and Shankweiler, 1980). However, interpretation of these results was complicated by the fact that the dyslexic and normal readers performed at different levels on the memory tasks (Hall, Ewing, Tinzmann and Wilson, 1981). In essence, the dyslexic readers' memory for the non-confusable items was 'at floor'. Their performance was so poor that it could not get any worse when confusable items were presented.

Subsequent studies that have equated task difficulty for the two groups have shown that dyslexic children and normal readers are equally sensitive to the effects of phonetic similarity (Johnston, 1982). However, their general level of performance has consistently been found to be only as good as that of younger children reading at the same reading level (Johnston, Rugg and Scott, 1987). Should, therefore, the significance of their memory problem be discounted? Whilst it is true that null results such as these are difficult to interpret, it is not at all clear why performance on short-term memory tasks should depend on reading experience. Thus, the finding that dyslexic readers are impaired relative to age-matched peers is of note. Furthermore, verbal short-term memory difficulties characterize adults with dyslexia (Snowling, Nation, Moxham, Gallagher and Frith, 1997), even when their reading problems are fully compensated (Paulesu et al., 1996). In short, there is no compelling evidence that verbal short-term memory reaches normal levels of performance as time progresses; the memory deficit cannot be dismissed as a facet of 'developmental delay'.

The simplest interpretation of the memory impairment in dyslexia is that dyslexic readers are less efficient than normal readers when required to recruit phonetic memory codes. Another way of framing this is that they have impaired representations of the phonological forms of words. This impairment in phonological coding restricts the number of verbal items they can retain in memory and has knock-on effects in working memory tasks. For example, to carry out a mental calculation it is necessary to store the sum temporarily whilst retrieving memory facts and algorithms. Consequently, many dyslexic children do poorly in mental arithmetic although their mathematical thinking can be good.

In addition to coding verbal items into phonetic form for short-term recall, successful memory performance depends on two further factors: rehearsal mechanisms that refresh the memory trace, and 'red-integration' procedures for reconstructing decaying memory representations (Hulme and Roodenrys, 1995). To illustrate these different memory processes, consider an experiment by Hulme, Maughan and Brown (1991) in which adults were required to recall lists of short, medium and long words and lists of matched nonwords of similar spoken duration to the words. They were also asked to articulate the items of different lengths from the memory span lists to measure speech rate. The speech rate task required participants to repeat pairs of words or nonwords as fast as possible, without error, and their average speech rate was determined across lists of four pairs of items. The results of the experiment are shown in figure 3.2.

First, it can be seen that memory span for short items is longer than for long items. This effect, known as the word length effect (Baddeley, Thomson and Buchanan, 1975), provides evidence for the use of speech-based codes in short-term memory. Since the capacity of short-term memory is limited, it is possible to hold fewer long than short words because they take up more space in the system.

Secondly, it can be seen that for both words and nonwords, there is a close relationship between speech rate and memory span. Speech rate is usually interpreted as an index of the maximum speed of rehearsal for the memory items; since short-term memory performance depends on rehearsal rate, speech rate places a constraint on memory performance across development (Hulme, Thomson, Muir and Lawrence, 1984).

Finally, there is a clear lexicality effect: memory for words is far better than memory for nonwords. This effect demonstrates that, over

37

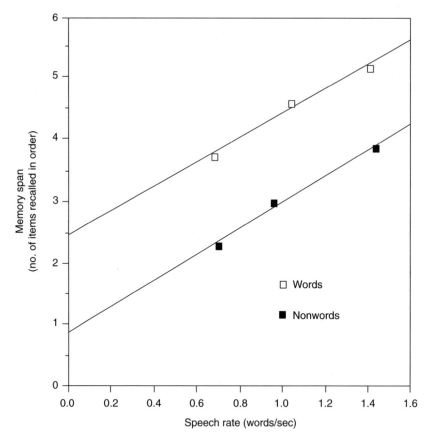

Figure 3.2 The relationship between memory span and speech rate for words and nonwords. Memory for words benefits from the availability of lexical representations

Source: adapted from Hulme, Maughan and Brown, 1991

and above the effects of rehearsal rate, there is a contribution from long-term memory to short-term memory performance. Words can be considered to have lexical entries or representations in long-term memory that nonwords do not possess. It seems that these long-term memory representations support the maintenance of words during short-term memory tasks. The general mechanism that is thought to be operating here is the reconstruction of memory traces. As the memory trace for a specific item fades, the system attempts to 'fill in' the missing phonetic information by drawing upon knowledge of phonologically similar words in long-term memory. This redintegration process works better for high-frequency than for low-frequency words and cannot play a significant role in memory for nonwords that do not have lexical representations (Hulme et al., 1997).

This view of the mechanisms of verbal short-term memory provides an interpretation of the memory impairments of dyslexic readers that can account for the persistence of these problems throughout development. Notwithstanding the problem dyslexics have in encoding verbal information into phonetic form, the proficiency of their short-term memory system depends on individual differences in speech rate and on the ability to draw upon long-term memory representations. As yet there has been relatively little work on dyslexia within this framework. However, poor readers have slow speech rates (McDougall, Hulme, Ellis and Monk, 1994) and, like young children, they are prone to make errors when articulating words at speed (Stone and Brady, 1995). Since dyslexic people also have difficulty in retrieving verbal information from long-term memory, this should reduce the efficiency with which they can lean on redintegration processes. Such a problem should affect learning to read by reducing a child's ability to blend sounds together during decoding (for example Baddeley, 1986; Torgesen et al., 1989). Moreover, if efficient blending requires a partial decoding attempt to be matched with a known lexical form (a word in the spoken vocabulary), a deficit in redintegration might be expected to have a direct impact on performance.

Verbal naming deficits

Naming tasks require the explicit retrieval of a verbal label from long-term memory. Clinically, dyslexic children often exhibit word finding difficulties: they frequently resort to long drawn-out descriptions to convey their ideas and sometimes they use words slightly inappropriately, for example 'uneven' for *uneasy*, 'installed' for *stalled*, 'pacific' for *specific* and 'portulant' for *corpulent*. Denckla and her colleagues (Denckla and Rudel, 1976a and b) were among the first investigators to note the diagnostic significance of naming problems which have since generated considerable interest among dyslexia researchers (see Wolf, 1997, for a review).

The naming skills of dyslexic readers have been examined using several different paradigms. Confrontation naming refers to the procedure in which participants are shown the picture of an object and are asked for its name (literally confronted with it). Naming to definition is a variant of this task and involves providing a name in response to the verbal description of an object.

The results of experiments using confrontation naming are somewhat equivocal, not least because levels of receptive vocabulary have not always been controlled. Typically, dyslexic children show more naming difficulties than controls, but the extent of their difficulty is not clear. Katz (1986) compared 8-year-old dyslexic children with average and good readers of the same age on an object naming test. The dyslexic children were less accurate in labelling the objects, and error rates were particularly high on low-frequency and polysyllabic words, even though they could often define these words correctly. The lack of a reading-age matched control group in this study makes the results difficult to interpret. It is plausible that low-frequency words are encountered mainly through reading rather than through everyday exposure to spoken words. If this is so, differential exposure to the more difficult words might account for the group differences that were observed.

Snowling, van Wagtendonk and Stafford (1988) followed up Katz's study by comparing 11-year-old dyslexic children on a picture naming task with age-matched and also younger controls aged 8 years who were reading at only a slightly higher level than the dyslexics. In line with Katz (1986), Snowling et al. found that dyslexic readers made more naming errors than normal readers of the same age, but they did no worse than younger controls. In a second experiment, they explored the nature of the dyslexic readers' problem further, using a tightly controlled matching procedure. Here each dyslexic child was matched with a normal reader according to their performance on a test requiring word definitions. They then completed two further tasks, one requiring confrontation naming and the other requiring matching a spoken word to a picture (see figure 3.3). Thus, with the two groups equated for vocabulary knowledge, their receptive and expressive language skills were assessed on independent tests.

The results were clear-cut. The dyslexic children performed as well as controls on the receptive vocabulary test that required picture–word matching. However, once again they were impaired on the picture

40

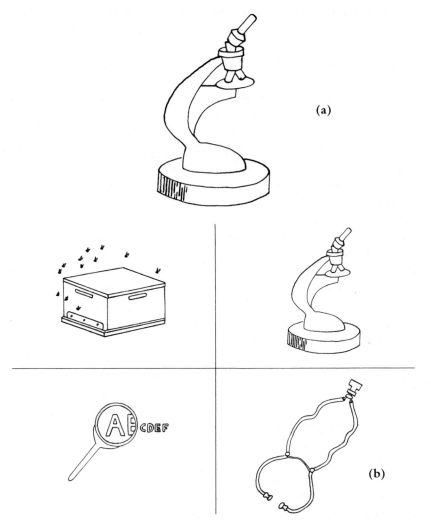

Figure 3.3 Stimuli for (a) naming and (b) vocabulary recognition for the item *microscope*

Source: Snowling, van Wagtendonk and Stafford, 1988

naming test. Together with Katz's (1986) findings, these results suggest that dyslexic readers have difficulty in retrieving the names of objects with which they are familiar. One way of thinking of this is that the memory representations for these words are adequately

41

specified in terms of their semantic attributes, but their phonological representations are either poorly specified or else inaccessible. Evidence in support of this hypothesis comes from a further experiment in our laboratory in which dyslexic readers made more semantic errors (for example *sword* → 'knife') in picture naming than RA-controls (Nation, Marshall and Snowling, in press). Importantly, a detailed error analysis also suggested that their naming errors were more strongly related phonologically to the targets than those of the control group, as measured by the proportion of phonemes shared between target and error (for example 75 per cent of phonemes are shared in the example *ladybird* → 'babybird'; 33 per cent are shared in *banana* → 'bat').

Swan and Goswami (1997) reported one of a minority of studies that have revealed naming deficits that are greater for dyslexic children than for younger reading-age matched controls (cf. Wolf and Obregon, 1992). In this study, they compared dyslexic readers with age- and reading-age matched controls, as well as with generally poor readers who did not fulfil the discrepancy definition of dyslexia. It seems likely that the group difference emerged because they used a carefully designed set of stimulus pictures, varying in the frequency and length of their spoken names, and the inclusion of several difficult items in their naming set made the task particularly sensitive. In line with previous research, Swan and Goswami reported that the dyslexic readers could define many of the words that they could not name, suggesting they had semantic representations for these items. Importantly, they also showed this was not the case for generally poor readers, whose main source of naming error was an absence of vocabulary knowledge for the items presented.

Evidence that phonological representations are poorly specified in dyslexic readers comes from their poor performance on naming-to-definition tasks, particularly those including long low-frequency words (German, 1979; Murphy and Pollatsek, 1994). Snowling, Van Wagtendonk and Stafford (1988) found that dyslexic readers could find fewer names of words following a spoken definition than age-matched controls, but when they did retrieve the word, they could do so as fast as their peers. This finding suggests that certain items can be retrieved efficiently, even by dyslexic readers, while others cannot. Griffiths (1999) elucidated this finding by tracking the time course of dyslexics' word retrieval in a naming-to-definition task.

In this experiment, dyslexic and normal readers named to definition a set of low-frequency unfamiliar words, such as *avocado* and *stethoscope*. When the accuracy of the two groups within the first 7 seconds following the definition was compared, there was no group difference; dyslexics performed like age-matched controls to whom they were matched in vocabulary knowledge. However, in the subsequent 8 seconds it was not uncommon for the normal readers to 'recover' from what has been described as the 'tip of the tongue' state, and to retrieve the target words. This happened much less often for the dyslexics, who were also less susceptible to facilitation from a phonemic cue or prompt at the end of each trial. Importantly, the word finding difficulties of the dyslexic readers could not be attributed to poorer semantic knowledge for the items, because they could define the target words as well as controls at the end of the experiment.

The findings from studies comparing the naming skills of dyslexic and normal readers suggest that dyslexic readers show a developmental dissociation between receptive and expressive vocabulary skill. Typically their vocabulary knowledge exceeds their naming performance, possibly because the phonological representations of words they know are not well specified. This lack of phonological specification may account for their failure to recover from the 'tip of the tongue' state. Furthermore, even phonemic prompts will be ineffective as retrieval cues if lexical representations are not organized into segments that correspond to the cues that are provided.

Rapid automatized naming

Rapid automatized naming (RAN) involves naming highly familiar objects under speeded conditions. The RAN task, used in early studies by Denckla and Rudel (1976a and b), involves naming items such as letters, digits or colour patches, arranged in matrices typically comprising 50 randomised stimuli in a 10×5 format. Assuming that error rates are low, the time to name the items is measured using a stopwatch, and group differences in the rate of naming are compared.

A consistent picture emerges from studies that have used the RAN task: dyslexic readers take longer to complete such tasks than children of the same age even though they are only required to name about five basic stimuli in each set (Wolf, 1986). Despite earlier conjecture that the problem might be attributable to the serial nature of this task

(Stanovich, Feeman and Cunningham, 1983), similar though less marked group differences have been found in studies using a discrete trial rather than continuous naming procedure (Bowers and Swanson, 1991). Moreover, the finding that adults with a developmental history of dyslexia also show rapid naming deficits (Felton and Wood, 1989; Pennington, Order, Smith, Green and Haitl, 1990) emphasizes that the findings are robust. What is less clear is how the rapid naming deficit seen in dyslexia should be interpreted.

Currently, two sorts of explanation for rapid naming deficits are under discussion. The first views this impairment, alongside other evidence of naming difficulties, as part of a pervasive problem at the level of underlying phonological representations (Snowling and Hulme, 1994). In short, although dyslexic readers possess adequate semantic representations of words they know, their representations of the phonological forms of words are impoverished. In this view, the relationship between reading and naming skill is similar to that between reading and other phonological processes (Torgesen, Wagner, Rashotte, Burgess and Hecht, 1997; Wagner, Torgesen and Rashotte, 1994).

The alternative account views rapid naming deficits as the consequence of an impairment of a timing mechanism (Wolf and Bowers, 1999); to the extent that dyslexic readers are slow to name highly familiar symbols, such as letters and digits, they will be slow to automate their reading processes and this will affect the fluency of their reading (Bowers and Wolf, 1993). Moreover, in an interesting proposal to which we will return, the rapid naming deficit might be closely tied to difficulties in establishing a sight vocabulary (Bowers, 1993; Wimmer, Mayringer and Landerl, 1998). Such problems would have deleterious effects, especially for the acquisition of exception word reading in English. Arguably, these difficulties would compound difficulties with phonological awareness, leading some dyslexic children to display serious reading problems as the result of a 'double deficit' in both naming speed and phonological skill (Wolf and Bowers, 1999).

Verbal repetition

Another area in which dyslexic children have difficulty is with speech production processes. Dyslexic children are often reported by their parents to have difficulty in saying certain words; 'baskwetti' for *spaghetti* and 'hopital' for *hospital* are common errors. As we saw in the case of JM, these difficulties may not resolve and some dyslexic adults can easily be tripped up by words such as *millennium* or *cerebral*. But are their difficulties outside of the normal range? Everyone makes speech errors and so it is important to ask whether these problems are more common for dyslexic than for normal readers.

With such clinical observations in mind, Snowling (1981) compared the ability of dyslexic readers and younger reading-age matched controls to repeat polysyllabic words, such as *pedestrian* and *magnificent*, and nonwords that were matched to them in terms of phonological structure (for example, *kebestrian, bagmivishent*). The design of this experiment was conservative; the dyslexic children were some four years older than the controls with whom they were compared on this spoken language task. Nonetheless, while they had no apparent difficulty with word repetition, the dyslexic children had relatively more difficulty repeating the nonwords.

To assess whether their difficulty might be due to a problem with the perception of such complex nonwords, an auditory discrimination task was constructed in which the child's task was to decide whether two nonwords were the same or different (for example, *fizidor–fizitor*). Where there were differences, these were only in terms of a single phonetic feature, making the discrimination difficult. Nonetheless, the two groups did not differ in their ability to discriminate the stimuli and it was proposed therefore that their repetition problem was likely to be with the segmentation processes required prior to establishing a new motor programme for articulation.

Problems of speech production in dyslexia were also reported by Brady, Shankweiler and Mann (1983), who showed that poor readers had more difficulty in repeating words presented in noise than age-matched controls, though the two groups performed like each other when the signal-to-noise ratio was favourable. The authors used these findings to argue that dyslexic readers needed a more distinct auditory signal in order to perform accurately than normal readers. However, the design of their study confounded aspects of speech perception and production, and because it did not include reading-age matched controls, the possibility that the normal readers were better able to recruit orthographic knowledge to facilitate their performance when auditory conditions were poor was not controlled.

To explore these possibilities, Snowling, Goulandris, Bowlby and Howell (1986) tested 10-year-old dyslexic readers who, like the participants in the experiment of Brady et al., were reading at the 8-year level. The performance of these children was compared with age-matched controls and younger reading-age matched controls. The procedure was modified in an attempt to pinpoint the difficulty of the dyslexic readers.

To examine the perceptual stage of processing, three levels of noise masking were used. Noise masking had the effect of making the speech signal less intelligible, rather like listening to a telephone call on a line on which there is interference. One-third of the stimuli were presented with a noise mask at the same level as the signal, one-third with a mask 3 decibels down on the signal and one-third with no mask at all. Second, in order to allow an assessment of the proficiency of phonological processing both when there was lexical support and when there was not, three sets of stimuli had to be repeated. In addition to the single-syllable words of high- and low-frequency used by Brady et al. (for example, *cake–dog; bale–dust*), a set of nonwords derived from the high frequency words was included (for example, *gake–tog*).

The results of this experiment differed from those reported by Brady and her colleagues in that there was no differential effect of noise masking between groups. Rather, the performance of both the dyslexic and normal readers deteriorated equally when there was noise masking. This pattern suggests that the dyslexic children did not have particular problems at the level of perceptual processing. The effect of word frequency was significant for all groups: high-frequency words were easier to process than low-frequency words, and nonwords were harder to repeat than words (see figure 3.4). When performance on high-frequency words was discounted to allow for possible ceiling effects, a significant group difference remained for low-frequency words and nonwords. Dyslexics performed worse than age-matched controls when repeating the low-frequency words (suggesting they had some lexical processing difficulties) but more strikingly, they repeated fewer of the nonwords correctly than either the CA-controls or the younger RA-controls. Moreover, they were the only group for whom repeating nonwords was significantly more difficult than repeating low-frequency words.

In order to interpret these results, it is important to be aware that there are two different mechanisms that can be invoked in order to

46

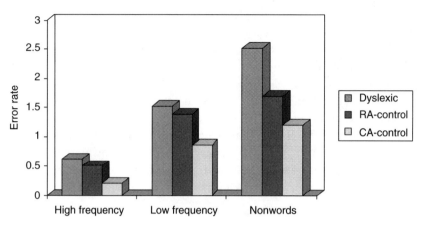

Figure 3.4 Numbers of errors made by dyslexic and normal readers when repeating high-frequency words, low-frequency words and nonwords
Source: Snowling, Stackhouse and Rack, 1986

repeat a verbal stimulus. If the stimulus is a word, then its articulatory motor programme can be directly accessed following perceptual processing. However, if the stimulus is either an unfamiliar word or a nonword that has no lexical representation, then the motor programme to articulate the item has to be constructed anew. High-frequency words are words that have been encountered often and therefore it is reasonable to assume that their lexical representations are easy to access and the motor articulation programmes will be easily retrieved and executed. Nonwords cannot be processed using this lexical mechanism. Instead, following perceptual processing, they must be subject to processes that include analysis and segmentation, prior to assembling a motor program for articulation. The finding that the dyslexics were not differentially affected by noise masking of the stimuli rules out a perceptual processing deficit as an explanation of their specific difficulty in repeating nonwords. It suggests instead that their deficit involves the system of analysis and segmentation processes that word repetition can bypass. In short, the phonological processes that are critical to nonword repetition are impaired in dyslexic readers.

Arguably, the consequences of a nonword repetition impairment might be far reaching. Gathercole and her colleagues (Gathercole and Baddeley, 1989; Gathercole, Hitch, Service and Martin, 1997) have proposed that nonword repetition (or phonological memory as they refer to it) is critical to vocabulary acquisition. Whilst it would be naive to deny the role of other processes, not least semantic and syntactic skills, in vocabulary development, this problem could contribute to the tendency for the vocabulary skills of dyslexic children to decline relative to age. The clinical impression that dyslexic individuals have difficulty learning foreign languages is also consistent with this view (cf. Service, 1992). In the longer term, difficulty in processing novel words for repetition could be expected to affect the nature of the lexical representations that are created for words, which, in turn, will have wide-ranging effects on all aspects of word retrieval.

Speech perception

A reasonable hypothesis that follows from the research we have reviewed so far is that the deficit in dyslexia is a consequence of deficits in basic speech processing abilities. However, a number of studies that have examined speech perception and spoken word identification in dyslexic readers have reported equivocal findings (Brady, 1997; McBride-Chang, 1996).

Studies investigating speech perception have commonly used a paradigm in which instances of words differing by a single phonetic feature have to be classified, for example *bath* and *path*. In fact, the initial consonants of these words differ by only a small change in the timing between lip closure and the onset of vocal cord vibration, known as voice onset time (VOT). By using synthetic speech, it is possible to manipulate the timing of this acoustic signal to produce a series of auditory stimuli that vary along the VOT continuum. Typically listeners categorize such stimuli as either 'bath' or 'path' with a sharp discontinuity between categorical boundaries, even though acoustically the changes are in fact more continuous. This phenomenon is known as categorical speech perception; each stimulus is perceived as either *bath* or *path*, not as a mixture of the two. Figure 3.5 illustrates categorical perception for the continuum [ba] [pa].

Brandt and Rosen (1980) investigated the perception of stop consonants, such as [ba] and [ga], by dyslexic and normal readers. Dyslexic children appeared to be extracting and encoding phonemic information like children at an earlier developmental stage. Likewise, Godfrey, Syrdal-Lasky, Millay and Knox (1981) found 10-year-old

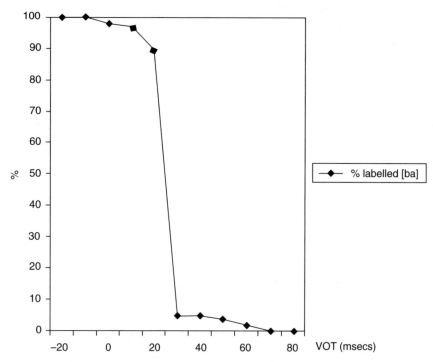

Figure 3.5 Typical speech identification function showing the classification of stimuli varying along the voice onset time (VOT) continuum. The figure shows the sharp shift in categorization of stimuli in the middle of the VOT continuum

dyslexic children to be inconsistent in their phonetic categorization of auditory cues, though not significantly impaired, and Hurford and Sanders (1990) reported reader-group differences in the discrimination of syllable pairs (for example, [gi]–[bi]) for second-grade but not fourth-grade good and poor readers.

One possible explanation for the inconsistency of findings regarding speech perception in dyslexic readers might be that not all dyslexic readers experience such problems, though some individuals do. With this in mind, Adlard and Hazan (1997) qualified their findings from comparisons of dyslexic readers with controls with an analysis of the performance of individuals on speech perception tasks. In the first part of their study they administered tests of synthetic speech discrimination and identification to 13 dyslexic children, comparing each with a reading-age matched and a chronological-age matched control. Each child was also given a battery of psychoacoustic tasks assessing non-verbal auditory processing.

Overall, group differences were slight, although the dyslexic group showed a higher error rate for the identification of stop consonants than nasals, and post hoc analyses revealed that four of the dyslexic readers had difficulty with the speech discrimination tasks. The performance of children in this subgroup was more than one standard deviation below that of controls on three out of four tasks. Interestingly, they also performed more poorly on tests of nonword reading and there was a trend towards weaker nonword repetition in this sub-group.

Along similar lines, Manis et al. (1997) compared severely dyslexic readers aged 12 years with age- and reading-age matched controls some four years younger on a categorical perception task in which instances of the words *bath* and *path* had to be identified. All three groups showed a relatively sharp boundary between [b] and [p] at about 21–26 ms of voicing delay. However, the slope of the identification function was shallower for dyslexics than CA-controls, reflecting a weaker categorical distinction. In fact, more dyslexics identified clear instances of [b] as [p] and vice versa. Arguably this pattern of performance suggests a 'labelling' rather than a perceptual impairment among dyslexics, a point to which we will return.

Manis et al. (1997) went on to divide the dyslexic readers into two sub-groups according to their performance on phonemic awareness tasks. The low-phoneme awareness group was significantly poorer than the high-phoneme awareness group in reading, as measured by word identification skill, but the two sub-groups did not differ in age and both were impaired relative to RA-controls in word attack skills. The group who had poor phoneme awareness had more difficulty distinguishing between [b] and [p] at the ends of the continuum than RA-controls, while the performance of the dyslexic readers with higher phoneme awareness was normal in the speech perception task. Further scrutiny of the data at the level of individual children revealed that only seven of the 25 dyslexics showed perceptual abnormalities. The functions of the three of these from the low-phoneme awareness group are reproduced in figure 3.6. Their erratic performance suggests that at least some of them had problems attending to or labelling the stimuli they perceived. The same was true of only one age-matched and three RA-matched controls.

50

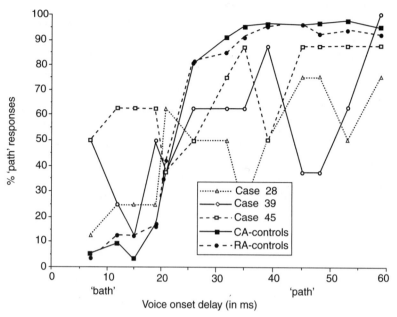

Figure 3.6 Speech identification functions for three dyslexic cases with low phonemic awareness, compared with CA- and RA-controls

Source: Manis et al., 1997

Thus, the interpretation of the findings from these studies is not straightforward. The tasks used to assess speech perception are highly demanding of attention and they may prove particularly difficult for dyslexic readers who have limited concentration. They may also be susceptible to strategic control, with some dyslexics being better able to bring other skills to bear, such as verbal labelling, to complete them successfully. Moreover, as Vihmann (1996) noted, performance of children on phoneme categorization tasks provides limited evidence concerning the skills relevant to the encoding of spoken words as they are heard in the context of other words in the speech stream. It is just such 'on-line' processing that is crucial throughout development for establishing phonological representations for items to be added to the spoken vocabulary.

The Phonological Representations Hypothesis

A final issue that needs to be raised before leaving discussion of the speech perception skills of dyslexic readers is that, given the importance of verbal communication, problems of speech perception experienced early in development might be quickly compensated. In line with this hypothesis, an analysis conducted by McBride-Chang (1995) of the relationships among speech perception, phonological awareness and word reading tasks in third- and fourth-grade children suggested that the best-fitting model between speech perception and reading was mediated through phonemic awareness (see also McBride-Chang, Wagner and Chang, 1997). McBride-Chang's model suggests the intriguing possibility that the origin of phonological processing deficits in some children might be in speech perceptual processes, but more studies will be needed to confirm or to refute this idea.

Spoken word identification in dyslexic children

To test the idea that one of the consequences of early perceptual difficulties is ill-specified or 'fuzzy' phonological representations, a number of studies have used the auditory gating paradigm. In the gating task, listeners hear relatively small segments of words and have to try to identify them from these partial inputs (Grosjean, 1980). In a typical gating experiment, the listener would initially be played the first 100 milliseconds of a target word. Subsequently they hear progressively longer segments of the word until finally the whole word has been presented. At each 'gate', the listener is encouraged to say what the target is, and to provide a confidence rating for their response. As might be expected, high-frequency words can be identified from less auditory input than low-frequency words, and it is also the case that words that have many phonetically similar neighbours require more input for accurate identification (Walley, Michela and Wood, 1995).

Rather few studies have used the gating paradigm with children, possibly because it is demanding in terms of attention. However, Walley, Michela and Wood (1995) showed that the point at which words could be identified changed with development, and kindergarten children needed to hear more of the word than first-graders. Metsala (1997) extended this work to show that children, like adults, were susceptible to the effects of word frequency and neighbourhood density, as defined by the number of words that differed by a single phoneme from the target. Moreover, high-frequency words from sparse neighbourhoods were identified more quickly than high-frequency words from dense neighbourhoods, whilst among low-frequency words, it was words from dense neighbourhoods that were identified more easily.

Elliott, Scholl, Grant and Hammer (1990) investigated the word identification skills of dyslexic children between the ages of 8 and 11 years using the gating task, comparing them with age-matched controls. Although the children with reading difficulties were poorer on fine-grained auditory discrimination tasks than controls, they performed as well as them on the gating tasks. Similarly, Metsala (1997), who compared dyslexic and normal readers of the same age using the gating task, failed to find overall group differences. However, dyslexic children required more input to recognize words of low-neighbourhood density, that is, those with few phonologically similar neighbours.

A recent study from our laboratory also failed to find dyslexic deficits in a gating task (Griffiths, 1999). In this experiment, dyslexic children were compared with both age-matched and younger reading-age matched controls in a gating task involving the identification of words varying in frequency and neighbourhood density. There were clear effects of word frequency and neighbourhood density on gating performance, and younger normal readers required more input than older controls. These findings confirm that the paradigm was sensitive enough to detect the effects of psycholinguistic variables as well as of developmental level. However, the dyslexic readers performed as well as CA-controls and better than RA-controls in all conditions of the experiment. This was as true of a sub-group with specific nonword reading deficits as of a sub-group who had better developed phonological decoding strategies.

Thus, like other studies of speech perception in dyslexia, the few studies that have used gating to compare the word identification skills of dyslexic and normal readers using the auditory gating paradigm have largely yielded null results. However, it is important to note that top-down information can be used to compensate for underlying phonological weaknesses in the gating task (Salasso and Pisoni, 1985). Indeed it is probable that semantic information about the target word becomes available at an early stage in the gating experiment, such that deficits at the level of phonological representation among dyslexics are masked.

So where does this leave us? We have argued that the deficits seen in dyslexic children's verbal memory, naming and repetition skills are a consequence of poorly specified phonological representations. Yet it has not been possible to trace the origins of these coding deficits to clear-cut problems in speech perception or spoken word identification. Current evidence suggests that the deficit in dyslexia is more marked in tasks that draw upon speech production than in those that draw on speech perceptual processes (for example Hulme and Snowling, 1992). Theoretically it is possible that the representations that underpin perceptual processes (input representations) are separate from those that are involved in speech production (output representations). Further progress in understanding the representational deficit in dyslexia will require more precise specification of the nature of these speech-based mechanisms.

Metaphonological deficits in dyslexia

By contrast to the rather subtle impairments observed in speech perception and production amongst dyslexic readers, the difficulties that dyslexic children experience on phonological awareness tasks are highly significant. Phonological awareness is a metacognitive ability that taps the organization of the phonological system and requires conscious reflection (Gombert, 1992).

The literature that relates explicit phonological awareness to reading ability and disability is extensive. From the age of around 4 years, children begin to be able to divide spoken words up into syllables so that, for example, they can split up the word *buttercup* into three units, namely *but*, *er*, *cup*. The ability to segment words into single speech sounds, or phonemes, does not emerge until much later, at around 5 to 6 years (Liberman, Shankweiler, Liberman, Fowler and Fischer, 1977). When children can segment words into phonemes, for example, *bat* → [b] [a] [t], then they are said to have achieved phonemic awareness.

Many influential theories of reading development regard the acquisition of phonemic awareness as essential if children are to abstract how written words relate to spoken words, and to develop the alphabetic principle (Byrne, 1998; Byrne and Fielding-Barnsley, 1989; Liberman and Shankweiler, 1979). In contrast, however, Morais, Cary,

Alegria and Bertelson (1979) were the first group to dissent from this view. In an important study carried out in Portugal, they presented adults who were just learning to read with an elision task in which they heard pairs of words differing by a single phoneme (for example *slit–sit*). The task was to indicate how one word could be changed into the other. In this case, the correct response was to take away the '*l*'. The findings were striking. The illiterate adults could not complete the task prior to enrolment in the literacy programme, but afterwards they completed it successfully.

Thus, Morais and his colleagues argued that phonemic awareness is not a prerequisite of reading, but rather a consequence of literacy. However, it should be noted that the task they used was quite difficult conceptually and it is likely that the non-educated participants in their study found it perplexing for reasons other than the phonemic level of analysis it required. Subsequent studies, notably those by Lundberg and his colleagues (Lundberg, 1994) have shown that some children who are non-readers demonstrate awareness of phonemes. It follows that the argument that phonemic awareness is a consequence of literacy is too strong, although the reciprocal influence of reading on phoneme awareness cannot be denied (Perfetti, Beck, Bell and Hughes, 1987).

A large variety of tasks have been used to assess phonological awareness. Some of the more straightforward versions include tapping out the syllables or phonemes in a word or 'finishing off' what the experimenter is saying in word completion tasks, for example when looking at the picture of a rabbit completing the word from the first syllable, [rab]? – [it], or supplying the last phoneme in response to the picture of a duck, [du]? – [k] (Stuart and Coltheart, 1988). Oddity tasks are more difficult and require the detection of the odd one out from a set of words presented either auditorially or with picture prompts (Bradley and Bryant, 1983). The odd one out can differ according to its rime (sun–gun–*rub*–fun) or its beginning as in alliteration oddity (sun–see–*rag*–sock). Even more challenging tasks tend to be used with older children. These include phoneme deletion, a task in which a sound has to be taken away from a spoken word, for example 'bice' without the [b] says 'ice' (McDougall, Hulme, Ellis and Monk, 1994), and spoonerisms, in which the task is to swap the initial sounds of two words, for example John Lennon → 'Lon Jennon' (Perin, 1983).

It will be clear from these examples that phonological awareness tasks require mental effort, and, in addition to tapping phonological skills, they vary in their cognitive demands. It is important to take account of this variation when interpreting the results of experiments that report differential patterns of impairment on phonological tasks. Importantly, while dyslexic readers fail some phonological awareness tasks because of deficits in phonological processing, they may sometimes succeed on others where they can bring to bear cognitive strategies, such as the use of orthographic codes, to compensate for their difficulties. A clear example of this was provided by Perin (1983) who noticed that a frequent error in spoonerizing 'Phil Collins' was to respond 'Chil Follins'. Here the initial letters, rather than the initial sounds had been swopped.

One of the first demonstrations of a deficit in phonological awareness in a selected group of disabled readers was reported by Bradley and Bryant (1978), who compared 12-year-old dyslexic children with younger RA-controls on tests of rime and alliteration oddity. Despite a four-year age advantage, the dyslexic readers made more errors on these tasks. They also had more difficulty on a task where they were required to generate rhyming words to go with a target.

Subsequent studies of groups of dyslexic children (for example Olson, Kleigel, Davidson and Foltz, 1985), groups of dyslexic adults (Pennington, Orden, Smith, Green and Haith, 1990) and single-case studies (Campbell and Butterworth, 1985; Funnell and Davison, 1989) have confirmed impairments in metaphonological skills, and it is common for significant deficits to be found in comparisons with younger reading-age matched controls (Bruck, 1990; Manis, Custodio and Szeszulski, 1993).

Very few studies have addressed the theoretically important issue of which level of phonological awareness is affected in dyslexic readers. Swan and Goswami (1997) compared the ability of dyslexic readers with that of CA- and RA-controls on tasks of syllable, rime and phoneme segmentation. The dyslexics performed less well than their age-matched peers but comparably to RA-controls in syllable segmentation and on a test of onset-rime similarity. However, in this study as in many others, the dyslexics were impaired on phonemic awareness tasks (Olson, Wise, Connors, Rack and Fulker, 1989). Similar findings were reported by Windfuhr and Snowling (submitted), who found that dyslexic readers were worse than age-matched controls on a rime

56

oddity task, but even worse than younger RA-controls in phoneme deletion.

An important feature of Swan and Goswami's study was that, prior to the phonological awareness tasks, the children had been required to name pictures depicting the words to be segmented. When performance on the segmentation task was adjusted to take account of naming problems, a slightly different picture emerged. In this re-analysis, segmentation performance was only assessed for words that the children had previously named correctly. When this was done, the dyslexic readers' scores were similar to those of age-matched controls in rime segmentation, but they remained impaired in phoneme segmentation. These results imply, on the one hand, that phonological segmentation requires access to lexical representations; Gombert (1992) would regard this as the 'epilinguistic' substrate. But segmentation at the phonemic level requires more besides. It appears from Swan and Goswami's results that the ability to analyse phonemic segments is a more critical determinant of reading ability (and disability) than segmentation processes that operate on larger units such as rimes.

Phonological learning

Before turning to a synthesis of the evidence on phonological deficits in dyslexia, it is worth noting that the undoubted importance of phonological awareness in the acquisition of the alphabetic principle may have drawn attention from the fact that reading acquisition is in fact a learning process. Indeed, in many ways, reading is an excellent example of paired associate learning. For instance, word-specific associations might be learned in this way as might letter–sound relationships.

Vellutino and his colleagues were among the first researchers to recognize this association, and a series of experiments conducted by this group revealed that the learning deficit of dyslexic readers was specific to tasks requiring the association of verbal labels with visual and verbal stimuli rather than more generally in associating visual shapes with each other (Vellutino, Scanlon and Spearing, 1995; Vellutino, Steger, Harding and Spearing, 1975).

Following on from this, Wimmer, Mayringer and Landerl (1998) incorporated a paired associate learning task into a battery

57

of tests used to compare dyslexic and normal readers of German. In this task, children had to learn three nonsense words as names for three unusual animals. Even though the reader groups were not differentiated in performance on tests of phonological awareness (which is acquired early among German speakers: Wimmer, 1996), the dyslexic children learned fewer of the nonsense names. In a replication of this study with English-speaking dyslexics, Windfuhr (1998) found that dyslexics took longer to learn the associations between four nonwords and four abstract shapes than younger RA-controls.

The mechanisms that account for the poor verbal learning of dyslexic readers are not yet understood. It could be that the problem is one of establishing new phonological representations because the deficit applies to phonological learning as well as to learning to associate visual and verbal stimuli. In some early work on dyslexia, Nelson and Warrington (1980) reported that it was more difficult for poor readers to learn the first ten words above their own ceiling on a picture vocabulary test than age-matched controls, suggesting a problem in consolidating new word knowledge into long-term memory. Aguiar and Brady (1991) found that poor readers were just as good as their peers at learning the meanings of new words but, consistent with the phonological deficit hypothesis, it was their names that they found difficult to remember.

In short, the hypothesis that dyslexic readers have poorly specified phonological representations can be invoked as an explanation of difficulties in the processes that are involved in learning new spoken words and in learning to read. The putative causal links among the different phonological processes we have discussed are depicted in figure 3.7. The different skills in which deficits are symptoms of dyslexia are shown in squares and the 'hidden' cognitive deficit in an ellipse. The validity of the model, and the relative importance of the different deficits in the causal chain, await future research.

Dyslexia as a Core Deficit at the Level of Phonological Representations

As we have seen, the evidence pointing to phonological deficits in dyslexia is strong. Indeed, the strength of the evidence is such that

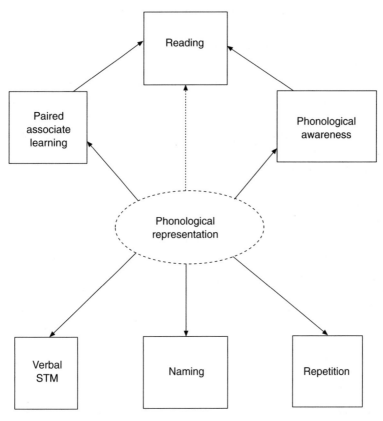

Figure 3.7 Causal links among the different phonological processes and reading

Stanovich (1986) proposed that dyslexia should be defined as a core phonological deficit. The adoption of this definition has been widespread with the decline in popularity of the discrepancy approach to diagnosis. According to what has become known as the *phonological core-variable difference model* (Stanovich and Siegel, 1994), poor phonology is related to poor reading performance, irrespective of IQ. Indeed, in a large empirical study of children varying in reading skills, Stanovich and Siegel (1994) reported that all poor readers differed from normal readers in skills close to the core of the deficit, for example in phonological awareness. However, discrepancy-defined readers only differed from other poor readers in skills further from the core, such as working memory and listening comprehension.

An important advantage of the core phonological deficit model of dyslexia is that it makes sense in terms of what is known about the normal development of reading. In addition, it unites findings on dyslexia from across the life-span (Morton and Frith, 1995). Although the majority of research on dyslexia has focused on school-age children, many of the phonological deficits in dyslexia persist into adulthood, and a growing body of studies concerning the precursors of dyslexia are consistent with this view (see Hulme and Snowling, 1997, for reviews).

Nevertheless, the core phonological deficit model of dyslexia leaves important questions unanswered. Primary amongst these is whether the phonological deficit in dyslexia that is associated with high IQ is the same as that associated with low verbal ability. Put another way, a child can have phonological difficulties for a number of reasons. Walley, Michela and Wood (1995) proposed that, as a child's spoken vocabulary increases, this leads to a re-structuring of their phonological representations from a global to a segmental organization. If this lexical restructuring hypothesis is correct, then poor vocabulary is likely to lead to phonological difficulties. In contrast, the classic dyslexic child who has poor phonological skills in the face of good receptive vocabulary might be the subject of a processing impairment that is quite different and impacts on reading in a different way. There are also other reasons why it might be necessary to continue to use IQ in the definition of dyslexia. IQ may act as a protective factor mitigating the effects of the phonological deficit on reading development in some children. In short, reading failure should be less marked when compensatory resources are available.

But as we have seen, dyslexic readers (like JM) show very consistent problems across a wide range of phonological processing tasks. Some of their difficulties emerge on tasks that require implicit access to phonological codes; others are seen on tasks that require the conscious manipulation of the segments of spoken words in phonological awareness tasks. The problems can be united under the hypothesis that dyslexic readers have deficits at the level of underlying phonological representations. Put simply, the way in which the dyslexic person encodes phonology is different from that of the normal reader. Snowling and Hulme (1994) hypothesized that children who come to the task of learning to read with well-specified phonological representations are well placed to establish links between the letters of printed words and the sounds of spoken words. We have seen that JM could not do this. The phonological representations hypothesis proposes that dyslexic children have poorly specified phonological representations. The hypothesis provides an account of their wide-ranging but related cognitive deficits, as well as of their difficulties in learning to read.

Chapter 4

Learning to Read and to Spell

We have seen that the deficits in dyslexia cluster on tasks that require dealing with the sounds of speech and have inferred that these deficits cause reading problems. To provide a framework within which to understand the impact of phonological deficits on the development of written language, we need to digress in this chapter to consider the normal development of reading and spelling skills. We begin by reviewing theoretical models of reading development that aim to capture the characteristics of reading as it changes over time, and discuss the critical role of phonological skills in learning to read. We then outline the principles of a computational approach to reading and focus on connectionist models that learn to read by creating mappings between orthography and phonology.

Learning to Read

Most children encounter their first printed words during everyday activities before going to school and many learn to recognize their own name or the name of their favourite chocolate bar with relative ease. The ability to read such *environmental print* should not be considered reading proper, for it is unlikely that young children will recognize these words outside of their usual context (Masonheimer, Drum and Ehri, 1984). Nonetheless, the knowledge that children gain from early encounters with print starts them off on the path to literacy. At about the same time, some children will be seen turning the pages of books, perhaps 'reading aloud' confidently, guided by the pictures they see. Such primitive reading attempts are important because they help establish the concept of what reading is – the extraction of meaning from the printed page.

In essence, learning to read involves integrating a system for processing written language with one that already exists for processing spoken language (LaBerge and Samuels, 1974). The process of learning to read extends over several years and involves both building a sight vocabulary and developing decoding skills. The goal of reading, however, is not merely to decode printed words but rather to understand text. Understanding what one reads requires the integration of meaning across sentences and makes use of contextual cues as well as inferences based on general knowledge. Put this way, learning to read represents a considerable challenge even for the child who comes to the task well prepared in terms of their spoken language competencies.

Stage models of reading development

A growth of interest in the development of children's reading skill occurred in the 1970s. Learning to read was referred to as an 'unnatural' act, and the difficulties children have in understanding the alphabet as a *cipher* were emphasized in theories of reading acquisition (Gough and Hillinger, 1980). Inspired by the Piagetian tradition, a number of stage models of reading development describing the child's progression from beginning reading to reading proper were proposed.

There was considerable commonality between the different stage models of literacy development that emerged (see figure 4.1. As we shall see later, Ehri's 1985 model has now been substantially modified and so its original version will not be discussed here). Marsh, Friedman, Welch and Desberg (1981) viewed the child as passing from a stage in which the main strategy for deciphering words was one of linguistic guessing, through a stage which they called 'discrimination net-learning' in which children use their visual memory to read. The next two stages were principally concerned with the acquisition of the decoding skills that allow children to sound out words they do not know. In the first of these, decoding was a left-to-right process; literally sounding out letters as they appeared and then blending them together, for example, [k]-[a]-[t] gives 'cat'. In the more advanced stage of hierarchical decoding, the child was observed to use more

Marsh et al.		Frith		Ehri	
Reading	*Spelling*	*Reading*	*Spelling*	*Reading*	*Spelling*
(1) Linguistic guessing		Logographic phase (1)		*Shared body of knowledge* ← Letter knowledge →	
(2) Discrimination net-learning			Alphabetic phase (1)	← Semiphonetic strategies →	
				← Phonetic strategies →	
(3) Sequential decoding	(1) Sequential encoding	Alphabetic phase (2)			
(4) Hierarchical decoding	(2) Hierarchical encoding	Orthographic phase (1)		← Morphemic strategies →	
(5) Morphophonemic analogy	(3) Analogies		Orthographic phase (2)		

(Ehri column side annotations: left — "Gradual increase in 'sight vocabulary' which is organized into orthographic neighbourhoods"; right — "Increasing knowledge of word-specific spellings")

Figure 4.1 Theories of literacy development: stages in the development of orthographic knowledge as viewed by Marsh, Friedman, Welch and Desberg (1980 and 1981), Frith (1985) and Ehri (1985). Time moves vertically down through the figure

advanced 'rules'. These included the *silent 'e' rule* that allows *make* to be pronounced [m] [A] [k] ('make') or the *soft 'g' rule*, that softens the *g* to [d] in *cage* giving [k] [A] [d] ('cage'). In the final stage, the child was thought to begin to use analogies at the level of morphology to read words. For example, the nonword *faugh* could be read as 'faff' by analogy with *laugh*. Marsh, Friedman, Welch and Desberg (1980) viewed the development of spelling as paralleling that of reading. Children first spell words by sequential encoding before moving through the use of hierarchical rules to the adoption of analogy strategies (see also Marsh and Desberg, 1983).

One of the limitations of Marsh's model was that it was entirely descriptive. Whilst illustrating the types of word that children could read and spell at various stages, it did not show how their performance related to their underlying cognitive competencies, nor did it differentiate between the strategies children could bring to bear when presented with new words and those that they relied on when they met familiar words.

A second model, proposed by Frith (1985), has had a considerable influence on the study of dyslexia. In Frith's model, children start out with a logographic approach to reading whereby they make use of their visual skills to read words by partial cues. To throw light on the way in which this first reading vocabulary is organized, Seymour and Elder (1986) studied the mistakes that children made in their reading at the logographic stage. Reading errors came predominantly from the set of words that had been taught to the children and there was a tendency for their mis-readings to be of the same length as the target items. One child read *policeman* as 'children', saying, 'I know it's that one because it is a long one'. There was also confusion between words with salient features in common. *Smaller* was read as 'yellow', 'because of the two sticks' (the *ll*) and *stop* was read as 'lost' because of the shared consonant cluster.

Several strands of evidence confirmed that logographic readers access semantic memory, where word meanings are stored. Some of the errors observed by Seymour and Elder were semantic in nature, for example, *room* was read as 'house' and *big* was read as 'cat' (having first been mistaken for *dog* because of the b/d confusion). In addition, there were word class effects, with verbs being harder to read than nouns. The importance of connections between the early sight vocabulary and semantics was also emphasized in a modification of Frith's model proposed by Morton (1989). In this formulation, logographic reading involved the same processes as picture recognition; in essence, the pronunciations of words were retrieved from an output system via connections with the verbal semantic system.

Logographic reading can function well as a system for recognizing printed words until the sight vocabulary expands to a point where much confusion between different words is apparent. In addition, a visual reading system is not conducive to spelling; while it is possible to read words globally, spelling requires letter-by-letter information. According to Frith's theory, children enter an alphabetic phase for spelling, motivated by the desire to write, and alphabetic skills are then transferred back to reading, where they allow children to read words they have not encountered before. Later advances in reading development depend upon the development of a specialized system of alphabetic mappings. However, as reading skills become more automatic, children rely more on orthographic relationships that transcend simple grapheme–phoneme correspondences and include the use of morphological spelling patterns. Thus, they move into the orthographic phase for reading before these skills are transferred to spelling.

Individual pathways in development

Despite the popular appeal of stage models of reading, they suffered from a number of limitations. First, they were poorly specified (this was particularly true of the later phases) and, in common with other models of this type, the mechanisms involved in the transitions between stages were unclear. Second, all of the models proposed an ordered sequence of stages or phases. This universal sequence was subsequently challenged by empirical data indicating that the course of reading development was not the same for all children. In fact, the reading strategies that children use depend upon the teaching regime to which they are exposed (Johnston and Thompson, 1989) and the language in which they are learning (Wimmer and Hummer, 1990). Strong evidence against a universal sequence comes from children learning to read in regular orthographies. In German, for example, where alphabetic skills soon reach a high level of competence (Wimmer, 1996), a logographic phase is not generally observed. A quite separate body of evidence suggests that developmental dyslexic readers can reach the orthographic phase of development without passing through the alphabetic phase (Campbell and Butterworth, 1985; Funnell and Davison, 1989; Snowling, Hulme and Goulandris, 1994).

It seems clear, therefore, that individuals can take different pathways on the way to becoming literate (for example Baron and Treiman, 1980). A modified stage model that allowed for individual variation in development was proposed by Seymour (1990; also Seymour and Bunce, 1992). In this 'dual foundation model', the orthographic system of fluent reading was seen as the merger of two earlier systems, a logographic system and an alphabetic system (see figure 4.2). According to Seymour, children need to have access to structures in a logographic lexicon with links to semantics, to account for the automaticity of later orthographic reading. In addition, phonological awareness and knowledge of alphabetic letter–sound correspondences is required to provide a foundation for the organized structure seen later in development in the orthographic phase. Individual differences in reading performance (say in dyslexia) might be understood in terms of difficulties within either one of these sub-systems. Similarly, individual differences in reading might reflect processing preferences rather than abnormalities of development.

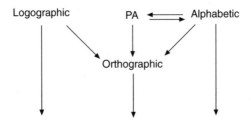

Figure 4.2 Schematic representation of the 'dual foundation' model of reading development

Source: Seymour and Evans, 1994

Acquiring the alphabetic principle

Our review of stage models of reading has revealed that a major challenge facing the child is to grasp the alphabetic principle; before they do this, they focus on the visual forms of words and how these link to meaning. In a highly original account of the foundations of literacy, Byrne (1998) suggested that one of the reasons that children do not immediately abstract the alphabetic mappings between print and sound is that they entertain the wrong hypotheses about the writing system. As their first exposure to print usually involves someone reading to them, it would be natural for them to imagine that the writing system maps on to meaning rather than on to sound. If alternatively they have the insight that the mapping is to sound as it is in alphabetic orthographies, then it is reasonable to ask, to what level of phonological representation? In principle, the mapping could be to the syllable, to the phoneme or possibly to another segment of the spoken word such as the rime, an idea we will return to in the next section.

In a series of ingenious experiments, Byrne (1996) demonstrated that young children start out thinking that the mappings from writing are at the level of the morpheme – the smallest unit of meaning. These experiments involved a three-stage process in which pre-school children were first taught pairs of words after which they were given two sets of transfer trials to investigate the hypotheses they held about the relationship between the printed and spoken forms of these words.

In the learning phase, children who could not yet read were taught the relationshps between the printed and spoken forms of pairs of words, such as *hat–hats* and *small–smaller*. Training continued until

67

the children reached the criterion of six errorless trials, which took about 10 minutes per pair of words. In the first transfer test, they were asked to distinguish new pairs of words analogous to the trained pairs, for example *cat–cats* and *mean–meaner*, again by selecting which written form matched the spoken form presented. Importantly, the children could be successful in this transfer test regardless of whether their performance was based on a phonological or a morphological representation of the critical letters because in the examples provided there was a one-to-one mapping between the morphemes and the phonemes. Thus, the '*s*' in *cats* represents both plurality (the morpheme) and [s] (the phoneme); the '*er*' in *meaner* represents both the comparative (the morpheme) and the phoneme [ə].

Eleven out of 12 children reached criterion on this transfer task, showing that they had been able to generalize knowledge gained during training to the reading of new items. However, the basis on which they were able to do this remained unclear; they could be using either letter–morpheme or letter–phoneme relationships. The second transfer test was more definitive. In this part of the experiment, the children had to distinguish between members of two further pairs of words but this time, success was only possible if performance was based on the phonological representations of the letters. The word pairs were *pur–purs* (phonetic versions of *purr–purse*) and *corn–corner*, the distinguishing features in both cases being phonological and not morphemic.

Most children failed the second transfer test, indicating that they had focused on the meaning function of the letter and had not abstracted the basic level of representation fundamental to the alphabetic principle, the phoneme. According to Byrne (1998), the child must abandon this morphological hypothesis to become a successful decoder. To do so requires both awareness of phoneme identity and knowledge of the letters representing the phonemes.

The importance of phonemic awareness and letter knowledge to early reading development can be seen clearly in a study by Stuart and Coltheart (1988), who proposed that the reading strategies children use are directly dependent upon the status of their phonological skills. In a small-scale but detailed longitudinal study, they followed the progress of a class of pre-school children through the early stages of learning to read, making assessments of their phonological awareness, letter knowledge and reading behaviour at regular intervals. An important finding was that the age at which children passed a phoneme segmentation task and knew at least half of the alphabet's letters predicted a change in the type of reading errors they made. From the point children reach this criterion onwards, Stuart and Coltheart showed children made systematic reading errors. In essence, the proportion of reading errors sharing first and/or first and last letters with their targets increased, with a corresponding decline in unsystematic errors that were not dictated by phonology.

The main thrust of Stuart and Coltheart's argument, like Byrne's (1998), was that children set up hypotheses about print on the basis of their phonological awareness. Children who are aware of the initial and final sounds of spoken words use this knowledge to predict how that word will look in print. The use of this strategy improves the accuracy with which they can decode words. In a subsequent series of training studies, Stuart, Masterson, Dixon and Quinlan (1999) demonstrated a relationship between children's phonological skills and the forms of words they are able to retain in their sight vocabulary. Thus, children's responses on forced-choice recognition tasks indicated that those who could segment initial or final sounds retained these in their orthographic representations of words they were taught. Furthermore, only children who could segment medial sounds were able to recognize medial vowel strings accurately. Interestingly, visual skills only predicted the acquisition of a sight vocabulary in children who could not segment.

The role of phonological skills: phonemes or rimes?

An alternative view to that which stresses the critical role of phonemic awareness to the early acquisition of reading is one which proposes that children's rhyming skills are the precursors of reading. The term 'rhyming' here is used in the formal sense to refer to a sub-syllabic level of phonological organization larger than that of the phoneme (Treiman and Breaux, 1982). (The terms rime and rhyme are used extensively in the literature on reading, not always in a consistent manner. Strictly, rime refers to the linguistic unit of the syllable containing the vowel and the succeeding consonant or consonants, for example, -*oat*, -*at*. Rhyme, in contrast, is used to refer to the shared phonetic similarity of the end sounds of at least two spoken words – *goat, coat, moat*. In practice it is not always possible to keep the use

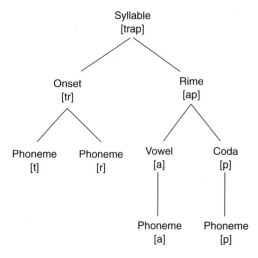

Figure 4.3 Hierarchical structure of the monosyllable *trap*

of the terms district because they overlap.) Figure 4.3 depicts the hierarchical view of the syllable, showing the intra-syllabic units of onset and rime. The onset of a syllable is the first phoneme or cluster of phonemes, with the rime comprising the vowel and the succeeding consonant or consonants (the coda). Thus, in a word like *croak*, the onset is *cr* and the rime is *oak*; in *mist*, the onset is *m* and the rime is *ist*.

With this hierarchical structure of the syllable in mind, Goswami and Bryant (1990) proposed that children's ability to recognize when words have common rimes and onsets leads them to form phonological categories. They argued that 'when [children] begin to read they soon recognise that words in the same category often have spelling patterns in common and this spelling sequence represents the common sound' (1990, p. 147). In short, children's awareness of the onset and rime distinctions in spoken words effectively directs their attention to how these sub-components of words are represented in print.

In several experiments, Goswami (1988) showed that even beginning readers could use lexical analogies to read words that shared orthographic rimes. Following a pre-test, the children in these experiments were taught a word such as *beak*, and told that this would provide them with a clue for reading some other words. They were then presented with words that either shared the rime unit (peak), the onset and vowel sequence (bean) or all of the letters but in a different order (bake). Goswami showed that children as young as 5 years could use analogies to solve this task; having learned *beak* the children were able to transfer their knowledge to read words sharing the same rime, for example *peak, weak*. Seven-year-olds, but not younger children, were also able to use beginning-analogies: they could read *bean* having been taught *beak*, but the benefit was not as great as for end-analogies.

To confirm the relationship between children's phonological knowledge and their use of analogy strategies, Goswami and her colleagues showed that children's performance on a rime oddity task was related to their use of end-analogies (Goswami, 1990), and their phoneme awareness was related to their ability to use beginning-analogies (Goswami and Mead, 1992). In a modification of this idea, Goswami (1993) proposed an 'interactive analogy model of reading development' according to which refinements in children's use of analogy with age developed as they attained awareness of increasingly smaller phonological units. In the earliest stages of learning to read, children's phonological awareness is restricted to onset and rime units, and analogies in reading are therefore made between words that share these units. As phonological awareness develops and children become more sensitive to phonemes, they begin to use this knowledge in their reading to make analogies based on grapheme–phoneme correspondences.

The work of Goswami and her colleagues has been influential both in pointing to children's ability to use lexical analogies at a much younger age than suggested by stage theorists, and in highlighting the association between children's reading strategies and their underlying phonological skills. However, some aspects of the theory have been challenged. There have now been several demonstrations showing that the analogy paradigm overestimates children's natural tendency to use analogies (Bowey, 1996, 1999; Muter, Snowling and Taylor, 1994; Savage, 1997), and Brown and Deavers (1999) have shown that children are more likely to use grapheme–phoneme correspondences than rime-based lexical analogies to decode nonwords, except when these are presented with 'clue-words'.

Furthermore, there is no direct evidence that early rime awareness drives the use of end-analogies. Muter, Snowling and Taylor (1994) failed to find a longitudinal relationship between rhyming skill at 4

71

years and the use of end-analogies at 6 years. However, at 6 years, children's rhyming skills were related to their ability to use lexical analogies in reading, suggesting that rhyming skills may be important later in development when a child's orthographic representations are more fully specified. Similar findings were reported by Duncan, Seymour and Hill (1997), who followed the progress of two groups of Scottish children from nursery school until the end of the second year of formal schooling. The children in Group A entered school with excellent rhyming skills, as a consequence of their pre-school experiences. Group A children outperformed Group B on tests of rhyme oddity and rhyme production. After seven months of schooling, both groups of children were asked to read a set of nonwords that contained familiar rime units. For the purpose of comparison, they also read non-words containing other linguistic structures that they had met in their classroom experience.

Contrary to expectation, children's pre-school rhyming skills did' not predict their success in the early stages of learning to read. Rather, reading achievement was significantly related to letter-sound knowledge. Moreover, nonwords containing rime units were read no better than those related to known words by smaller segments, for instance the onset, medial or final sounds of the words. In fact, the use of rime analogies in reading appeared in the second year of reading only, by which time some children displayed a bias in favour of rime units in the reading of nonwords (Seymour, Duncan and Bolik, 1999).

Taken together, the findings from a growing number of studies suggest that knowledge of the rime-based regularities of words appears to develop slowly, in contrast to knowledge of grapheme–phoneme rules (Bowey and Underwood, 1996; Coltheart and Leahy, 1992; Laxon, Masterson and Coltheart, 1991). This evidence does not rest easily with the notion that children use analogies based on large units in their early reading attempts. While it is clear that they can do so if encouraged in specific circumstances, it does not seem a natural option.

The development of word recognition: item-based models

Regardless of the units of analysis that children use to guide their decoding attempts in reading, it is clear that they must move beyond the alphabetic principle to become fluent readers. Share (1995) has argued that every successful decoding encounter with an unfamiliar word provides an opportunity to acquire word-specific orthographic information that is critical to the development of skilled word recognition. In this sense phonological recoding can be considered part of a 'self-teaching device' that furnishes the learner's orthographic representations. Phonological recoding in and of itself is, however, insufficient. As we shall see later, the learner also needs to be able to use contextual information to disambiguate partial decoding attempts so that, on an item-by-item basis, their word recognition system develops. A spin-off is that the phonological recoding mechanism becomes increasingly 'lexicalized', taking it beyond its basic function of translating letters into sounds for use in deciphering words containing a wide range of spelling patterns and morphological consistencies.

Another model of the development of 'sight word' acquisition is that proposed by Ehri (1992) as a reformulation of her original stage-model of reading (Ehri, 1985). This theory views children's reading skills as an emergent property of the interaction between their phonological representations and the print to which they are exposed (Ehri, 1995). In Ehri's conceptualization, the influence of children's phonological knowledge on their word learning is first witnessed as they begin to read using phonetic cues. At this stage in their development, children use what knowledge of letter names or letter sounds they have in order to access the pronunciations of words in memory. In so doing they begin to form connections between the spellings and the sounds of spoken words and to develop primitive orthographic representations.

The findings of an experiment by Ehri and Wilce (1985) support the idea of phonetic cue reading. In this study, beginning readers were taught a set of nonwords which either had systematic links to their pronunciations (for example, the acronym 'grf' for *giraffe*), or else were arbitrary (for example, 'xbt' for *giraffe*). Those children who possessed some letter-sound knowledge read the nonwords with systematic spellings better than those with arbitrary spellings. In an extension of this work that achieved better control over the visual similarity of the two sets of stimuli, Rack, Hulme, Snowling and Wightman (1994) replicated the finding that children with minimal letter knowledge, but who could not decode nonwords, learned to read acronyms that were phonetically close to their target pronunciation (for example, 'bvr' for *beaver*) more quickly than those that were phonetically distant (for example, 'bzr' for *beaver*). Both sets of findings support the idea that children establish links between spoken words and words in their early sight vocabulary, without resorting to the use of letter–sound translation rules.

The third phase in Ehri's scheme involves well-specified mappings between the letters in printed words and the phonemes in spoken words. Since the orthographic representations for words are fully specified in this phase, children no longer make the errors characteristic of phonetic-cue reading. Ehri saw the transition between the second and third phases as gradual and quantitative rather than qualitative in nature.

Learning to Spell

Although most models of literacy development allude to the development of spelling, the majority of evidence used to support them comes from children's reading. It is important to discuss spelling development in its own right because the view that it is simply the converse of reading is mistaken. Furthermore, spelling poses much more of a problem to dyslexic people than does reading, where compensatory strategies can more easily be brought to bear.

Children's early scribblings suggest that they have an idea of how print should look before they know any letters. Like early reading, early writing may serve to establish the function of the medium to convey messages. As soon as children learn the names of letters, the nature of their writing changes and they begin to use letter-name knowledge to construct simple words. Good examples are 'gnys' for *genius* (Bissex, 1980) and 'efnch' for *adventure*. At first, children might only write one letter to represent a salient sound in a word, for example 's' for *dress*, or 'l' for *elevator*. Next it is typical for boundary sounds to be used although medial sounds are still ignored, as in 'bk' for *back* or 'mp' for *map* (Ehri, 1985). Later, semiphonetic spelling errors occur in children's transcriptions of more difficult words. Commonly consonant clusters are reduced, as in the spellings of 'fez' for *friends* 'hep' for *help* and 'tet' for *tent* (Reed, 1971), and sometimes the features of consonants that signal whether or not they are voiced are confused, for example, the phonemes [p] and [b] are often substituted in spelling: 'plousis' for *blouses*, 'bobe' for *bumpy*, as are [f] and [v]: 'tref' for *twelve*.

Linguistic considerations account for the particular way in which clusters are simplified in spelling. Nasals ([n] or [m]) that follow vowels cause young children particular difficulty. These represent an interesting case because, from a phonetic point of view, it is the vowel in words such as *bank* and *bump* that is perceived as nasalized although the orthographic convention requires writing the consonant 'n' or 'm'. Snowling (1982) showed that nasal consonants which follow vowels are more likely to be omitted from clusters in which the final consonant is unvoiced, for example, writing *bent* as 'bet', than when the final consonant is voiced, as in *bend*.

The important point made by these examples is that the spoken language system, and the child's awareness of it, influences the acquisition of spelling. Changes in the child's ability to decompose syllables into phonemes makes a significant contribution to the proficiency of their spelling. By the close of what has been described as the alphabetic phase, the child can spell with complete phonetic accuracy. However, in an opaque orthography such as English that contains many exceptions that do not follow sound–spelling rules, there is still much to be learned before orthography is mastered.

By far the most extensive study of young children's spelling development was carried out by Treiman (1993), who examined changes in children's free writing during their first year in school. Treiman's detailed analyses confirm that, from the outset, children rely heavily upon phonology, soon replacing the strategy of spelling by letter names with that of spelling using letter sounds while continuing to delete specific parts of words that are difficult for them to segment. Contrary to a stage-like conceptualization of learning to spell, Treiman also showed that children are sensitive to orthographic conventions from a very early stage. Thus, they rarely violate constraints on the positions of graphemic patterns in spellings; they might spell *cake* as *kack*, but never as *ckak*. They also soon come to understand that morphemes such as *ed* are spelled consistently, irrespective of their pronunciation. So, *jumped* which ends with the sound [t] is spelled the same at the end as *liked* which ends with the sound [d].

Impressive evidence of children's sensitivity to morphological constraints comes from their spelling of 'flaps'. A 'flap' is the phonetic term for the pronunciation of the medial consonant in words such as *dirty* and *attic* in American English. The phonetic value of the 't' is in each case [d]. Treiman, Cassar and Zukowski (1994) showed that kindergarteners produced more correct spellings of words containing flaps if the flap signalled a morphological boundary (as in *dirt + y*) than when it did not (as in *attic*), indicating a sensitivity to the word's morphological constituents.

Nunes, Bryant and Bindman (1997a and b) documented children's increasing command over orthographic conventions. In a three-year investigation of children's spelling of morphemes, they showed that children first generalize their knowledge of the regular past tense ending '*ed*' to irregular verbs, before over-generalizing it to 'non-verbs', for example *soft → sofed*; *next → nexed*. Importantly, children's mastery of the proper usage of '*ed*' was predicted by their performance on morpho-syntactic awareness tasks six months earlier. One of these tasks required children to make word analogies ('heal is to healthy as wealth is to ——?'), and the other involved sentence analogies ('Tom helps Mary. Tom helped Mary. Tom sees Mary. Tom —— Mary?'). Thus, children's ability to represent grammatical distinctions in spelling appears to be related to their grasp of these distinctions in spoken language.

Taken together, the evidence from studies of the development of spelling indicates that exposure to written language through reading is not enough to ensure proficient spelling. Rather, phonological skills are required together with attention to the meaning and syntactic functions of words in the spoken language. It follows that children's spelling difficulties will best be understood in relation to impairments of their underlying language system.

Longitudinal Studies of Learning to Read and Spell

The demonstration that phonology provides a foundation for ortho-graphic representations can be taken as evidence for a link between phonological development and the acquisition of literacy. One of the most influential longitudinal studies examining the relationship between children's early phonological skills and their later reading achievement was conducted by Bradley and Bryant (1983). This study followed the progress of some 400 children from 4 to 8 years of age.

At the beginning of the study, each child was administered three sound categorization tasks, two requiring the detection of rime oddity, one the detection of alliteration in strings of three words. Their memory span for these word strings and their vocabulary was also measured. Four years later, the reading and spelling skills of these children were assessed and their attainments related to their earlier performance on the tests of sound categorization. There was a strong relationship between the children's phonological awareness at 4 years and their reading and spelling achievement at 8, even when the substantial effects of IQ, memory and social class were controlled. Moreover, the relationship between phonological awareness and literacy development was specific – individual differences in phonological awareness at 4 years did not predict mathematical performance at 6, so it was not simply a predictor of general academic achievement.

At around the same time, Lundberg and colleagues (Lundberg, Olofsson and Wall, 1980) reported some of the first evidence of the universality of these findings from a cross-linguistic perspective. One of the interesting features of the work of Lundberg's group is that it had been undertaken in Scandinavia where, at the time, reading instruction did not begin until the age of 7 years. It was, therefore, possible to assess phonological awareness in individuals who were cognitively mature but (unlike British or American pre-schoolers) had not yet begun to read. The criticism that metalinguistic tasks place heavy cognitive demands on pre-school children cannot be levelled against these studies. Nonetheless, the strong relationship between phonological awareness prior to literacy instruction and subsequent reading achievement was replicated. It is a robust finding that has since been confirmed by a large number of studies (Byrne and Fielding-Barnsley, 1989; Ellis and Large, 1987; Share, Jorm, Maclean and Matthews, 1984; Stanovich, Cunningham and Cramer, 1984; Tunmer and Nesdale, 1985).

However, it needs to be borne in mind that the relationship between phonological skills and reading development is not unidirectional (Morais, 1991). Rather, reading plays a reciprocal role in promoting phonological awareness (Cataldo and Ellis, 1988; Perfetti, Beck, Bell and Hughes, 1987) and, as soon as children start to learn to read, this experience alters the way in which they represent the speech sounds of spoken words. In a striking example of this, Ehri and Wilce (1980) showed that although the words *pitch* and *rich* each contain three phonemes, adults think that *pitch* contains an extra [t] sound because it contains the letter 't'. Similarly, Seidenberg and Tannenhaus (1979) showed that it takes longer to judge that *ache* and *lake* rhyme than *take* and *lake* because they have different orthographic representations.

The Structure of Phonological Abilities

Since the strong relationship between phonological awareness and learning to read has been established, researchers have turned their attention to the more specific question of which phonological skills are causally related to reading. This question turns on the structure of phonological abilities and remains debated. Whilst some authors have argued that phonological skills are the reflection of a single underlying ability (Bowey, 1996; Stanovich, Cunningham and Cramer, 1984; Wagner and Torgesen, 1987), others have argued for separable, though related, phonological ability factors (Hoien, Lundberg, Stanovich and Bjaalid 1995; Lundberg, Frost and Petersen, 1988; Yopp, 1988).

Muter, Hulme, Snowling and Taylor (1998) found that two independent factors accounted for performance on phonological awareness tasks in 4- to 6-year-old children. The first factor, Segmentation, received loadings from syllable and phoneme tasks, and the second factor, Rhyme, accounted for performance in rhyme detection and rhyme production. Segmentation was a better predictor of reading performance than Rhyme in this group of children, both concurrently and longitudinally. A follow-up study carried out when these children were 9 years old indicated that early segmentation ability predicted reading outcome through reading at 6, and also made an independent contribution to the development of spelling skill at 9 years (Muter and Snowling, 1998a and b).

Wagner, Torgesen, Laughan, Simmons and Rashotte (1993) proposed a more differentiated structure of phonological abilities after administering an extensive battery of phonological tasks to a group of kindergarten and second-grade children. The tasks included four phonological analysis tasks, namely, phoneme elision, where the child is required to repeat a word and then to say what would be left after a phoneme has been removed, phoneme segmentation, rime oddity, and first sound categorization; and three phonological synthesis tasks, namely blending of the onset-rime components of words, blending phonemes into words, and blending phonemes into nonwords.

As well as these measures of explicit phonological awareness, implicit processing was measured using working memory, discrete naming of isolated digits and letters and serial rapid naming tasks. The use of a technique known as confirmatory factor analysis uncovered four correlated phonological ability factors among kindergarten children. These were Analysis/Working Memory, Synthesis, Isolated Naming and Serial Naming.

Wagner, Torgesen and Rashotte (1994) went on to investigate the predictive validity of these factors in a longitudinal study of 244 children from kindergarten to second grade. Each of the phonological factors predicted children's later success in learning to read; however, they were redundant with respect to each other. Thus, in analyses of the simultaneous influence of these variables, only phonological analysis influenced first-grade reading, and only phonological synthesis influenced second-grade reading.

Although it is informative, factor analysis is an imperfect tool for analysing the nature of the phonological skills that support reading development. In addition to the methodological difficulties associated with studies that vary in sample size and use tests that vary in their reliability, it is important to be aware that the structure to be uncovered depends on the types of task used to assess component skills. Underlying much of the work on phonological skills and learning to read has been the implicit assumption that the key to reading development lies in performance on metaphonological tasks – tasks that require children to reflect consciously on the structure of spoken words. An alternative view that is gaining precedence, as we saw in chapter 3, is that such tasks are merely indirect tests of how the brain represents phonology, in short, of underlying phonological representations (Fowler, 1991; Snowling and Hulme, 1994). It follows that children who do well on tests of phonological awareness have access to well-specified representations, in contrast to those who have difficulties at a representational level (Elbro, 1996; Hulme and Snowling, 1992). This brings us full circle to the deficits that underlie dyslexia.

The role of letter knowledge

Another powerful predictor of reading achievement is letter knowledge: how many letter names or sounds a child knows (Bond and Dykstra, 1967; Chall, 1967). While there is some evidence that children's letter knowledge interacts with their segmentation skills to promote reading and spelling development (Muter, Hulme, Snowling and Taylor, 1998), how best to understand its role remains unclear.

There is no doubt that knowledge of letter names or sounds provides an important foundation for children's reading and spelling development. At the simplest level, children who already know their letters have less to acquire on the road to literacy (Adams, 1990). More specifically, decoding or writing a new word requires some translation between letters and sounds, and children require knowledge of letter sounds to create mappings between the orthographic representations of words and their phonological forms (Ehri, 1992; Rack, Hulme, Snowling and Wightman, 1994). What is not clear is why some children learn letters before others. Undoubtedly, the literacy environment in a child's home is an important factor, and some children are taught letters at nursery school while others are not. It is also possible that children with good phonological skills have a greater capacity to learn the names and sounds of letters. If this is the case, then the predictive relationship between letter knowledge and reading may be just an example of a more general relationship between phonological learning ability and learning to read (Windfuhr and Snowling, submitted).

Connectionist Models of Learning to Read

An implicit assumption in many discussions of reading development and dyslexia is that children have at their disposal two strategies for reading words: a direct or visual strategy that they use to read familiar words, and a phonological strategy for reading unfamiliar words that fall outside of their sight vocabulary. This idea has its origins in dual-route models of reading (Coltheart, 1978). However, more recent developmental models, such as that of Ehri (1995), have moved away from thinking of the child as learning to use separate reading systems. Rather, Ehri's model embraces the notion that a single orthographic system evolves over time, shaped by children's experience with print in interaction with their underlying phonological representations (cf. Brown, 1997; Goswami, 1986; Metsala, Stanovich and Brown, 1998).

Another way of conceptualizing reading development has been within a set of models typically referred to as connectionist or parallel distributed processing (PDP) models. The development of PDP models has offered a new framework within which to interpret and explain a wide range of human cognitive phenomena, including aspects of child language acquisition, speech production, memory and reading (McClelland, 1988). The models are implemented as computer simulations and therefore they have to be computationally explicit. Although they are not programmed with rules, they abstract statistical regularities from the information they are presented with and exhibit rule-like behaviour. Models of this sort offer an excellent metaphor for the processes involved in learning to read. However, it must be borne in mind that such models do not set out to capture conscious reading strategies that readers may adopt. Nor do they allow for the different ways in which specific teaching interventions might affect the process of learning.

Consider again for a moment the process of learning to read. Setting up a reading system requires children to learn how letter strings map onto sequences of phonemes. At the same time, the normal child abstracts the relationships between single letters or letter groups (graphemes) and phonemes. This is, in effect, a process similar to that implemented in connectionist models. The essential feature of these models is that representations of words are distributed across many simple processing elements in input and output systems. These elements gradually become associated with each other just as during reading acquisition children gradually learn the associations between letter strings in written inputs and sequences of phonemes in spoken outputs. Part of the problem in learning a language such as English is that these mappings are not entirely consistent, although they are far from arbitrary. Children, like adults, are sensitive to the quasi-regularity of English spelling (Treiman, Mullenix, Bijeljac-Babic and Richmond-Welty, 1995). As a consequence, they learn to read regular words more easily than exceptions and retain this advantage as fluent readers. By comparison, languages such as German and Italian are much more consistent in their mappings from spelling to sound. Not surprisingly, children appear to find learning to read in these languages easier than in English (Cossu, 1999; Wimmer, 1996).

A critical feature of PDP models which makes them ideally suited to the study of development is that they can learn (Plunkett, Karmiloff-Smith, Bates, Elman and Johnson, 1997). Learning is based upon simple associative principles. When patterns have been associated previously, this is recorded by weighting the links between units or 'connections'. Hence, connections that are activated frequently accrue larger weights or connection strengths. As a consequence, they pass on activation more strongly to the units to which they provide input. Before learning begins, the majority of connections between elements in the model are not associated. This naive state is modelled by setting the weights on the connections to random values. Next, during a training phase, the weights are gradually altered according to a formula called a learning algorithm. This learning algorithm essentially has the role of reducing the error between the activation across the input units and the activation computed across the output units. In other words, it makes the model behave more accurately.

In summary, the knowledge that a PDP model acquires during the course of associating strings of graphemes and phonemes is stored as weights on connections. This knowledge base can be drawn upon when the model is faced with a new word. Effectively then, the knowledge within connectionist networks generalizes. With respect to reading, there is no need to posit a separate system for processing new or novel items. This is particularly relevant for the development of the reading system because a crucial 'self-teaching device' (Share, 1995) is inherent in the architecture of the models.

Seidenberg and McClelland's framework

The most influential word recognition model of this sort was proposed by Seidenberg and McClelland (1989). This 'triangle' model contained sets of representations dealing with orthographic, phonological and semantic information, interconnected by sets of hidden units as shown in figure 4.4. However, the part of the model first implemented (referred to here as SM89) was a three-layer network with orthographic input and phonological output units connected by a set of intermediate or 'hidden' units (depicted in bold in the figure).

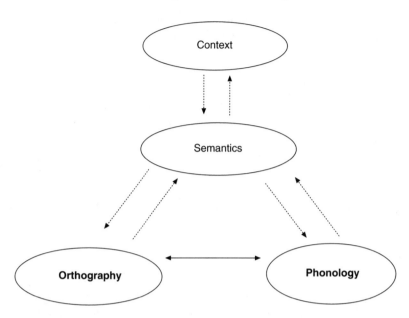

Figure 4.4 The framework for single-word processing from Seidenberg and McClelland (1989)

The SM89 model is a network that learns to associate letter strings with pronunciations. The letter strings are coded as activations distributed across orthographic units in the input layer, connected to phonological units in the output layer via a set of 'hidden' units. In the orthographic layer, graphemes are encoded as sets of triples, so that each individual item is represented flanked by its immediate neighbours. For example, the word *net* is represented as_*ne*, *net*, *et_*. In the phonological layer, phonemes are also encoded using triples of phonetic features (for example, stop, vowel, fricative). Any word containing such an ordered sequence of features in its phonemes will activate this unit. For any word presented there will be many units activated in the input units, and many units activated in the output representations. The important point, however, is that the *pattern* of activation across these units will be unique for each word.

The SM89 model was trained on a corpus containing the majority of English single-syllable words. At the beginning of learning, the weights on the connections were random; these were gradually altered using a learning procedure called the *back propagation* algorithm. On each trial, presentation of a letter string was converted into a pattern of activation across the orthographic units that was fed to the hidden units and on to the phonological units. There was also feedback to the orthographic input units from the hidden unit layer, but not from the phonological output units. Thus, the model had two sources of output for a given letter string, one at the orthographic layer, and one across the units in the phonological layer. These two output scores were compared to the desired outputs to provide an error score. The learning rule then altered the weights on the connections to reduce this error score so that the model's output and the desired output were gradually brought into line. It is possible to think of this in effect as the model 'learning' to read the words in the training corpus.

An additional feature of the training is that words were presented to the model in proportion to their frequency of occurrence in the English language. This strategy mimics the fact that readers encounter some words more frequently than others, and affords the model more chance of learning highly frequent than infrequent words.

The SM89 model simulated several aspects of human word recognition. Following the training regime, performance on the trained words had reached a high level. All of the trained words were then presented to the model to provide what might be considered an 'assessment of its reading skill'. The performance of the model could then be compared against data from experiments involving human participants.

The model showed the classic effects of word frequency and spelling–sound regularity on reading accuracy, even though it did not have an inbuilt system of 'rules'. It read high-frequency words (on which it had been more extensively trained) better than low-frequency words, and it read regular words better than exception words. Such regularity effects were larger in low-frequency words than in high-frequency words. These findings are important: they indicate that the classic effects of frequency and regularity derive from the same source, and they reflect statistical regularities in the relationship between orthography and phonology. Furthermore, the effects can be simulated in a single system that has neither a lexicon nor letter–sound translation rules.

A critical feature of this model, and others like it, is that after training to associate many input patterns (written words) with output patterns (spoken words), it was able to generalize to words it had not been explicitly taught to read, including nonwords. Whilst on the one hand the behaviour of the SM89 model was impressive, it was not without its critics. Foremost among them were Besner, Twilley, McCann and Seergobin (1990) who pointed out that, whilst the model could recognize 97 per cent of words from the training set at the end of learning, it produced correct pronunciations for only 70–75 per cent of nonwords. This level of performance was much less good than would be typical of normal adult performance; it could read words well, but its nonword reading was far from perfect.

The structure of the model's phonological representations was also a concern for quite different, conceptual reasons. Hulme, Snowling and Quinlan (1991) noted that the model's phonological representations at the start of learning were unstructured. As we have seen, this state of affairs is quite unlike that of the child coming to the task of learning to read, who ideally will have segmentally organized representations. From the point of view of reading acquisition, then, the implemented SM89 model fell short of psychological plausibility, though the framework offered a very fruitful approach to the study of reading development.

A 'second generation' model within the same general framework was proposed by Plaut, McClelland, Seidenberg and Patterson (1996). Importantly, this revised model overcame the problems that had limited the ability of SM89 to read novel letter strings. Essentially, the representation of each element in the letter or phoneme string was dependent on its local context because triples of features were coded. This meant, for example, that the knowledge that 't' maps to the phoneme [t] was dispersed across the different units activated by the words, such as *top*, *step*, *lit*. In the same way that children do not immediately abstract phoneme invariance from their encounters with print (Byrne and Fielding-Barnsley, 1989), this feature affected the model's ability to 'decode'. To overcome this limitation, Plaut et al. (1996) adopted a form of representation that contained the phonemes and graphemes as entities, rather than as triplets of features. When tested on nonword reading, the Plaut et al. (1996) model out-performed SM89, with performance approximating that of adult readers. Thus, as anticipated, the improved forms of representation led to better generalization to nonword stimuli. This is important from the point of view of reading development. As predicted by developmental theories,

85

generalization within the reading system was better when training began with well-structured representations. By analogy, children learn to read most effectively when they come to the task with well-specified phonological representations and they demonstrate this by performing well on tests of phonological awareness.

The role of semantics in learning to read

Although few would deny that the aim of reading is to extract meaning from printed words, it is surprising that the majority of models of reading development have been silent regarding the role of semantics in the learning process. It is an everyday observation that children will tend to read concrete words, such as *sun* and *frog*, but may confuse words that are equally easy from a decoding point of view, such as *him* or *from*. The difference is that the latter words are abstract, their semantic representations are not well specified and it seems that, without this 'hook' to hang them on, they can be difficult to learn. In line with this observation, Laing and Hulme (1999) showed that beginning readers found learning to read acronyms for words easier if their referents were spoken words of high rather than of low imageability.

A similar criticism could be levelled at the SM89 implementation, which did not deal with meaning. However, Seidenberg and McClelland (1989) did note that a semantic mechanism would need to be implemented in order to describe the reading process fully. More recent models of this type have attempted to implement a system of semantic representation, notably that of Plaut et al. (1996). We will go into details of this model later. Suffice it to say that the models of reading development we have discussed have focused on the creation of mappings between orthography and phonology and have not taken account of the role of semantics in this process. We have seen that children's reading development is heavily dependent upon their phonological skills. While there remains debate about the structure of phonological abilities and particularly about the mechanism through which phonology influences orthographic development, it is generally accepted that there is a causal relationship between phonological skills and reading ability. In chapter 11, we will return to the issue of semantics and in particular, how semantic resources may bootstrap learning to read.

Chapter 5

Dyslexia: A Written Language Disorder

The models of literacy development that we have reviewed all carry the assumption that phonological skills play a critical role in learning to read. While it might be possible to learn to read and write in logographic scripts, such as Chinese, without recourse to such skills (but see Ho and Bryant, 1997), phonological awareness acts as a catalyst to the development of decoding skills in English children (Byrne, 1998), and spelling proficiency also hinges on it (Treiman, 1993).

In this light, it is inevitable that the dyslexic child who comes to the task of learning to read with poorly developed phonological skills will encounter problems. In this chapter we discuss the effects of a phonological deficit on the course of reading and spelling development.

Why is Reading Difficult for the Dyslexic Child?

One of the basic tasks the child confronts in learning to read is to set up a system of links between print and sound that exploits the alphabetic principle. The alphabetic principle is crucial to the development of proficient reading skills because it provides the child with a 'self-teaching' device that enables them to decode unfamiliar words (Jorm and Share, 1983; Share, 1995). A child who understands the alphabetic principle, and who has learned to read *hat* and *fin*, can abstract the correspondences between the letters and the sounds in these words. This process will provide them with implicit knowledge of the alphabetic mappings $h \rightarrow$ [h], $a \rightarrow$ [a], $t \rightarrow$ [t], $f \rightarrow$ [f], $i \rightarrow$ [i] and $n \rightarrow$ [n] and allow them to read letter strings they have not seen before, such as *hit, fat, fan, tan*. In a reciprocal fashion, alphabetic skills can be used to spell simple words that conform to consistent phoneme–grapheme rules.

As we have seen, the abstraction of alphabetic mappings requires the child to be aware of the phonemic segments of spoken words (Byrne, 1998). Given the phonological deficits seen in dyslexic children, it follows that they should be at least slow, and at worst fail, to develop alphabetic skills. Frith (1985) put this simply when she stated that, in its classic form, dyslexia represents 'arrest at the logographic phase of development'; children who do not have the requisite phonological skills do not make the normal transition into the alphabetic phase. As we will show, this does not mean they will fail to read altogether; they may learn to read a large number of words 'by sight' by expanding the logographic lexicon (Seymour and Evans, 1994).

From the perspective of connectionism, there is an alternative way of framing the dyslexic child's reading problem. According to this view, children who come to the task of learning to read with well-specified phonological representations can develop a rich network of connections between orthography and phonology. But dyslexic children who have deficits at the level of phonological representations face the task of trying to read from a foundation that is not optimal for the creation of orthography–phonology mappings. By default, the dyslexic child has to create 'coarse-grained' mappings that are adequate for the establishment of associations between whole words and their pronunciations but does not support the development of fine-grained links between grapheme and phoneme sequences. In other words, they do not allow the child to generate a self-teaching device. The obvious consequence is that dyslexic children will have difficulty decoding words they have not encountered before.

It is worth pausing for a moment at this point to reflect on the performance of SM89, the connectionist model of reading that we have already discussed. It will be recalled that, following training on words, this model was poorer at reading nonwords than a proficient adult reader because its powers of generalization were limited. In short, its nonword reading ability was out of line with its reading skill. This pattern of performance is precisely what is predicted for dyslexic children who have to learn to read with poorly specified phonological representations.

The limited nonword reading skill of SM89 was traced to a problem with the representational scheme used in the 'input' and 'output' units. In concrete terms, having learned $p \rightarrow$ [p] from *pat*, this knowledge did not help the model to pronounce the *p* in *cap* where it appeared in a different position. Given the phonological deficit in dyslexia, this is just the kind of problem a dyslexic child is likely to experience; a dyslexic child who learns to pronounce *pat* as 'pat' will, when faced with *cap*, have to learn this anew.

Nonword Reading Skills in Dyslexia

The most direct way of assessing a child's decoding skill is by asking them to read nonwords they have not encountered before, such as *tegsib, nalsnop*. In 1980, Snowling (1980) investigated how children's nonword reading skills developed as their reading age increased. This cross-sectional study involved dyslexic children with severe reading impairments who attended a hospital reading clinic. At the time they were studied, they were reading at between the 7- and the 10-year levels of ability and their performance was compared with that of normally developing children who were matched on the basis of a single-word reading test (RA-controls).

The paradigm chosen was nonword matching. The letter strings were all single-syllable nonwords containing four letters, corresponding to either three (*torp*) or four (*sint*) phonemes. Successive stimuli were presented without a delay either visually (in print) or auditorily (spoken) and the children had to decide if they were the same or different. If they were different, the difference was subtle and involved transposing the middle two letters (for example, *torp* $\rightarrow$ *trop*; *sint* $\rightarrow$ *snit*).

Altogether there were four conditions in the experiment requiring matching between the auditory and the visual forms of words. Importantly, the dyslexic and normal readers did not differ in the two within-modality conditions. For present purposes, the condition of most interest was the one in which a visual string had to be matched to a spoken form, a task requiring nonword decoding although a spoken response was not required.

Performance on this visual–auditory matching condition improved as reading age increased in the normal readers (figure 5.1). This is just

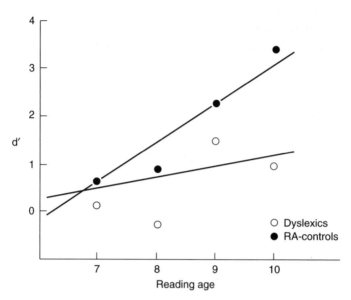

Figure 5.1 Recognition of visually presented nonwords in the auditory modality (d′) by dyslexic and normal readers according to reading age. Performance of the control but not the dyslexic group increases with reading age

Source: drawn from Snowling, 1980

as expected if learning to read is accompanied by an increase in phonological reading strategies. In marked contrast, dyslexic children showed little improvement in nonword reading as their reading skill developed. It seemed that the dyslexic children were learning to read in an atypical way by building their sight vocabulary without also developing their decoding skills. As in the SM89 model, the knowledge gained from learning to read words had not generalized to reading novel words. An alternative explanation was possible, however. Perhaps the dyslexics *were* able to use phonological reading strategies, but not at the speed required of them for nonword matching in this experiment.

To tease apart the two alternative explanations of the results, a second experiment examined nonword reading in dyslexic readers who varied in reading skill (Snowling, 1981). The better dyslexic readers and their controls were reading at around the 9-year level; the poorer readers were reading at the 7-year level. This time the phonological complexity of the nonwords was manipulated so that half contained one and half contained two syllables. Within each syllable there were up to two consonants clusters. The children read the nonwords aloud and the time it took them to do this was measured.

In line with the findings of the previous experiment, the dyslexic readers were both slower and more error prone than their controls when reading the nonwords aloud. A new finding was that phonological complexity affected performance: dyslexics did not differ from RA-controls on the one-syllable nonwords but they did on the two-syllable ones. It was clear that the dyslexic readers could use phonological reading strategies to some extent provided there were no time constraints, and this time, there was an improvement in nonword reading skill with reading age.

More recently, we carried out a longitudinal study in which we followed the progress of dyslexic and normal readers for two years (Snowling, Goulandris and Defty, 1996). At the beginning of the study, the children were matched pairwise for reading age. At this stage the dyslexics, who were much older than the controls and had benefited from remedial help, were also marginally better in nonword reading. Two years later, the picture was dramatically different: the dyslexic children showed nonword reading impairments; their phonological reading skills had not kept pace with development.

It should be noted before proceeding that there have been a number of failures to replicate the findings of nonword reading difficulties in dyslexia (Beech and Harding, 1984; Johnston, 1982; Treiman and Hirsh-Pasek, 1985). Rack, Snowling and Olson (1992) suggested possible reasons for these discrepant findings, including variations in IQ between dyslexic and normal reader groups, differences among studies in the age of the dyslexic children tested, the teaching the dyslexic children had received and the difficulty of the nonwords used.

To examine the role of these various factors systematically, van Ijzendoorn and Bus (1994) carried out a meta-analysis of 16 studies of the nonword deficit. Meta-analysis is a technique that can be used to pool the results from several studies, some of which may lack the 'statistical power' necessary to detect group differences in performance. In line with the hypotheses of Rack et al., variations in IQ between dyslexic and normal readers in different studies was a factor determining whether or not a group difference emerged. This interesting finding suggests dyslexic children may develop different reading strategies depending upon their IQ level. A related point was that although the age of the dyslexics tested did not seem to matter, the discrepancy between their age and reading level did suggest that the more severely disabled readers had greater difficulties with nonword reading. In contrast, whether or not they had received intervention did not explain differences in 'effect size' between studies, nor did the type of nonword stimuli used. Overall, however, there was strong evidence that dyslexic children had a nonword reading deficit, which led van Ijzendoorn and Bus (1994) to conclude that 'more than 400 studies with null results would have to be available to bring the combined probability level [of finding the nonword deficit] down to insignificance' (p. 274).

The Regularity Effect in Dyslexia

It is worth reflecting at this point on the probable consequences of the nonword reading deficit in dyslexia for subsequent reading development. A considerable amount of empirical research on dyslexic reading has been conducted within the dual-route framework of reading in which words can be read visually via a direct route to meaning and pronunciation or phonologically via the application of grapheme–phoneme rules (Coltheart, 1978). Within this framework, regular words can be read either by the direct or the phonological route, giving them a processing advantage over irregular words that can only be read by the direct route.

Connectionist formulations of reading reject the notion that regular and irregular words are processed by different sub-systems of reading. Rather, these models are sensitive to the statistical regularities inherent in the orthography of the words on which they are trained. The connection strengths for patterns that occur frequently are therefore greater than for those that occur less frequently, and it is this that leads to regularity and consistency effects in reading.

The finding that regular words are read more easily than irregular words is robust throughout development and characterizes adults' reading of low-frequency but not high-frequency words. One critical difference between regular and irregular words is the consistency of their rime units; orthographic rimes with a single pronunciation (for

92

example, -*ain*) are processed more easily than those where more than one pronunciation can be given to the same letter string (for example, -*eak*) (Backman, Bruck, Hèbert and Seidenberg, 1984; Coltheart and Leahy, 1992; Laxon, Masterson and Moran, 1994). Thus, Treiman, Mullenix, Bijeljac-Babic and Richmond-Welty (1995) examined 6- to 11-year-olds' reading of 56 words varying in the consistency of their rime units (for example, the *eak* in *break*) and in their onset-vowel strings (for example, the *bre* in *break*). Performance on this task improved with age from first grade onwards and, although children's reading was affected by rime consistency, there was no significant effect of onset-vowel consistency.

Within the dual-route framework it has been usual to infer that a difficulty in reading novel words will slow down the expansion of a sight vocabulary. In short, if dyslexic children do not possess a 'self-teaching device', then the development of word recognition in these children will be compromised. In fact, the only option would be for all words to be learned 'visually' (using the 'direct' route), and as a consequence, dyslexics should show no advantage for reading regular words that can be handled by both visual and phonological strategies (the direct and indirect routes) over irregular words that must be learned using the visual reading system (the direct route).

Within the connectionist framework, however, the nonword reading deficit in dyslexia cannot be considered a 'cause' of the word reading impairment. Rather, the difficulty in reading nonwords marks the failure of the reading system to generalize the knowledge it has gained from associating the orthographic strings within words with their pronunciations. The nonword reading deficit is therefore a consequence of other limitations in the system, most likely an effect of having developed coarse-coded mappings (Brown, 1997). It follows from this that provided dyslexic readers set up mappings between printed and spoken words that vary in the consistency of their spelling-sound components, there is no reason for them to be less sensitive to a word's regularity than normal readers with the same amount of reading experience.

Some of the early studies of dyslexic reading suggested that the regularity effect was reduced in dyslexic children (Frith and Snowling, 1983). However, studies that used words carefully selected to control for relevant variables such as frequency, concreteness and age of acquisition failed to replicate these findings (Brown and Watson,

1991). Moreover, a recent meta-analysis reviewing 17 studies of the regularity effect in dyslexia has confirmed that dyslexic readers are generally just as sensitive to the effects of orthographic regularity as controls matched for reading level (Metsala, Stanovich and Brown, 1998).

The finding of a normal regularity effect alongside deficient nonword reading skills in dyslexia is important. It tells us that, although the dyslexic reading system is characterized by problems of generalization, it learns in the normal way. Nonetheless this is a little surprising. After all, dyslexic children have phonological learning difficulties (as exemplified by their poor paired associate learning). Learning to map orthographic onto phonological forms is a prima facie example of paired associate learning. So how can their reading of regular and exception words be normal?

It turns out that this is not such a conundrum. To understand the apparent contradiction, it is important to remember that in the experiments demonstrating the regularity effect among dyslexic readers, the comparison group has been RA-matched controls some years younger than the dyslexics. Therefore, it is not the case that dyslexic readers learn specific print–sound associations at the same rate as normal readers. A second point is that learning to read is supported by vocabulary knowledge to a larger extent than is sometimes acknowledged. This top-down influence on single word reading almost certainly helps children to achieve a pronunciation for words they can only partially decode (Share, 1995). To take an example, when faced with the new word *postage* it is likely that a child will decode this as 'post-age'. A child with a good vocabulary will quickly reject this response, refining it to settle the correct pronunciation 'postage'.

To pursue this idea, we presented children with nonwords to read aloud either with or without context (Pring and Snowling, 1986). The nonwords were all *pseudohomophones* that when read aloud sounded like words, for example *nirse*, *nite*. The choice of these nonwords allowed us to construct pairs that were either presented preceded by a word that provided a semantic cue (for example, *doctor–nirse*) or by an unrelated prime (for example, *doctor–nite*). We also included control pairs in which the nonwords were preceded by a neutral string of crosses (for example, *xxxx–nirse*; *xxxx–nite*; JM's perfomance in this same experiment is discussed on p. 9 above).

Like JM, all of the children we tested benefited from the availability of the semantic cue, and particularly the less proficient readers.

This finding might be interpreted as indicating that semantic activation 'pushed' the pronunciation of the nonword towards the level required for a response to be made. In the same experiment, we had included nonwords differing in their 'word-likeness' to assess the effect of graphemic complexity on performance. The nonwords chosen differed either by one or by two graphemes from their targets (following Taft, 1982). Thus *nurce* differed from the target *nurse* by a single grapheme (*se → ce*) whereas *nirce* differs by two graphemes (*se → ce*; *ur → ir*). We called these '1g' and '2g' items respectively; the 1g items were closer to the words they were based on than the 2g items.

The first finding of interest was that 1g nonwords were read more easily than 2g items. This is what would be expected on the basis of a connectionist account; generalization to novel words containing similar spelling–sound relationships would be better because the connection strengths would be greater. However, the availability of a semantic cue facilitated the decoding of 2g items more than 1g items.

The most straightforward interpretation of this finding is that, when decoding is slow, the child draws upon the support of vocabulary knowledge to facilitate the reading of novel words. This need not be a conscious strategy though sometimes it is. We would suggest that our experiment artificially mimicked the process through the provision of semantic cues.

The tendency of young readers to use semantic support to facilitate decoding highlights the interactive nature of the reading process, particularly in the early stages of development (Stanovich, 1980). It also has implications for an understanding of dyslexia. Dyslexic children have difficulties in reading nonwords, yet they are still sensitive to orthographic consistencies, as revealed by the regularity effect. It seems likely that at least part of the explanation for this unusual dissociation is that their word reading benefits from semantic support. Just as the reading deficit in dyslexia can be traced to poorly specified phonological representations, the availability of well-specified semantic representations may provide a vital compensatory strategy for them. A knock-on effect, much less discussed, is that if dyslexic readers continue to read using large orthographic units, not only will their nonword reading suffer but also their phonological representations will tend to remain global rather than becoming segmental in form.

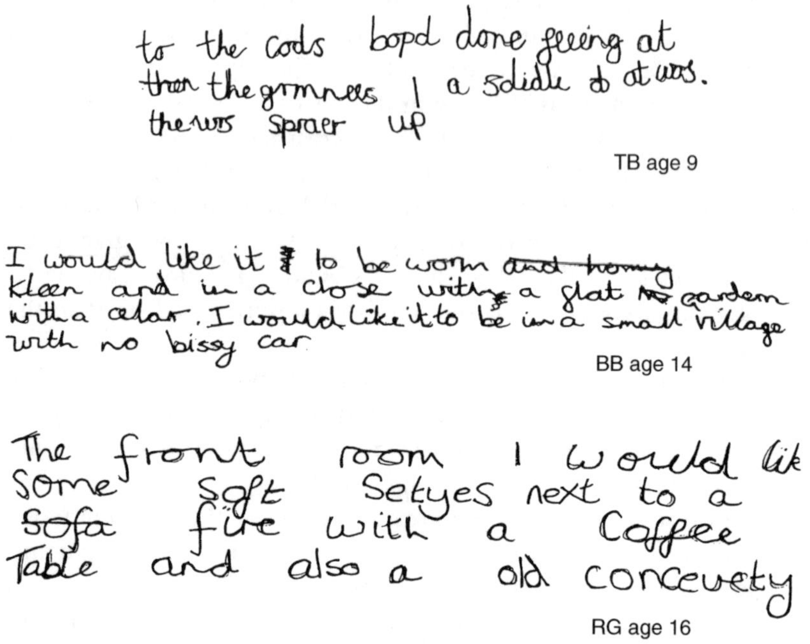

to the cods bopd done feeeng at
ther the grmnces | a sdidle d at wos.
the wos spraer up

TB age 9

I would like it to be worm and hommy
kleen and in a close with a glat no garden
with a celar. I would like it to be in a small village
with no bissy car

BB age 14

The front room I would lik
Some soft setyes next to a
sofa fire with a coffee
Table and also a old conceuety

RG age 16

Figure 5.2 Spelling in free writing by three dyslexic children from the same family

Spelling in Dyslexia

Although dyslexic children are sensitive to the statistical regularities of the orthography, their ability to deal with its inconsistencies when spelling words is almost always impaired. From the earliest stages of learning to spell, children who have difficulty reflecting on the sound structure of words will be disadvantaged, and in the absence of a firm foundation in phonology, the acquisition of orthographic knowledge is compromised. Figure 5.2 shows extracts from the writing of three dyslexic children from the same family. All of the children had phono-logical problems, and, although they differed in age when assessed, it can be seen that they all had severe spelling difficulties. Indeed, one of the very significant and persisting consequences of a phonological processing deficit is a difficulty with spelling (Bruck, 1990).

To aid discussion of the spelling difficulties associated with dyslexia, it is useful to begin with a simple task analysis. As we saw earlier, children take their first steps into spelling by writing down the sounds they perceive in spoken words. Strong sounds are the first to be represented (for example, stop consonants and fricatives like *d* and *s*) with weak sounds, like the nasals *n* and *m* only beginning to be represented later. Gradually, the child's knowledge of orthographic conventions and morphological regularities improves, but fundamentally, it is their awareness of the phonological structures that provides a skeleton for the monitoring of these graphemic elements (Caravolas and Bruck, in press). If dyslexic children have phonological difficulties, then this will affect their ability to spell words phonetically, which and is the foundation for their orthographic skill.

In a study designed to assess dyslexic readers' difficulties with phonological spelling strategies, we asked dyslexic children, reading at the 7-year level, to spell a series of 30 words of one, two and three syllables (Snowling, 1994). Using a corpus of errors made by a group of 7-year-old normal readers for comparison, the dyslexic children's spelling errors were classified as phonetically acceptable (for example, 'kiton' for *kitten*, 'coler' for *collar*) or unacceptable (for example, 'sigregt' for *cigarette*, 'tetr' for *tent*). Although the dyslexics spelled as many words correctly as the younger controls, there were significant differences in the kinds of errors they made. In line with our prediction, the dyslexics made a preponderance of phonetically unacceptable (dysphonetic) errors, while the phonetic accuracy of the spellings of the normal readers was much better (see figure 5.3).

The raised incidence of phonetically unacceptable errors made by the dyslexic children shows that they have more difficulty with the use of phonological spelling strategies than would be expected given their reading experience. Similar results were reported by Bruck (1988) and Bruck and Treiman (1990), and Kibel and Miles (1994) noted that dyslexic children had particular difficulty in spelling consonant clusters within words. However, as Treiman (1997) has argued, it would be incorrect to assume that the attempts of dyslexic children to spell are not phonologically motivated. In particular, some ways of classifying spelling errors may be misleading. Sometimes errors that are semiphonetic, for example, *blanket* → 'bankit', have been classed as dysphonetic and this can mask their phonetic similarity with the target

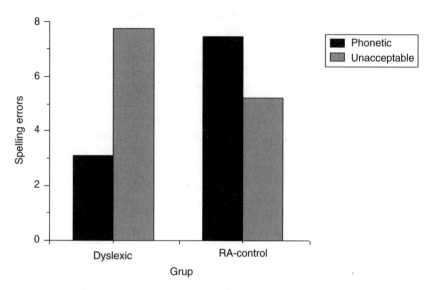

Figure 5.3 Histogram showing the distribution of phonetically accept-able and unacceptable spelling errors made by dyslexic readers and RA-controls

Source: Snowling, 1994

word. Indeed, even quite bizarre spellings can be analysed to reveal correspondences between phonology and orthography.

Snowling, Goulandris and Defty (1996) used a strict method for scoring the phonetic accuracy of children's spelling attempts. One point was given for each phoneme of the target word transcribed correctly, with one point being deducted where phonemes were misordered. In this way, a phonemic accuracy score, reflecting the pro-portion of phonemes spelled correctly, was calculated for each child from their spelling attempts. This approach avoids the problem of judging subjectively whether or not a spelling error is phonetic. Using this method, the spelling errors of the dyslexic children were less pho-netic than those of children of the same age but as phonetic as those of younger reading-age matched controls. These results are consistent with the idea that, even in relation to their limited reading skills, dyslexic children are poor at linking speech and spelling at a fine-grained level.

Table 5.1 High-frequency words varying in syllable length with stress on either the first (Stress 1) or second (Stress 2) syllable

Two-syllable		Three-syllable	
Stress 1	*Stress 2*	*Stress 1*	*Stress 2*
butter	police	officer	department
curtain	delight	industry	direction
pepper	event	uniform	beginning

Continuities between Problems of Speech and Spelling

To assess the extent to which problems of spelling might be traced to poorly specified phonological representations, Snowling, Hulme, Wells and Goulandris (1992) focused upon the spelling difficulties of JM, the child described in chapter 1. In this study, JM spelled a set of words designed to examine the effects of word frequency, syllable length and syllable stress on performance (see table 5.1).

To carry out a detailed analysis of JM's spelling errors, they were compared with those made by six dyslexic children from the same class as him, who spelled as many words correctly as he did. Spelling errors were classified into three categories. Phonetic errors portrayed the sound sequence of the words correctly, for example *blankit/blanket*, semiphonetic errors were minor errors of phoneme–grapheme correspondence or consonant cluster reduction with the overall phonetic sequence being represented accurately, for example *banket/blanket*, *membship/membership*. Finally, dysphonetic errors contained multiple errors involving phoneme–grapheme correspondence, omission and/ or sequencing, which did not portray the sound sequence correctly, for example *bagid/blanket*.

JM made 16 per cent phonetic, 18 per cent semiphonetic errors and 66 per cent dysphonetic errors. His performance was quite different from that of the other dyslexic children, who made between

36 and 97 per cent phonetic errors, (59 per cent on average), and between 2 and 57 per cent dysphonetic errors. Furthermore, at least some of his errors were plausibly related to problems with speech production (output phonology). These included errors in which the voicing feature of at least one consonant was misrepresented ('con-tanker' for *conductor*, 'megcanit' for *mechanic*; the phonemes [t] and [d] differ in voicing as do [g] and [k]), those in which the sequence of sounds was misordered ('derege' for *degree*, 'shapoon' for *shampoo*) and those in which segments were omitted ('hoile' for *hotel*, 'dierant' for *direction*).

It is interesting to note that throughout his development JM had experienced difficulty producing the voiced/voiceless distinction in his speech, i.e. differentiating sounds like [b]–[p]; [g]–[k]; [d]–[t]. Arguably, the distinction might not be well represented in his phono-logical system. This hypothesis led us to make the strong prediction that JM would confuse in his spelling the voicing features within words. Specifically, if voicing was not a salient feature of his phono-logical representations of words, this would cause confusion when spelling words differentiated by this phonetic feature.

We selected a set of words of two to four syllables in length, con-taining the consonants corresponding to the phonemes [k], [g], [t], [d]. The list included items such as *maggot, trader, crocodile, cater-pillar, helicopter* and *medallion*. We first made sure that JM could read the words, and then we asked him to spell those that we were confi-dent he was familiar with. We compared his performance with that of a much younger group of spellers whose spelling age was similar to his; this provided a very conservative test of our hypothesis. In line with previous findings, the majority of the normal children's spellings were either phonetic, for example *crocodile* → 'crocadile', *mackintosh* → 'macintosh', or semiphonetic, for example *conductor* → 'conduter' and *indian* → 'indin'. In contrast, the majority of JM's errors were dysphonetic, for example *gardener* → 'grander', *helicopter* spelled as 'hiolicoper'.

Of central interest was the way in which JM transcribed the voiced and voiceless consonants in his spellings. Altogether five of his errors resulted in a substitution of k/g or t/d, for example, crocodile → cocktell, conductor → contert, mackintosh → matindoss. Six of the spelling-age controls made voicing errors. However, these were infre-quent; in four cases there was only one example, and two children, who both spelled fewer of the sample words correctly than JM, had more difficulty. They both made three voicing errors.

A small proportion of voicing errors are to be expected in the spelling of young children, especially when they are asked to spell words with which they are relatively unfamiliar in spoken form. Given that JM was older than children in the comparison group, it is likely that he was more familiar with the words used. In spite of this advantage, he experienced more difficulty with the transcription of consonants with which he showed uncertainty in his speech.

So, having set up the difficult task of demonstrating continuities between JM's speech processing difficulties and his spelling problems, we found that his subtle difficulties with the voice/voiceless distinction were recapitulated in his spelling. It was not that JM pronounced a word wrongly and then went on to spell it in this incorrect way, but rather that the tendency to have problems with particular phonological features that characterized his phonological (speech) system also affected his spelling from time to time. In short, JM confused the spelling of voiced and voiceless consonants more often than to be expected, and there was a much greater tendency for him to spell polysyllabic words dysphonetically than even other dyslexic children of similar spelling age. JM's progress in spelling was exceedingly slow, despite excellent remedial provision. It seems that his poor representations of the sound patterns of spoken words left him without a framework on which to 'hang' orthographic information.

Specific Spelling Problems

The term dyslexia has sometimes been applied to individuals who have spelling difficulties in the absence of reading problems (Nelson and Warrington, 1974). Clinically, these children tend to have higher Verbal than Performance IQ and they usually make phonetically accurate spelling errors.

The special instance of children with such specific spelling problems was investigated most extensively by Frith (1978 and 1980). It remains a moot point as to whether these individuals were dyslexic children who had grown out of their reading problems or whether they really had never had reading difficulties. Using experimental methods and error analysis, Frith (1978) distinguished between good readers who were good spellers (Group A) and good readers who were poor spellers (Group B). In line with clinical reports, Group B spellers spelled phonetically. They had particular difficulty knowing when it was appropriate to double consonants (begi*nn*ing) and how to represent the 'schwa vowel', for example, the 'er' sound in 'cat*a*pult'. The uncertainty of Group B spellers was also reflected in their poor performance on tests where they were forced to select the correct spelling from two plausible alternatives, for example *successful/succesful*; *necessary/necessery*. They also did less well than Group A in proofreading tasks and in nonword reading.

What seemed on the surface to be a spelling difficulty might thus be reconstrued as a subtle reading problem. Frith and Perin (reported in Frith, 1984) sought further evidence for this using a search task in which adolescent poor spellers had to detect and cross out every instance of an *e* they came across in a text they were scanning (known as an 'e-cancellation' task). Target words contained two types of *e*. Important *e*'s were crucial for word recognition, as in the word *left*, while unimportant *e*'s were in words that could be identified without noticing the *e*, as in *lifted*. As it happens, important *e*'s are in stressed syllables, usually at the beginning or the middle of words, whereas unimportant *e*'s usually represent *schwa* or are silent and occur at the ends of words. If all of the letters in words are attended to, even if only fleetingly, then all of the *e*'s should be cancelled. However, for readers who focus in on only the more salient parts of the word, many unimportant *e*'s should be missed.

The results of the experiment supported the claim that poor spellers do not read in a detailed way. Good and poor spellers cancelled as many important *e*'s as each other, but poor spellers missed many more unimportant *e*'s. It seems that they attended mostly to salient letters that had a systematic relationship with the word's pronunciation. The strategy suffices for reading, which can proceed using only partial cues, but is insufficient to ensure satisfactory spelling performance. Thus, Group B spellers read by eye but are forced to spell 'by ear' (Frith and Frith, 1980) because they do not abstract letter-by-letter information during reading sufficient to allow the proficient development of orthographic knowledge.

The findings from a number of case studies suggest that a subtle difficulty with visual processing may contribute to the difficulty of spelling for children who can read well but not spell well. Seymour and MacGregor (1984) described the case of RO, whose reading was on the face of it normal. However, when words were presented in vertical rather than horizontal format, his performance deteriorated significantly more than that of other children. While he could read words holistically, he appeared to have difficulty with multi-letter segments of words. Seymour and MacGregor coined the term 'visual-analytic' dyslexia to describe RO's difficulty. RO resembled one of Frith's Group B spellers in that he had mastered alphabetic skills but failed to pass into the orthographic phase of spelling (Seymour, 1986).

This was also true of JAS, an undergraduate with specific spelling problems (Goulandris and Snowling, 1991). Although able to read fluently, JAS was unable to decide which of two homophones signalled a given meaning (for example, a vegetable – *leak* or *leek*?). At the stage in development when she was assessed, her phonological skills were normal but, like RO, she appeared to have visually based deficits. In particular, her memory for visual materials and her ability to copy were poor.

More recently, Romani, Ward and Olson (1999) have reported the case of AW, a student with specific spelling problems who showed no obvious sign of reading impairment. However, AW's ability to analyse printed words was poor; he was particularly slow to complete lexical decision tasks when the distractors were visually similar to words, suggesting that, habitually, he used a 'holistic' reading strategy. In contrast to JAS, AW had good memory for visual configurations. However, like her, he had very poor visual sequential memory, and his inability to learn letter sequences appeared to be at the core of his spelling problem.

Cases of people who can read well but who spell poorly highlight that reading and spelling are not identical processes. Reading can proceed using partial cues, whereas spelling requires complete orthographic knowledge. For this reason, it is much easier to compensate for a reading problem than for a spelling problem. Moreover, the incidence of Group B spellers suggests it may be possible to mask a reading deficit, perhaps by relying on semantic support, though its effects on spelling cannot be hidden. This is particularly true in an irregular orthography such as English where, in order to spell well, the child has to learn not only how sounds map on to spelling, but also about the inconsistencies in these rules that make the writing system 'opaque'.

In this chapter we have seen that the dyslexic child's poorly specified phonological representations have a significant impact on their ability to decode and to spell phonetically. With fundamental problems in acquiring skills that are the foundation of subsequent orthographic development, dyslexic children are forced to develop atypical reading and spelling strategies. Nevertheless, dyslexic children, like normal children, differ from one another in their reading, spelling and other cognitive skills – we now turn to consider individual differences in their pattern of reading skill.

Chapter 6

Individual Differences in Dyslexia

The evidence we have reviewed so far falls into two parts. First, we have seen that the cognitive impairment in dyslexia is a phonological deficit. Second, we have seen that the reading and spelling of dyslexic children is characterized by a difficulty with phonological strategies that are the foundation of literacy development. In fact, Vellutino and Scanlon (1991) observed that the majority of dyslexic children, some 83 per cent, have difficulties with phonological decoding. However, dyslexic children who do not seem to fit this picture and use alphabetic skills well in reading and spelling are a puzzle for the phonological deficit theory. On the face of it, these children pose problems for the theory that dyslexia can be traced to a deficit at the level of phonological representations. This chapter considers the possibility that there are sub-types of dyslexia, each with a different etiology, and asks if a unitary theory of dyslexia is tenable. It begins by reviewing some traditional approaches to the classification of dyslexic children and proceeds to discuss contemporary approaches to the study of individual differences in dyslexia.

The Classification of Dyslexic Children

The attempt to classify dyslexic children into different sub-types has a long history. From a clinical perspective, Kinsbourne and Warrington (1963) used patterns of sub-scores on the Wechsler Intelligence Scales as a means of classification. Children with a Performance IQ at least 20 points lower than their Verbal IQ scores who had associated problems with finger differentiation and right-left orientation were described as having developmental *Gerstmann syndrome*. Children with the opposite pattern, higher Performance than Verbal IQ, were described as having *language-retardation*.

Mattis, French and Rapin (1975) also used a neuropsychological approach to classify dyslexic children into three sub-groups. The largest sub-group, 48 per cent of the sample, had problems with speech articulation, graphemic motor skills and poor sound blending, and were described as having 'articulatory and graphomotor dysco-ordination' difficulties. A second sub-group were considered to have a 'language disorder', and the smallest sub-group showed problems of visual discrimination, visual memory and visuo-spatial difficulties.

An alternative and more objective approach to the classification of dyslexic children involves the use of multivariate statistical techniques. Using factor analysis, Doehring and Hashko (1977) identified three sub-groups of dyslexic children on the basis of reading-related skills. The first group had severe oral reading difficulties but performed well on visual and auditory matching tasks. A second group demonstrated slow auditory–visual letter association skills and a third group with slow auditory–visual association of words and syllables had difficulties with phoneme analysis, blending and sequencing.

Unfortunately neither the clinical approaches nor these clustering techniques revealed distinct and homogenous subtypes (cf. Naidoo, 1972) and, typical of other studies, Petrauskas and Rourke (1979) reported that between 20 and 50 per cent of children in their sample could not be readily sub-typed. A further problem is that from a theoretical perspective, these methods failed to specify the nature of the reading disorder that the children manifested.

Reading and spelling profiles in dyslexia

The importance of differentiating dyslexic children according to the kinds of problems they have with reading and writing has long been recognized by educators (Johnson and Mykelbust, 1967; Mykelbust and Johnson, 1962). An influential approach to sub-typing that started from analysing the reading and spelling errors made by dyslexic children was that of Boder (1971 and 1973). Boder's technique was simple. She began by presenting children with words to read aloud and noted those that were read automatically. She assumed that these words were already part of the child's sight vocabulary. When a word was not read immediately, she allowed 15 seconds for the child to

Table 6.1 Examples of the spelling errors made by dysphonetic dyslexics for words which they can and cannot read

Known words		Unknown words	
Target	*Error*	*Target*	*Error*
almost	alnost	promise	ponet
awake	awlake	rough	rofot
front	fornt	forge	fogt
laugh	lnonl	tomato	tonto

Source: drawn from Boder 1971 and 1973

attempt to decode it using phonic skills. She then gave a spelling test comprising words they had read correctly (known words) and words they had been unable to decode (unknown words).

More than 60 per cent of the children Boder studied showed what she described as *dysphonetic dyslexia*. They had a limited sight vocabulary and experienced difficulties with word attack skills including phonic analysis and synthesis. They were said to spell 'by eye' alone and were unable to spell words unless they were in their sight vocabulary (see table 6.1). A second, smaller group (10 per cent) of the children had difficulties in building up a sight vocabulary. This *dyseidetic* group read laboriously 'by ear', being unable to memorize the visual shapes of words so to read them as a whole, and all of their misspellings were phonetic (see table 6.2). Boder also identified a third group, comprising 22 per cent of her sample, that showed errors typical of both the dysphonetic and dyseidetic groups. These children were the most severely handicapped since they could not draw upon either visual or phonic skills.

Boder's approach was well motivated and offered clinicians the opportunity to devise remedial programmes to suit the individual needs of dyslexic children, although it was not rigorous methodologically. A shortcoming was the failure to take into account the differing reading levels of the children, and it could be that children in the mixed group were simply less good readers than those in the dysphonetic and dyseidetic groups. In addition, since the analysis

107

Table 6.2 Examples of the spelling errors made by dyseidetic dyslexics for words which they can and cannot read

Known words		Unknown words	
Target	*Error*	*Target*	*Error*
and	annd	blue	bllw
mother	muthr	talk	tok
dinner	dinnr	other	uther
work	wrk	ready	redee

Source: drawn from Boder 1971 and 1973

of individual differences proceeded from the errors the children made, the lack of control over the words which different children read and spelled was problematic because it can often be the case that different types of word produce different types of error.

Boder's work was nonetheless pioneering and caught the interest of cognitive psychologists who believed that a rigorous description of the reading and spelling strategies of dyslexic children was the key to understanding the causes of their difficulty. A more formal approach, influenced by mainstream cognitive neuropsychology, began in the 1980s and is the foundation of much current research. It is to this method that we now turn.

Analogies between acquired and developmental reading disorders

Cognitive neuropsychologists who study the reading skills of neuro-logical patients have described a variety of ways in which the adult reading system can fractionate following brain damage (see Ellis, 1994 for a review). Two contrasting patterns of breakdown involve the selective impairment of either the phonological pathway, specialized for the reading of novel words, or the lexical or semantic pathway that is involved in the reading of exception words (Coltheart, 1978; Plaut, McClelland, Seidenberg and Patterson, 1996). Patients with phono-logical dyslexia have impairments of the phonological reading system.

They typically show poor reading of nonwords in the context of good reading of familiar words, and they make predominantly dysphonetic spelling errors. Patients with surface dyslexia can no longer recognize many words that were once familiar by sight. However, they retain the ability to sound out words to a degree, using the alphabetic properties of English. As a consequence of this strategy, they are prone to make 'regularization' errors on irregular words in English, such as *yacht*, or *colonel*, by decoding them as though they were regular letter strings. They also tend to spell phonetically.

The first case of phonological dyslexia in childhood was described by Temple and Marshall (1983). HM was a 17-year-old dyslexic girl who was reading around the 10-year level. HM produced all the characteristic symptoms of an acquired phonological dyslexic; she had difficulties reading novel words as well as long regular words and her reading errors included visual 'paralexias', for example, *press* → 'pass'; *cheery* → 'cherry'; *attractive* → 'achieve' and derivational errors, for example, *imagine* → 'image'; *appeared* → 'appearance'. Despite her decoding difficulties, HM read exception words well. In fact, she did not make many regularization errors and did not show the ubiquitous advantage of regular over irregular words. When she mis-read words, her attempts tended to include components of other words, suggesting she was trying to use visual analogies.

Within the same framework, Coltheart, Masterson, Byng, Prior, and Riddoch (1983) described the case of CD, a 15-year-old dyslexic with a reading age of around 11 years. CD showed the pattern of deficit characteristic of acquired surface dyslexia. Consistent with this description, she read regular words better than irregular words and many of her reading errors were regularizations, for example *quay* → [kway]; *come* → [kome]. However, in one respect CD's reading was not typical of surface dyslexia. Although she was observed to read phonologically, her phonological reading skills were not actually very proficient and her reading of nonwords was poor.

Further parallels between acquired and developmental dyslexia were reported following these initial case studies. Prior and McCorriston (1984) described NM, an 11-year-old boy who resembled a 'letter-by-letter reader'. This reading disorder in its classic form is known as 'alexia without agraphia'. NM was reading at the 6–7-year level and the only method he had for pronouncing printed words involved first spelling out the letters using a mixture of letter sounds and names.

Using this technique he could read regular words better than irregular words.

Putative cases of deep dyslexia in children have also been described. Deep dyslexia is an acquired reading disorder in which patients are left with severely impaired reading skills. The cardinal feature is the tendency to make semantic errors in reading, for example, reading *boat* as 'captain' or *lorry* as 'car'. Patients read concrete words better than abstract words, tend to omit function words, such as 'for' and 'the', and are unable to read nonwords (Coltheart, Patterson and Marshall, 1980).

Johnston (1983) reported on CR, an 18-year-old girl who read only at the 6-year level. In single word reading she was more accurate with concrete than abstract words and of the 382 reading responses she made, five were semantic errors. Thus, she read *office* → 'occupation'; *down* → 'up'; *seven* → 'eight'; *chair* → 'table'; *table* → 'chair'. Siegel (1985) also reported a series of cases of children whom she described as 'deep' dyslexic. All were reading at the 6–7-year level, like CR, and were unable to read nonwords. The errors that Siegel interpreted as 'semantic' included substitutions of pronouns (he/she) and function words (of/for). There were also verb substitutions, *walk* → 'run'; *like* → 'walk', as well as frank semantic errors: *wheel* → 'ball'; *gentleman* → 'grandmother'.

One problem with these case reports is that they failed to take a developmental perspective. As Seymour and Elder (1986) showed, semantic errors are not unusual in the reading of children at the early logographic stage, and it is quite clear that all of these deep dyslexic children were reading at the beginner level. Moreover, the rate at which they made semantic errors was very low and probably not significantly greater than chance. An exception was KJ, a case of developmental deep dyslexia reported by Stuart and Howard (1995), who made 24 per cent semantic errors in single word reading and was completely unable to use phonological reading strategies. KJ also showed word class effects typical of deep dyslexia, though she made a higher proportion of omission errors than adult patients. As the authors noted, this was an inevitable consequence of the fact that these words had never been part of her reading vocabulary. From a developmental perspective, Stuart and Howard proposed that KJ was learning to read using an isolated semantic pathway. In a therapy study, she was able to learn concrete nouns better than matched function words.

However, this routine was defective because she also made semantic errors in speech production and comprehension tests. KJ's case illustrates an unusual developmental reading disorder, and presents a convincing case of deep dyslexia in a child. However, she, like the other cases reported, had severe learning difficulties, with a full scale IQ of 54 (CR's IQ was 75; Siegel's cases had IQs in the range of 76 to 100). The difference in IQ levels between these children and classic discrepancy-defined dyslexic readers is important. It highlights the potential role of semantic skills in modifying the effects of decoding deficits on reading behaviour. It seems that the deep dyslexic children were unable to recover from their difficulties with decoding because they lacked support from vocabulary. Their cognitive profile of phonological difficulties coupled with semantic impairments is not typical of developmental dyslexia and exerts a distinctly different influence on the development of reading.

Thus, cognitive neuropsychology offered a principled approach to the classification of dyslexia, by reference to a model of reading. However, one of the main limitations of the first case studies within this framework was the absence of reference to the performance of appropriately matched control groups. It is important for case studies to proceed in the knowledge that there is also variation in the reading skills of normal readers. This normal developmental variation must be taken account of before concluding that a particular set of reading behaviours is the hallmark of a specific sub-type of dyslexia.

The case series approach

A further requisite of cognitive-neuropsychological case studies of children's reading difficulties is that they should be couched in developmental terms. From a developmental perspective, Frith (1985) proposed that it is possible to conceptualize dyslexia in its classic form as a failure to proceed to the alphabetic phase of development. The profile of phonological dyslexia exemplifies this phase of development well. Subsequently, however, literacy acquisition may often proceed after developmental arrest. The profile of surface dyslexia might then emerge as the child begins to proceed in reading following a developmental delay. Alternatively, surface dyslexia could be the result of a distinct deficit in progressing from the alphabetic to the orthographic stages of literacy development.

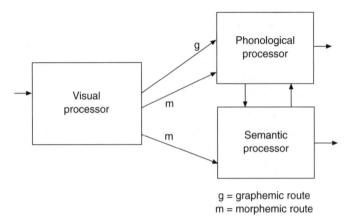

Figure 6.1 Schematic representation of functional model of basic reading processes

Source: adapted from Seymour, 1986

Seymour and his colleagues (Seymour, 1986; Seymour and Mac-Gregor, 1984), recognizing the limitations of the standard cognitive-neuropsychological approach, modified it to investigate individual differences in dyslexic reading with data from normally developing readers as a backdrop. In his first studies, Seymour made reference to a 'functional' model of reading comprising a visual processor, a phonological processor and a semantic processor. This model is depicted schematically in figure 6.1.

In Seymour's model, the visual (or graphemic) processor was a system specialized for the analysis of print and for detecting familiar graphemic forms, such as letters or groups of letters. The phonological processor was a speech production system in which the spoken vocabulary was stored in phonemic level representations, and the semantic processor was the system which possessed knowledge of semantic features and was used for comprehension. These processing units were connected via processing routes. The morphemic route to semantics was used in the translation of groups of letters to words when reading for meaning; the morphemic route to phonology operated on similarly sized units but was used when producing a vocal response for a printed word, and the grapheme–phoneme translation route was used to assemble the pronunciation of a novel word.

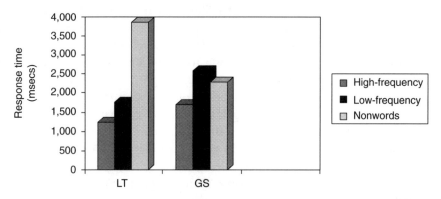

Figure 6.2 Figure showing the response times of LT, a phonological dyslexic, and GS, a morphemic dyslexic, for words of high and low frequency and non-words

Source: drawn from Seymour and MacGregor, 1984

The analysis of individual differences in dyslexia within this framework involved assessing a sample of 21 poor readers on a large battery of tasks designed to test the proficiency of the different processing systems of the model using accuracy and reaction-time data. It is not possible to do justice to the rich data sets that Seymour (1986) discusses in the monograph that reports the results of these explorations. However, one notable feature of this work was that data were presented not only on the proficiency of the different processes but also on their efficiency, as revealed by reaction time (RT) measurements. Differences in processing efficiency for different classes of words, such as words and nonwords, proved to be informative in the analysis of individual differences.

Seymour and MacGregor (1984) illustrated the variability in performance observed in the sample by discussing the cognitive profiles of children with distinctive problems. The first of these, LT, was presented as typical of a series of children who, like JM, showed 'developmental phonological dyslexia'. Though 18 years of age, LT was reading only at the 11-year level. Her nonword reading was much slower than her word reading (see figure 6.2) and her error rate for nonwords was much higher (her error rate in nonword reading was about 30 per cent). Furthermore, neither her reading accuracy nor her rate was affected by the regularity of the words she attempted.

In contrast, GS was typical of children in the series who had an impairment of what was described as sight word extension. GS was 13 years of age and was reading at the 10-year level. His word reading was slow and he took almost as long to read a high-frequency word as to assemble the response for a nonword (figure 6.2 shows his data compared to those of LT). Examination of the distribution of his reaction times to words of differing length suggested that he read in a serial letter-by-letter fashion, such that processing time was a function of the length of the words he was given regardless of whether or not a spoken response was required. Using this approach GS read regular words more accurately and faster than irregular words, which he tended to regularize.

Seymour and MacGregor (1984) chose not to describe GS and others like him as surface dyslexic, though he showed this profile of reading and spelling. Rather, they chose the term 'developmental morphemic dyslexic' to reflect the fact that he had difficulty in using the morphemic routes to phonology and semantics and was forced, therefore, to rely on a piecemeal approach.

At the close of this first series of case studies, Seymour (1986) concluded that there was heterogeneity within the dyslexic population, without distinct sub-types. Pure cases of phonological and morphemic dyslexia were rather rare, and many dyslexic children had multiple impairments of the reading sub-systems. Nonetheless, it did seem clear that, broadly, two patterns of disability could be discerned, one in which children had difficulty with phonological aspects of reading, the other in which morphological aspects were affected. With data from a second case-series of younger dyslexic readers, Seymour and Evans (1994) suggested it was possible to trace these patterns of reading impairment back to malfunction in the reading system as it developed, termed the 'foundation' level. The foundation level comprised letter-sound knowledge and both logographic and alphabetic processes. Within this model 'alphabetic dyslexia' referred to children who had difficulty in applying the alphabetic principle. It was assumed that these children would later become phonological dyslexics. Other children had difficulty in learning to treat words as multi-letter segments and were deemed to have 'logographic dyslexia'. It was assumed that these children would be slow to acquire a sight vocabulary and would become morphemic dyslexics.

The regression approach to sub-typing

A different approach to the classification of dyslexic children into sub-types relative to patterns of normal reading performance was described by Castles and Coltheart (1993), who studied a sample of 53 dyslexic children. Fundamental to this approach was the use of regression to identify dyslexic children whose reading of either nonwords or exception words falls outside of the expected range for their age. The first step in this procedure is to examine how different reading skills co-vary with each other in a population of normal readers. In so doing, it is possible to define confidence limits indicating the range of expected variation in that skill domain amongst normal readers. This is shown in figure 6.3a for the regression of irregular word reading on age. The second step is to identify children in the dyslexic sample whose reading performance falls outside of this normal range (see figure 6.3b).

Castles and Coltheart initially focused on individuals for whom a single 'component' reading skill was outside the normal range. On this criterion, eight (15 per cent) of their sample could be classified as having a specific deficit in nonword reading (phonological dyslexia), and ten (19 per cent) as having a specific deficit in exception word reading (surface dyslexia). Using a less stringent method, Castles and Coltheart went on to identify the proportion of individuals who were outside the normal range for *both* component skills, but more so for one than the other ('soft' sub-types). Using this criterion, they were able to classify 55 per cent of their sample as phonological and 30 per cent as surface developmental dyslexics.

The method chosen by Castles and Coltheart to identify sub-types of dyslexia made reference to a normative sample of children of the same age as the dyslexics. These children, by definition, read at a higher level than the dyslexics. One problem with this approach is that the relative efficiency of different reading strategies may be bound to the overall level that the reader has attained. If this is the case, then extrapolation from the reading patterns of children at one level to another may not be an appropriate way of defining abnormal patterns of reading (Snowling, Bryant and Hulme, 1996; Stanovich, Siegel and Gottardo, 1997).

To get around this problem, Manis, Seidenberg, Doi, McBride-Chang and Petersen (1996) adapted Castles and Coltheart's (1993)

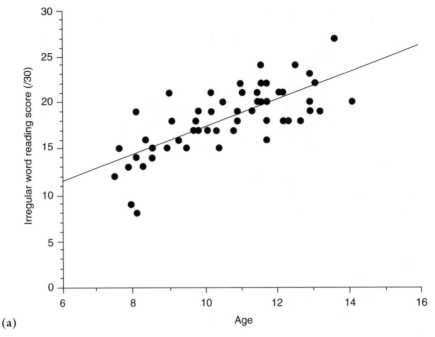

Figure 6.3a Castles and Coltheart's (1993) method for classifying dyslexic readers. (a) Irregular word reading by the control group

approach to examine sub-types of dyslexia using a more rigorous reading-age matched design. Following this procedure, they identified relatively few children who demonstrated dissociations between nonword and exception word reading, once reading age was taken into account. In fact, the incidence of surface dyslexia dropped to negligible proportions. Moreover, as many as 75 per cent of the sample showed a normal pattern of reading performance. A similarly low incidence of sub-types was reported by Stanovich, Siegel and Gottardo, (1997), with 74 per cent of children showing component reading skills within the normal range.

An important feature of the Manis et al. (1996) and Stanovich et al. (1997) studies is that these investigators went on to compare the children conforming to the description of phonological dyslexia with those considered to show the surface profile on tests of phonological and orthographic processing skill. The phonological task required the child to listen to a nonword and say what came immediately before or

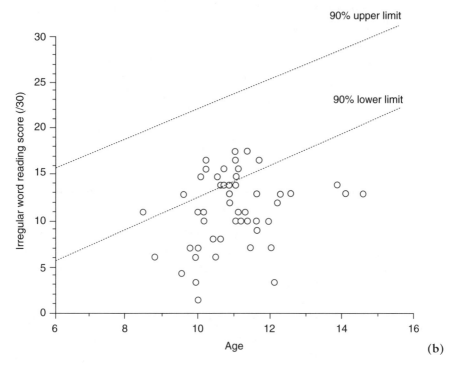

Figure 6.3b Castles and Coltheart's (1993) method for classifying dyslexic readers. (b) Irregular word reading by the dyslexic group, with 90 per cent confidence limits shown. Those whose irregular word skills fall outside of the confidence limits for the regression of irregular word reading on age were classified as surface dyslexic

after a target phoneme, for example, which sound comes before the [t] sound in [skwupt]? The orthographic choice task required the child to decide which of two visually presented letter strings was a correctly spelled word, for example, *streat/street*. In both studies, children identified as showing a phonological dyslexic profile showed poor phonological awareness skills when compared with younger reading-age matched controls. In contrast, the performance of children with a surface dyslexic profile was indistinguishable from that of the controls, even on tasks measuring orthographic skill.

The most straightforward interpretation of these results is that surface dyslexia is characterized by a delayed pattern of reading development, whilst developmental phonological dyslexia represents a

117

developmental reading disorder. A similar conclusion was reached by Snowling, Goulandris and Defty (1998), who carried out detailed case studies of two children conforming to each profile. It should be noted, however, that this conclusion does not address the important question of what accounts for by far the largest majority of dyslexic children, those who cannot be classified into a distinct sub-type. A comprehensive theory of dyslexia should specify not only the cognitive deficits that underlie the disorder (Morton and Frith, 1995) but also the factors that lead to variation in its behavioural manifestations.

Predictors of nonword and exception word reading skill among dyslexic readers

In a study carried out by Yvonne Griffiths and myself involving a sample of 59 dyslexic readers, we took a slightly different approach to the investigation of individual differences (Griffiths and Snowling, submitted). Our starting point was the knowledge that phonological awareness is an excellent predictor of individual differences in normal reading development, and that dyslexic children showing different reading profiles have been found to differ in phonological skills. In addition, we noted that it is not unusual in development for children to compensate for basic deficits by drawing on compensatory resources. Thus it is important to bear in mind that children differ not only in the severity of their phonological deficit but also in the proficiency of other cognitive skills, such as visual memory or semantic processing abilities.

With this idea in mind, we decided to use a multivariate approach to determine the concurrent predictors of individual differences in component reading skills among dyslexic children. We first assessed each dyslexic child's ability to read nonwords and exception words as well as their vocabulary knowledge. We then proceeded to investigate their performance on two tests of phonological awareness – phoneme deletion and rhyme production – and on three phonological processing tasks – nonword repetition, verbal short-term memory and speech rate. We also assessed their ability to reconstruct sequences of abstract visual shapes in a visual memory span task, and their speed of perceptual processing using the Coding and Symbol Search sub-tests of the WISC-III (Wechsler, 1992). We included the latter two tasks to test the hypothesis that some dyslexic children suffer a double deficit affecting both phonological awareness and processing rate (Bowers and Wolf, 1993).

In line with the results of many previous studies, we found that, as a group, the dyslexic readers showed a nonword reading impairment but were no worse at exception word reading than younger reading-age matched controls. There were substantial correlations between measures of phoneme awareness and both nonword reading and exception word reading in both groups of children. However, once overall reading attainment was controlled, regression analyses did not identify unique predictors of exception word reading. In contrast, several important factors were related to nonword reading proficiency. Put another way, a number of different cognitive skills appeared to be involved in the development of individual differences in decoding.

In line with expectation, phonemic awareness was strongly related to nonword reading in both normal reader and dyslexic samples. This finding confirms that the ability to decode novel words depends upon children having good segmentation skills. Furthermore, three additional factors were important for dyslexic readers (normal readers were not tested on the full range of tasks and therefore their data could not be examined in this way). Phonological processing skills were the strongest predictors of nonword reading, but these were not the only sources of variation. Both visual memory and speed of perceptual processing were important factors that accounted for unique variance in nonword reading over and above the very significant influence of phonology.

The results of this study were broadly in line with the conclusions of Manis et al. (1996) and Stanovich et al. (1997). In our study, we were able to classify 16 children (27 per cent) as having a phonological dyslexic profile, and only one child resembled a surface dyslexic. However, to the extent that such children might be considered extremes on a distribution of nonword reading skill (phonological dyslexics being bad at nonword reading and surface dyslexics good), we were able to predict the position on this continuum of an individual child by the proficiency of their underlying processing skills; children with a surface dyslexic-like profile had relatively good phonological ability, while those with a phonological dyslexic profile had more severe phonological deficits. There were additional predictors too. The ability to remember sequences of visual items was associated with better decoding skill. In addition, speed of processing influenced the reading profile: children with a slow speed of processing tended to be better nonword readers, at least in terms of accuracy.

These findings should not be taken to deny that clinically, it is possible to observe quite marked differences in reading profile. Indeed, in our sample we found children who showed rather clear-cut patterns of deficit. NW and CHD were two such children whom we assessed when they were 10 years old (Snowling and Griffiths, in press). Both were well behind in their reading development and their spelling was more impaired. CHD showed many of the features of phonological dyslexia. Although his exception word reading was at the same level as that of NW, he could read only 31 per cent of the nonword set given to both boys and he made relatively fewer regularization errors. In contrast, NW showed many of the features of surface dyslexia. His nonword reading was relatively good considering his overall level of reading ability, while his exception word reading was more impaired. A large proportion of his reading errors were regularizations, for example, he read *sword* as [swɔd].

The patterns of reading behaviour demonstrated by CHD and NW were associated with distinctive patterns of behaviour on the other cognitive tasks they were given (see table 6.3). As might be predicted from his better nonword reading, NWs phonological skills were stronger than those of CHD. However, CHD's strengths were in visual memory and speed of processing, two skills that he may have been able to draw upon to compensate for his phonological problems when learning to read. We suggest that these resources may have been important in allowing him to develop his sight vocabulary to a level in advance of that of his nonword reading skill. In turn, this produced the nonword reading deficit typical of phonological dyslexia.

The cases of NW and CHD illustrate how two dyslexic readers of similar age and reading at the same level may show markedly different behavioural profiles. Some dyslexic children, like CHD, show phonological impairments when compared with younger reading-age matched controls. Such children are most likely to develop decoding deficits. Others, like NW, show phonological deficits only in relation to age-matched peers. They are more likely to acquire decoding skills, but relatively slowly for their age. But as we have shown, it is not the impact of the phonological deficit alone that determines individual differences in reading behaviour. The findings of the regression analyses described above suggest that the phonological deficit observed in

Table 6.3 Performance of NW and CHD on cognitive processing tasks

Cognitive processing task	NW 'Surface profile'	CHD 'Phonological profile'
Phoneme deletion (% correct)	63	46
Nonword repetition (% correct)	82	63
Verbal memory span (no. of words recalled)	3.5	3.3
Speech rate (no. of words articulated per second)	2.6 (normal)	1.8 (slow)
Visual memory span (no. of shapes recalled)	2.5	3.5
Speed of processing (centile score)	4	66

dyslexia may be moderated by other cognitive skills, such as visual memory and speed of processing. In the case of CHD, the influence of poor phonology on reading outcome may to an extent have been compensated for by strong visual memory capacity. Thus, his impaired nonword reading was coupled with better exception word reading skill. On the other hand, NW's slower speed of processing brought with it a better chance of developing phonological reading strategies. Whilst this made for better decoding in his case than for CHD, it was not conducive to exception word reading and resulted in an excess of regularization errors (cf. Bowers, 1995).

Connectionist models also provide a framework for thinking about the role of visual memory and speed of processing as factors that modify the impact of a phonological deficit on learning to read. In a recent modification of SM89 implemented by Harm and Seidenberg (1999), the phonological network was pre-trained before learning trials began, in an analogous way to that in which a child's phonological development proceeds prior to the start of learning to read. Harm and Seidenberg (1999) simulated phonological dyslexia by reducing the network's capacity to represent phonological information. A more severe impairment of phonological representation was created by also severing connections within the phonological layer. In an analogous manner, dyslexic children who have more severe phonological processing impairments have worse decoding skills as measured by nonword reading.

Harm and Seidenberg's simulations also showed that the more severe the phonological deficit, the more the network had to draw upon general processing resources. Visual memory might be thought of here as part of a more general processing resource. Within this view, differences in general processing capacity can moderate the extent to which poor phonology disrupts the ability to learn to read. Put simply, children with good visual memory like RE and JM can, to a degree, use visual skills to compensate for their phonological deficits.

Current connectionist models are silent as to the role of speed of processing in the determination of patterns of reading behaviour. However, Wimmer, Mayringer and Landerl (1998) have linked slow speed of processing with a difficulty in establishing memory representations for printed words, possibly because of a mistiming of sources of activation (cf. Bowers and Wolf, 1993). In such cases, children can learn to decode but only by slow and laborious means.

It is proposed, therefore, that the course of reading development is not predetermined in children with phonological deficits. If their phonological deficit is severe but they have good visual memory skills, they are likely to develop the 'phonological dyslexic' profile. However, if they have poor visual memory or their speed of processing is slow, they are more likely to read novel words slowly and laboriously but nevertheless accurately, but to have difficulty in acquiring exception word reading skills, the profile characteristic of 'surface dyslexia'.

Of course, visual memory and speed of processing are not the only skills which could, in principle, modify the reading strategies children use. Stanovich, Siegel and Gottardo (1997) suggested that low levels of exposure to print may be a potential cause of the surface dyslexic pattern, since it is only possible to build word recognition skills if given the opportunity to recode irregular as well as regular words (Share, 1995). Thus, differences in reading profile associated with dyslexic 'sub-types' are exacerbated when it is the case that the children who can decode actually read little and fail to develop a sight vocabulary (Snowling, Bryant and Hulme, 1996).

We will return to the idea that dyslexic children differ in the cognitive resources they can use for compensation in chapter 11. For the

122

present it is hypothesized that individual differences in reading behaviour can be viewed as the outcome of an interaction between the phonological deficit and other cognitive skills. As Castles, Datta, Gayan and Olson (1999) have also argued with support from behaviour-genetic analyses, the variation in reading skills among dyslexic readers is perhaps best captured as distributed on a continuous dimension of reading skill, with those who show a phonological dyslexic profile at one extreme and those who show a surface dyslexic profile at the other. But it is important to stress that the severity of the core phonological deficit has a major influence on the reading (and spelling) profile that emerges. This is a hypothesis that we will explore more fully in the next chapter.

Chapter 7

The Severity Hypothesis

Although we have seen that it is difficult to identify clear sub-types of dyslexia, this is not to deny that there are individual differences among dyslexic children. In particular, dyslexic readers differ in the extent to which they can use phonological reading and spelling strategies. We now turn to explore the idea presented at the close of the last chapter, that variations in severity of a dyslexic child's phonological deficit determines their reading profile. A second issue we shall address is how 'severity' should be conceptualized in terms of underlying phonological representations. As discussed in chapter 4, it is difficult to ascertain the causes of poorly specified representations, and their likely origin in speech perceptual processes is as yet unproven. On the other hand, there is good evidence of deficits in speech output processes that plausibly depend upon these representations. Furthermore, Hulme and Snowling (1992) suggested that children set up mappings from orthography to phonology by linking to output rather than input representations (Stothard, Snowling and Hulme, 1996). We begin by discussing whether in principle different types of phonological impairment, whether they are at the input or output stage of processing, could have different impacts on literacy development. We go on to consider how the severity of a deficit might affect prognosis before discussing the impact of a pervasive phonological disorder on reading and spelling skills.

Qualitative Differences in Phonological Development

The hypothesis that individual differences in the nature of a phonological deficit could have an impact on the development of reading

Table 7.1 Examples of the reading errors made by dyslexic children of reading ages 6 and 7 years

Logographic	sign/sing
	bowl/blow
	spade/space
	breath/bread
	cask/cash
	pint/pink
Lexical-sounding	flood/fault
	choir/clot
	bleat/built
	lettuce/lettering
	organ/olive
	grill/grit

Source: Snowling, Stackhouse and Rack, 1986

and spelling skills was explored some years ago by Snowling, Stackhouse and Rack (1986). Our study used Frith's (1985) model of literacy acquisition as a framework for examining the association between cognitive deficits and patterns of reading difficulty observed. It involved three dyslexic children reading at the 6- to 7-year level, and four older dyslexics who had attained a reading age of at least 10 years. All the dyslexics had poor nonword reading skills and were classified as showing developmental phonological dyslexia. For the purpose of developmental comparison, the study also included two groups of normally developing readers, 7- and 10-year-old RA-controls.

Consistent with Frith's hypothesis, the dyslexic children, particularly those of low reading age, appeared to be arrested in the *logographic* phase of development. Thus, their reading was inherently inaccurate, with a preponderance of visual (or logographic) errors (see table 7.1). There was a notable absence of the regularization errors that are seen frequently among controls, though many of the reading errors reflected partial decoding attempts (lexical-sounding errors). In all cases but one, nonword reading skills were impaired relative to reading-age matched controls; the exception was a boy who had received extensive tutoring. In a similar vein, the spelling skills of the dyslexics were poorer overall than those of the controls, and there was

Table 7.2 Examples of the spelling errors made by dyslexic children of reading ages 6 and 7 years

Normal immaturities	packet/pak
	trumpet/tumput
	finger/fing
	lip/lap
	adventure/adencher
	contented/contened
Segmentation errors	fish/fine
	traffic/tatin
	polish/phins
	instructed/insted
	bump/bunt
	geography/gorhy

Source: Snowling, Stackhouse and Rack, 1986

a marked tendency for spelling errors to be dysphonetic. These included *fish* → 'fine'; *polish* → 'phins'; *instructed* → 'insted' and *geography* → 'gorhy'.

A more detailed analysis of the children's spelling errors revealed that they were not just like those of younger children who frequently make semiphonetic errors. Only 30 per cent of the dyslexics' errors were of this type. The remaining 70 per cent suggested difficulties due to problems with phoneme segmentation and/or sound–letter translation (see table 7.2).

We also collected data about the phonological processing skills of the seven dyslexics. The tasks we used included auditory discrimination, rhyme detection, syllable and phoneme segmentation, nonword repetition and verbal short-term memory. We reasoned that some variation in performance between the dyslexic readers was to be expected on these tasks as progress to the alphabetic phase could be hindered for a number of different reasons. This was indeed the case. All of the dyslexics could segment by syllable but they had difficulty with tasks tapping rhyme and phoneme segmentation. They also all had verbal memory deficits. The poorest reader of the group, TW, had difficulty with auditory discrimination and two of the others, JM and KF, had speech production difficulties.

Table 7.3 Examples of spelling errors made by three children with developmental dyslexia

Target spelling	TW	AS	JM
sack	canpe	sed	sag
trap	mupter	tapt	tap
tulip	peper	tlep	tilup
traffic	teryer	tatin	tafit
packet	tcunin	pak	pagit
polish	pcst	phins	bols
refreshment	threesleling	raften	refent
adventure	hadleguns	avat	afvoerl
membership	boatsery	mabrshep	meaofe
contented	earpun	continted	codter
catalogue	catofleg	canolog	catolog

Source: Snowling, Stackhouse and Rack, 1986

In short, the cases we examined all had similar reading profiles but they experienced subtly different phonological impairments. If it is true that spellings provide a 'window on children's phonological representations' then these differences should translate into idiosyncratic patterns of spelling performance. We therefore went on to investigate whether individual differences in spelling pattern could be related to variations in phonological processing. We focused on the dyslexics of lower reading ability as we reasoned that it would be easier to detect if there were a relationship between the type of impairment and the spelling pattern observed earlier in development, rather than later when compensatory processes had come into play (see table 7.3).

TW's phonological problems were with what might be termed 'input phonology'; she performed poorly on the auditory discrimination task. When listening to the examiner dictating the words to be spelled, she would typically look very carefully at her face, making use of information she could lip-read. Her spelling strategy was interesting in view of this. She had more difficulty in writing down the first phoneme of a word than the other dyslexics. In fact, she tended to write down the last phoneme first and, as a result of using lip-read information, she sometimes substituted consonants for others made in the same place in the mouth, such as writing *m* for [b].

AS had more classic dyslexic difficulties including problems with phoneme segmentation and verbal memory. In contrast to TW, she tended to spell the beginnings of words correctly but to have more difficulty with the endings. This problem seemed related to a memory limitation; she was unable to segment the word in its entirety before her memory for it declined. Although many of her errors were semiphonetic, her overall tendency was to produce dysphonetic versions of the target words, especially the longer ones where her short-term memory problems impeded the transcription process significantly.

As we have already discussed, JM had problems with 'output phonology', and to an extent, his speech production and spelling difficulties appeared to be related. He had inordinate difficulty spelling three-syllable words which he had trouble pronouncing (*membership* → 'meaofe'), and significant difficulty with the voicing features of phonemes, as seen, for example, in the way he spelled *sack* as 'sag'.

The findings of these case studies suggested that varying patterns of spelling performance seen among the dyslexic readers may indeed be related to the nature of phonological deficit they experienced. However, what was not clear was whether it was the *nature* of the deficit that was important, or rather, whether its *severity* was the critical factor. In developmental disorders it can often be difficult to separate these two aspects of variation. In practice, children whose deficits are more severe relative to the norm are often also those who show more pervasive deficits.

In an attempt to tease apart the influence of the nature versus the severity of a phonological impairment, let us compare the reading and spelling profile of JM with that of another dyslexic, MB, who had a similar type of phonological impairment implicating output phonology, though it was less severe.

A case evaluation of the 'severity' hypothesis

MB had severe literacy problems and, at the age of 12 years, he was some four years behind in reading attainment. His spelling was also impaired. Like JM, MB had been slow to speak, and he had received speech therapy from 2 years of age. He attended a language unit for a year before transferring to an opportunity class in which he received intensive help. Following a period of education in a school for children with moderate learning difficulties, he was placed in a school specializing in the teaching of dyslexic children, which was where he was being educated when we saw him.

The similarity of MB's difficulties to those of JM were striking. Both boys had good vocabulary knowledge but specific difficulties with word finding. MB's naming errors included circumlocutions, such as when shown the picture of a *koala bear* saying 'lives in America' [Australia – author's interpretation] and naming *stethoscope* as 'heliscope'. We have already documented JM's poor phonological processing skills. Like him, MB had great difficulty with a task in which he was required to produce rhyming words to a target. Not only did he produce fewer rhyming words than other children of the same age, but he also tended to lose track and to produce phonologically incorrect responses. In response to *clown*, he produced 'sound, found, clown, shed, cloud, sound'. In response to *star*, he produced 'car, far, clock, shark, stars, store, stallion'. MB also had difficulty on a test of sound categorization requiring rhyme detection. Here he had to say which was the 'odd one out' of four auditorily presented items, for example, 'sun, gun, *rub*, fun' (Bradley and Bryant, 1983). He made five out of 16 errors on this test, a score outside of the normal range for children of similar reading skill.

Importantly for our comparison, MB scored within the same range as JM when asked to repeat nonwords, gaining a score that was significantly below age expectation. However, the two boys differed qualitatively in their pattern of speech errors. Analysis of JM's speech showed that generally his errors were further from their targets than those made by MB. More of JM's errors contained multiple substitutions, there was inconsistency in his responding and considerable dysfluency in his planning of speech output. To give just two examples: when asked to repeat *fenneriser*, JM's response was [fɛnʔ(·)fəhɛʔ(·)f·fənɛn:(·)fənɛnifsfð]; MB's response was 'venneriser'. When asked to repeat 'glistering', JM's response was [kl[.]glɪstɹɪn[.]glɪstəɹɪn]; MB's was [glɪstrɪn].

The errors that the dyslexics made when repeating nonwords were classified to capture these differences. Responses in which there were several consecutive attempts at the target were classified as planning errors, for example, *fenneriser* → [fɛnʔ(·)fəhɛʔ(·)f·fənɛn:(·)

fənɛnifsfð], and because these were serious errors, we gave them an error score of 2. Similarly, multiple substitutions were regarded as serious, for example *empliforvent* → [empəfəmənt], *blonterstaping* → [plɔntəs'tefɪn] and were given an error score of 2, while single substitutions errors were scored as 1, for example *fenneriser* → [vɛnəɹɪsə], *tafflest* → [təfləs.].

Overall, JM made 6 planning errors, 6 multiple substitutions and 4 single substitutions (a total error score of 28). MB, on the other hand, made 3 planning errors, no multiple substitutions and 10 single sub-stitutions (a total error score of 16). Thus, JM's output phonological deficit was more serious than that of MB. While the two dyslexic boys experienced similar phonological processing difficulties (the *nature* of their disorder was the same), they differed in severity. We were then in a position to compare their written language skills. If the nature of the phonological deficit is critical to outcome, both boys would be expected to show the same reading profile. However, if it is the severity of the deficit that is important, JM's profile should be the more atypical.

We have already seen that JM presented with a clear-cut phonolog-ical dyslexic profile; he read words better than nonwords and he was a dysphonetic speller. Our evaluation of MB began with an assessment of his ability to read sets of regular words (*grill, task, market*) and irregular words (*flood, dove, police*) matched for frequency and letter length. In contrast to JM, MB was sensitive to the regularity of the words he was presented with and read more regular than irregular words. Furthermore, many of his attempts at irregular words were regularizations, for example, he read *sword* as [swɔd] and *swan* as [swɑ́n]; JM had never made these phonologically based errors. MB was also able to read nonwords, at least as well as younger reading-age matched controls. In short, MB was better at using phonological reading strategies than JM and, by contrast, he resembled a surface dyslexic.

We next turned to examine MB's spelling and to compare his errors with those of JM. The first indication that MB also had problems spelling phonetically came from his poor performance on a nonword spelling test where he only managed to spell 27 per cent of complex items correctly. His errors included *tegwop* → 'tekwop'; *romsig* → 'romsick', and his performance compared unfavourably with that of normal readers of similar reading skill, who spelled 65 per cent correctly.

Further evidence for MB's difficulty with phonological spelling strategies came from a qualitative analysis of his spelling errors. More than 57 per cent of his spelling errors on a test of one- to four-syllable words were dysphonetic. He spelled *finger* → 'thinger', *cigarette* → 'securte', *adventure* → 'affench' and *politician* → 'potishone'. At a similar stage in his development, JM had made 75 per cent non-phonetic spelling errors when attempting the same set of words. So, although the two boys had different reading problems, they had similar difficulties with spelling, though MB's were less marked than those of JM. These findings argue for a closer and more direct relationship between impairments in output phonological representations and spelling than reading performance. Arguably, this is the same pattern of association that we saw earlier in the three young phonological dyslexics, TW, AS and JM. It represents further evidence for continuities between speech and spelling. It seems that both processes require relatively direct access to phonological representations (Stackhouse and Wells, 1997).

The detailed comparison of JM and MB provides support for the idea that it is the severity more than the nature of the phonological processing deficit that places constraints on reading and spelling development (Snowling, Goulandris and Stackhouse, 1994). To test this hypothesis further, it would be necessary to contrast the effects of an isolated deficit in input phonology with those of a specific output deficit such as that which characterized JM's performance. In a case study that went some way towards this, we assessed LF, a child with poor input phonology but normal speech production who had poor phonological awareness (Stothard, Snowling and Hulme, 1996). The interesting aspect of LF's case was that she was in many respects a normal reader. Although LF was poor at decoding, consistent with her difficulties with phonological awareness, her word recognition system developed normally during the four years in which we studied her, and she did not have spelling problems. In interpreting LF's success in learning to read despite deficits in phonological awareness, our speculation was that she had been able to establish mappings between the spellings and sounds of words because she possessed well-specified output representations.

Learning to read and spell with a phonological disorder

Our proposal is that children who have deficits in output phonology are particularly vulnerable to dyslexia. However, neither JM nor MB had an obvious speech difficulty that would lead them to be classified clinically as speech-impaired. On the other side of the coin, findings regarding literacy outcomes of children who do have primary speech disorders are mixed, with some studies reporting that reading difficulties ensue (Bird, Bishop and Freeman, 1995) and others that this is not an inevitable outcome (Catts, 1993). A reasonable reading of this literature is that it is the nature of the speech disorder and its severity at the time when the child is learning to read that are critical factors. Indeed, there is accumulating evidence that speech disorders that are associated with difficulties at the level of phonological representation have a more deleterious impact on literacy development than those that are more peripheral or articulatory in nature (see Stackhouse, 2000 for a review). The crux of the matter is that a child whose speech production is poor because of problems executing articulatory gestures but who has normal phonological representations will be able to set up alphabetic mappings between spellings and underlying speech sounds in the normal way. In contrast, a child whose speech disorder is associated with pervasive phonological deficits will be at the same disadvantage as a dyslexic child in learning to read, because of impairments at the level of phonological representations. MC was one such child studied by Joy Stackhouse and myself (Stackhouse and Snowling, 1992). We shall discuss his case here to illustrate the profound limitations such problems can place on the development of written language skills.

Although of average intelligence, MC's speech had been unintelligible during his early school life. He also had a history of fluctuating hearing loss although during the course of our study his hearing was within normal limits. MC was tested during two time-periods. At the beginning of the study he was aged 10 years 7 months and at follow-up, four years later, he was 14 years 5 months. During this time he was educated in a language unit where he received daily speech therapy and reading and spelling tuition. In spite of this assistance, MC made very little progress with his literacy skills. When first assessed his reading age was 7 years 7 months and four years later it was 7 years 8 months. Spelling measured at 6 years 8 months at the first time of test and had increased to 7 years 9 months four years later. We will focus first on his profile at the beginning of this period of investigation.

To quantify the extent of MC's phonological processing difficulties, he was administered tests tapping auditory discrimination, auditory lexical decision and phonological awareness. MC had more difficulty than reading-age matched controls on all of these tasks. In short, he had phonological problems affecting both input and output phonology as well as phonological awareness. His difficulties were noticeably more severe and more pervasive than those of the dyslexic children we described earlier, including JM.

To investigate MC's reading and spelling development, he was asked to give the names and sounds of the letters of the alphabet. When first assessed his letter-name knowledge was good but he had difficulty both in producing and in writing letter sounds. To investigate his use of lexical and phonological reading strategies, he read sets of regular and irregular words and nonwords similar to those used in our previous studies. MC's word reading was towards the lower end of the normal range and he did not show a regularity effect. In addition, he failed to read any of the nonwords correctly.

Over 50 per cent of MC's reading errors were visually-based (for example *pint* → 'paint', *flood* → 'foot', *drug* → 'drum', *grill* → 'glue', *lime* → 'lemon'). The next highest proportion of errors, some 35 per cent, were attempts to read words by sound, but these were largely unsuccessful and he made only two regularizations. We next turned to investigate his spelling performance by asking him to spell the one, two and three syllable words which had also been give to JM and MB. Given MC's serious output deficit, this comparison offered a further test of the severity hypothesis. In line with prediction, MC made very serious spelling errors which were not characteristic of the normal group. Only a minority of his spelling errors resembled the mistakes made by young normal children; these were spellings of *lip* → 'lepp', *bank* → 'back', *kitten* → 'keten'. The great majority of his spelling errors were dysphonetic; he spelled *bump* → 'borr'; *trap* → 'thew'; *sack* → 'satk', *instructed* → 'nisokder'.

While MC could transcribe the initial consonant of words correctly 90 per cent of the time, he could only maintain the syllable structure on 45 per cent of occasions. Observation of him while he was spelling, together with an analysis of his errors, suggested he was attempting to spell words sound by sound. Although this was a strategy fostered by

133

Table 7.4 Spellings of three-syllable words by MC, a child with a phonological disorder

Target spelling	MC
membership	mabsttb mabspht splt sthp
September	sabarber smber
cigarette	satesatarhaelerar
umbrella	rberhertelrarlsrllles
understand	rarato sandrarde
refreshment	lpohet
adventure	arterer
catalogue	catcolg catdog gog
instructed	nisokder
contented	kitr

Source: drawn from Stackhouse and Snowling, 1992

teaching, it was generally unsuccessful. His difficulties were plausibly related to severe problems with segmentation processes. For example, he would often only attempt the first and last sound in a two-syllable word (for example *tulip* → 'tottper', *packet* → 'pater') and three-syllable words were frequently reduced (for example *contented* → 'kitr', *refreshment* → 'lpohet'). Although these responses at first appeared bizarre, a consistent pattern emerged. MC was able to identify initial and final sounds, but not sounds embedded within the words.

It seems very likely that aberrant speech processes were intruding on MC's attempts to spell by ear. Indeed, some of his speech difficulties were recapitulated in his spelling. For instance, there was a tendency for intrusive sounds to be included (for example *sack* → 'satk', *puppy* → 'pats') and for consonant changes involving stops to be made (*polish* → 'porter'). Clusters such as [sp], [spl], [tr] and [str] were an added complication for MC. Even complex spelling errors were also interpretable in relation to his speech difficulties (see table 7.4). He spelled *cigarette* → 'satersatarhaelerar'. This error can be deciphered with the knowledge that he made repeated attempts to segment and spell parts of the word. This 'searching' behaviour when spelling has a parallel in disordered speech, namely articulatory searching or 'groping'. The error *cigarette* → 'satersatarhaelerar' provided another illustration of this phenomenon. Here MC first attempted to transcribe the first and the last syllable twice (*cig* → 'sa', *ette* → 'ter', *cig* → 'sa', *ette* → 't'). He then attempted the middle syllable (*gar*) four times – 'ar' 'hael' 'er' 'ar'. Similarly, *umbrella* → 'rberhertelrarlsrlles' reflected repeated attempts to get the second syllable (*brel*) – 'r' 'be' 'rhe' 'rte', one attempt at the final syllable (*la*) – 'l', two more attempts at the second syllable – 'ra' 'r', and so forth.

Spelling error analysis is by necessity subjective. However the important point is that, although on first examination, MC's spelling errors appear bizarre, knowledge of his speech difficulties provides a way of interpreting them. Close examination of his responses suggested they reflected attempts to use a 'sound-by-sound' spelling strategy which was compromised by severe segmentation and speech difficulties.

Four years later, MC's reading performance was similar to that of very much younger reading-age matched controls and he showed a regularity effect. However, he persisted in making predominantly visual errors (62 per cent). By this stage, MC could read nonwords to some extent, although here too, the majority of his errors, some 56 per cent, were lexicalizations (for example *rask* → 'risk', *swad* → 'swam', *kiscuit* → 'kissed'). MC indeed had severe and persisting reading difficulties. Turning to his spelling, MC's errors were still predominantly dysphonetic. However, they were not as perseverative as before and he was better able to retain the syllabic structure of the words he spelled. Thus, he wrote *basket* → 'bastit', *biscuits* → 'bisecet', *scarecrow* → 'scerwar', *fire engine* → 'firenegel' although on other occasions the phonological skeleton was reduced (for example *cigarette* → 'sicerk', *membership* → 'minship', *umbrella* → 'urmpt'). MC also used a strategy of spelling by word components to some extent. This allowed him to spell *catalogue* → 'catlong', *adventure* → 'addever' and *refreshment* → 'readfashmet'. It is probable that he had developed this strategy to get around the difficulty he had in accessing the phonemic segments of spoken words. It may be recalled that JM had also used this compensatory strategy to some extent.

MC's case demonstrates that the consequences for literacy development of a severe and pervasive phonological impairment can be extreme. At 10 years of age, although of average intelligence, he was still only a beginning reader; he relied exclusively upon a small sight vocabulary, his knowledge of letter–sound rules was imperfect and he could not read nonwords. In addition, his use of phonological spelling strategies was grossly deficient and his progress over time was lamentably poor, despite intensive intervention. In fact, MC had been fairly resistant to intensive speech therapy and a phonic teaching regime. Even though he had been taught letter–sound translation rules, he was unable to apply these in reading and spelling because his phonological system was too impaired to support the acquisition of literacy along normal lines. MC would not be defined as dyslexic because his primary impairment was in spoken rather than written language. However, in cognitive terms, his difficulties were similar to, but more extreme than, those of a dyslexic child such as JM. His case underlines the importance of phonological representations to the acquisition of literacy skills.

Output phonology and orthographic development

The study of children with the profile of developmental phonological dyslexia at the single-case level confirms the picture that emerges from group studies, that phonological deficits constrain not only the development of decoding skills in these children but also the rate at which word recognition develops. The inability of these children to develop orthographic representations precludes accurate spelling performance. The default option is to use phonetic spelling strategies but these processes are also compromised because of deficits at the level of output representation, exacerbated by short-term memory deficits.

An obvious limitation of single-case studies, however, is that they present *associations* between cognitive deficits and orthographic impairments. Although developmental associations are incapable of demonstrating causal relationships, they are important because they can highlight the dependence of changes in one cognitive system on the acquisition of skills in related domains (Bishop, 1997). The single-case studies presented here suggest that the severity and pervasiveness of a child's phonological difficulties – in particular, the integrity of output phonological representations – is a major determinant of the success they will have in acquiring phonological reading and spelling strategies. According to this view, children who have milder deficits in phonological processing can acquire the use of phonological reading and spelling strategies, albeit later than their peers, and may resemble surface dyslexics (Snowling, Goulandris and Defty, 1998). The 'severity' hypothesis postulates that the reading and spelling problems in all dyslexic children depend upon phonological deficits; however, the form of the reading and spelling problems observed will depend critically upon the severity of the underlying phonological impairment. This is a simple view that may be wrong. It needs to be refuted before separate causes are invoked to explain the different behavioural manifestations of dyslexia.

Is a Unitary Definition of Dyslexia Possible?

Studies that have attempted to classify dyslexic children illustrate a wide range of different behavioural symptoms of dyslexia. However, none of the proposed taxonomies has been successful in assigning all dyslexic children to a sub-type. Even theoretically motivated distinctions, such as that between developmental phonological and developmental surface dyslexia, leave a substantial majority of dyslexic children unclassified. However, it is rare to find a dyslexic child who does not have some kind of phonological problem if they are tested using sensitive enough measures. A unitary definition of dyslexia with phonological impairments at its core therefore still seems tenable, provided it is acknowledged that, as in any developmental disorder, different cognitive sub-systems are in constant interaction (Karmiloff-Smith, 1998). With respect to dyslexia, it seems likely that the failure to learn to read (and spell) along normal lines is a direct consequence of phonological deficits. However, children who differ in the severity of their phonological deficit differ in outcome. As we will discuss further in chapter 11, these differences interact with other factors, such as the semantic and visual abilities that are used as compensatory resources to determine individual differences in both the severity and surface form of dyslexic children's reading and spelling disorders.

Chapter 8

Biological Bases of Dyslexia

Although as we have seen in the previous two chapters, dyslexia can manifest itself in a variety of ways, there may nonetheless be a single cause, a phonological deficit, which is modified by other cognitive skills. It is now important to address the question of what, at the biological level, causes the phonological processing disorder that is the proximal cause of dyslexia. This chapter begins by considering the evidence that dyslexia has a genetic origin before turning to its brain correlates.

The Heritability of Dyslexia

It has been known for many years that reading difficulties tend to run in families. Orton (1925) was one of the first to propose that spoken language difficulties were also common among the family members of dyslexic children. As evidence from dyslexic families has accumulated, it has become possible to estimate the risk of dyslexia for an individual from the knowledge of their affected relatives. Recent estimates indicate that the risk to a son of being dyslexic if he has a dyslexic father is about 40 per cent, if he has a dyslexic mother it is about 36 per cent. For a daughter the risk is somewhat less, at about 20 per cent regardless of which parent is affected (Gilger, Pennington and DeFries, 1991).

It is tempting to infer from these figures that heredity has a role in the transmission of a dyslexic disposition. However, these kinds of data are insufficient. Families share similar environments as well as heredity so this evidence does not necessarily imply that genetic factors are involved.

A stronger case for the role of heredity is made by studies that compare concordance rates in twin pairs. Concordance refers to the proportion of pairs in a sample of twins in which both twins show the same condition. There are two types of twin: identical twins (monozygotic: MZ) who share 100 per cent of their genes, and fraternal twins (dizygotic: DZ) who share on average 50 per cent of their genes. If dyslexia were perfectly heritable, then co-twins in a monozygotic pair would always be affected, and thus the concordance for monozygotic (MZ) twins would be 100 per cent. Reported concordance rates vary between samples but tell a consistent story. There is a higher probability of both twins being dyslexic if they are monozygotic than if they are dizygotic, implying that genetic factors are involved.

However, concordance rates are more suited to the assessment of genetic influences on categorical disorders, such as diseases, than on behavioural traits such as reading. It is easier to decide if both twins have a particular disease than to decide if they are 'dyslexic' or not, because there is disagreement surrounding the diagnosis of dyslexia. To take account of the fact that reading varies continuously, and assuming that dyslexia can be considered at the extreme of the continuum, behaviour geneticists have developed a statistical technique that allows an estimate to be made of the relative influence of heredity and environment on the behaviour of twins (DeFries and Fulker, 1985). In research on dyslexia, the behaviour of interest is usually reading; the approach, based on regression, is complex mathematically but its logic is really quite simple.

When a twin is selected as reading disabled, he or she is referred to as a proband. It is reasonable to assume that the co-twin of a proband will read better than the referred or indexed child. In fact, the reading of the co-twin is likely to be more similar to the average level expected for children of this age. Formally, it is said to 'regress' towards the population mean. This is illustrated in table 8.1, which shows the average performance of affected twins and their co-twins as measured by a composite score for reading and spelling performance; the values are expressed here in terms of standard scores where 0 is the average for the normal population.

It is important to understand that the amount of regression – the movement towards average – is under the control of a combination of genetic and environmental factors. It follows that among monozygotic twins who are genetically identical, regression will be less for the

Source: adapted from DeFries, Alarcon and Olson, 1997, p. 27

Table 8.1 Mean performance on literacy tests for identical (MZ) and same-sex fraternal (DZ) twins in which at least one twin is dyslexic

	Proband	Co-twin	(Population average)
Identical (MZ)	−2.72	−2.51	0
Fraternal (DZ)	−2.65	−1.71	0

co-twins, whereas among dizygotic twins, co-twins will regress further towards the population mean and their reading skills will diverge more from those of the probands. Put simply, if a trait is heritable, then monozygotic twins should be more similar for that trait than dizygotic twins. By assessing the amount of variation in reading skill between co-twins in large twin-samples, it is possible to assess the relative contributions of genes and environment to reading.

Very influential work on the heritability of dyslexia has been conducted by John DeFries, Richard Olson and their colleagues in Boulder, Colorado (DeFries, 1991). As the basis for this work they have recruited a very large sample of twins in which at least one member of each pair is dyslexic. The screening tests administered to the twins on referral included measures of intelligence, reading, spelling and related cognitive tasks, and these have provided a rich source of data for heritability analyses as well as molecular genetic studies. For the moment we will focus on the behaviour-genetic analyses.

Estimates of the genetic contribution to reading (heritability) range from 0 to 1, where 1 would indicate that all of the variance between co-twins is under the control of genetic factors. Using a similar procedure it is possible to assess the amount of variance that is due to environmental factors. In their initial work, DeFries, Fulker and LaBuda (1987) found significant heritability for reading recognition and spelling deficits, but not for reading comprehension. A slightly different conclusion was reached by Stevenson, Graham, Fredman and McLoughlin (1987), who investigated a UK sample of 13-year-old twins. In this study, the effects of genetic factors were more marked for general intelligence and spelling performance than for reading.

A possible difference between the findings of the Boulder group and those of Stevenson and colleagues was in the age of the children tested. Plausibly, spelling is less susceptible to the effects of remediation, and hence individual differences at older ages between twins in spelling are more likely to reveal genetic influence than variations in reading ability. To test this idea, De Fries, Alarcon and Olson (1997) assessed the genetic aetiology of reading and spelling deficits separately in 194 younger twin pairs (aged 8 to 11 years) and 146 older twins (aged 11 to 20 years). Heritability estimates decreased as a function of age for word recognition (0.64 vs 0.47) but increased for spelling (0.52 vs 0.68), with developmental differences being marginally significant in both cases.

Heritability of reading sub-skills

An important contribution to understanding the causes of dyslexia has come from the behaviour-genetic investigation of reading sub-skills by the Colorado group. To assess phonological decoding skill, two basic techniques have been used. The first is a nonword reading task in which measures of both speed and accuracy are taken. The second is a task in which children have to use phonological decoding skills to decide which of two letter strings sound like a word (for example, *caik–dake*). To assess orthographic reading skills, exception word reading is measured as well as a task in which children have to decide which of two phonologically similar letter strings is a word, for example *rane–rain*; *sammon–salmon* (Olson, Kliegl, Davidson and Foltz, 1985). To assess the phonological skills that underlie reading, Olson and his colleagues have used a range of tests including rhyme judgement and Pig Latin, a task in which children have to remove the first letter of a spoken word and put it at the end, followed by 'ay' (*sack* → 'acksay').

In their early work, Olson and colleagues reported that there was a greater genetic contribution to measures of phonological decoding than to orthographic reading skills (Olson, Wise, Connors, Rack and Fulker, 1989). They also reported that phonological reading skills shared genetic variance with phonological sensitivity measures, such as rhyme and phonemic awareness. However, as the size of the twin sample has increased, the picture has changed. More recently, Olson, Forsberg, Wise and Rack (1994) reported heritability estimates in the

141

same range for phonological decoding (0.59) and orthographic skills (0.56). The contribution of environmental factors to these component skills was 0.29 and 0.27 respectively. Arguably, this is what might be expected from cognitive models of reading development; phonological skills are the foundation of orthographic knowledge and opportunities to read are vital for the development of word recognition.

In contrast, estimates of the genetic contribution to reading comprehension are typically much smaller than to single word reading, while the environmental contribution is greater. It can be inferred that what appears to be genetically determined is phonological processing ability, and this underlies the development of both phonological decoding and orthographic reading skills. Furthermore, the processes associated with the development of word recognition are more constrained by genetic factors than processes involved in understanding text once it has been decoded.

To account for the larger environmental contribution to reading comprehension than to word recognition, Olson, Forsberg, Wise and Rack (1994) hypothesized that the knowledge of vocabulary and language concepts required for satisfactory reading comprehension depends largely on the shared educational and home environment experienced by twins. Another potentially important variable is the amount of exposure children have to text, be it in books, in comics or in magazines. Even a child with excellent phonological skills would not learn if they did not practice reading, and dyslexic children are more prone to turn away from reading than children without reading difficulties.

Stanovich and West (1989) pioneered a set of measures for estimating print exposure. These tests simply involve asking participants to choose the names of authors that they know in the Author Recognition test or of books in the Title Recognition test. The trick is that half of the items in each case are fictitious; they are neither names of real authors nor names of real books (see figure 8.1). By assessing sensitivity to real names, it is possible to derive a measure of print exposure which picks up individual differences in reading skill even when other important variables such as IQ and phonological awareness are controlled (Cunningham and Stanovich, 1991). Consistent with the idea that print exposure taps environmental variance in reading ability, Olson, Forsberg, Wise and Rack (1994) reported a non-significant heritability estimate of 0.21 for performance on a Title Recognition

(a) *Author Recognition Test*

Dean Koontz	Michael Harshorne
A. C. Leach	Stephen King
Paul Dobson	John Steinbeck
Anthony Lunch	Enid Blyton
Dick King-Smith	Charles Dickens
Betsy Byars	Carolyn Young
Judy Blume	Rosie Gunning

(b) *Title Recognition Test*

Space Brownies	Forever
B.F.G.	Great Expectations
Animal Farm	Lord of the Rings
Pride and Prejudice	Macbeth
Without Wishes	Reasons for Trying
Squashed Bananas	Dreams of New York
1984	The Babysitters Club

Figure 8.1 Extracts from tests of print exposure devised for a UK sample of 15- to 16-year-olds. The task is to tick (a) the correct author names (b) the correct book titles

test, whereas the estimate for the contribution of environmental variance was much greater at 0.60.

Heritability of individual differences in dyslexia

An extension of the behaviour-genetic approach to the analysis of individual differences involves assessing the relative contribution of genetic and environmental influences to a child's reading profile. To capture the variation between children who show a phonological dyslexic profile at one extreme and those who show a surface dyslexic profile, Castles, Datta, Gayan and Olson (1999) created a sub-type dimension. The starting point was to take measures of orthographic coding by assessing exception word reading, and of phonological coding by assessing nonword reading, from each child in a sample of 967 dyslexic twins aged 8 to 18 years. The next step was to create a standardised (z) score for exception word and nonword reading for each child. By subtracting the z score for orthographic coding from the z score for phonological coding, it was possible to describe each child's relative standing on this sub-type variable. Finally, after reading level was controlled, the top and bottom third of the distribution were classified as showing different reading profiles.

This procedure resulted in the identification of 322 children who resembled 'phonological dyslexic' readers and 322 who resembled 'surface dyslexic' readers. The classification was validated independently by performance on further phonological and orthographic choice tasks, and a test of phoneme deletion. Since word recognition taps phonological skills, which are poor in 'phonological dyslexia', as well as orthographic skills which are poor in 'surface dyslexia', it was natural for Castles et al. (1999) to assess the heritability of word recognition for the two sub-groups separately.

Among 'phonological dyslexics', the heritability estimate for reading was 0.67 and the estimate of environmental variance was 0.27. In contrast, among 'surface dyslexics', the heritability estimate for reading was 0.31 and the estimate of environmental variance was 0.63. Castles et al. (1999) concluded that there is a strong genetic component to phonological dyslexia, 'associated with a fundamental and possibly inherited spoken language deficit' (p. 89). Their conclusions about surface dyslexia were more speculative. Although they noted that the different etiology for the surface dyslexic pattern supports the partial independence in development of phonological and orthographic skills, the surface dyslexics were also impaired to a degree on phonological tasks. In line with the severity hypothesis proposed in chapter 7, the severity of the underlying phonological deficit appeared to be an important determinant of reading style in this study too.

In similar vein, Olson, Gayan, Datta and DeFries (1999) reported heritability analyses for dyslexic readers classified according to other variables such as IQ and processing speed. Speed of processing was indexed here by performance on four measures including cancellation tasks and coding. Moreover, the slow speed of processing sub-type showed a group deficit in orthographic coding. This finding complements those we reported in chapter 6 showing that poor nonword reading is associated with slow speed of processing (Griffiths and Snowling, submitted). For present purposes, it is interesting to note that the heritability of word recognition was higher among children with fast processing speed, and the environmental contribution to individual differences was higher among children with slow speed of processing.

The Genetic Basis of Dyslexia

The behaviour-genetic approach provides a powerful technique for assessing the validity of cognitive theories of dyslexia as well as for analysing the likely antecedents, both genetic and environmental, of individual differences in reading. Since the findings of this approach suggest that the disposition to be dyslexic is heritable, it is reasonable to question what accounts for its transmission between generations from the same family.

Before discussing this issue, it is important to stress the complexity of reading as a behavioural trait. Different skills are involved in word decoding and word comprehension, and phonological decoding skills are at least partially separable from orthographic knowledge. It would therefore be highly unlikely to find that dyslexia was associated with a single gene. Rather, several gene loci are likely to be involved and geneticists are at an early stage in understanding these.

The human karyotype consists of 46 chromosomes, 23 from the mother and 23 from the father. These chromosomes contain sequences of DNA comprising the human gene complement. Because of the very large number of genes in the human genome, looking for the chromosome locations of those associated with dyslexia would, metaphorically speaking, be like 'looking for a needle in a haystack' unless some clues could be found. Fortunately clues or 'markers' are available. The effects of some sequences of DNA are already understood, typically those involved in the transmission of well-understood diseases. These DNA sequences can be stained to provide markers to help in the search for the genes linked with dyslexia in affected family members.

The first gene markers for dyslexia were found on the long arm of chromosome 15 (Smith, Kimberling, Pennington and Lubs, 1983) and replications suggest these genes are implicated in some 30 per cent of families (Grigorenko et al., 1997; Schulke-Korne et al., 1997). More recently, gene markers have been identified on the short arm of chromosome 6 in other families (Cardon et al., 1994; Fisher et al., 1999; Gayan et al., 1995; Grigorenko et al., 1997). Interestingly, these markers are in the same region as the genes implicated in autoimmune diseases that have been reported to show a high degree of association with dyslexia (Behan and Geschwind, 1985). Finally, a translocation on chromosome 1 has also been suggested (Rabin et al., 1993). This finding has not yet been replicated.

Precursors of dyslexia in the pre-school years

With genetic studies of dyslexia as a backdrop, a new methodology has emerged that allows researchers to study the manifestations of dyslexia before the child fails to learn to read. The basic approach is to investigate pre-school children who are at high risk of dyslexia because they have a first-degree affected relative and then to conduct retrospective analyses examining the pre-school period after the children have been classified according to reading status. The major advantage is that it allows an assessment to be made of the manifestations of dyslexia before a child has experienced reading failure, and to a degree it avoids clinical bias.

Scarborough (1990) reported a pioneering study that followed the progress of a small sample of 34 children at genetic risk of dyslexia from age $2\frac{1}{2}$ to 8 years. More than half of these children (some 65 per cent) could be classified as dyslexic at 8 years. The next step was to carry out analyses that compared their early language skills with those of normal readers selected from the control group who had no family history of reading difficulty, as well as children from high-risk families who had turned out to be normal readers.

Contrary to the prevailing view that dyslexia is caused by a specific phonological deficit, Scarborough's findings revealed a changing pattern of language difficulties over time for children who later became dyslexic, with language skills outside of the phonological domain also being affected. At 30 months, children who went on to be dyslexic used as wide a range of vocabulary items in their conversation as the comparison groups, but their use of grammar was more restricted and they had more difficulty with speech production. At 36 and 42 months, the dyslexic children's vocabulary skills were less advanced than those of controls, and syntactic difficulties persisted (Scarborough, 1991). Finally, at 5 years, just as these children were starting school, they had poorer knowledge of letters and poorer phonological awareness than their peers.

It is difficult to assess how well Scarborough's findings can be generalized to the population of dyslexic readers at large. The sample size was small and conclusions were based on data from only 20 dyslexic children. However, following on from her work, several studies of children at genetic risk of dyslexia have been initiated, some of them starting in the very early years (Locke et al., 1997; Lyytinen, 1997).

The evidence available so far is broadly consistent with the phonological deficit hypothesis, though surprisingly few studies address the speech and language precursors of the observed deficits in phonological awareness. In the United States, Lefly and Pennington (1996) followed 73 high-risk and 57 low-risk children from the beginning of kindergarten to just before entry to first grade. In kindergarten, high-risk and low-risk groups differed in letter knowledge, detection of initial consonant differences, rime oddity and rapid naming, and during the second year, the groups also differed in phonemic awareness. Likewise, Byrne, Fielding-Barnsley, Ashley and Larsen (1997) found that problems of phonological awareness at $4\frac{1}{2}$ years, together with limitations of letter knowledge and knowledge of print, were precursors of reading difficulties in a sample of Australian children; and in Denmark, Elbro, Borstrom and Petersen (1998) found that whether or not children at risk of dyslexia became dyslexic depended upon their letter naming and phoneme identification skills in pre-school, together with a measure of the precision of their articulation skills.

In 1992, Alison Gallagher, Uta Frith and I commenced a UK study of children at genetic risk of dyslexia. Altogether we saw 71 children who had a first-degree relative who was dyslexic (in most cases a parent). The first assessment was conducted just before their fourth birthday, and they were followed through to 8 years of age. At each point in time, we compared the at-risk group with controls from families matched in terms of socio-economic circumstances and mother's educational level.

At 6 years of age, some 58 per cent of the at-risk group scored more than one standard deviation below the mean of the control group on literacy tasks (Gallagher, Frith and Snowling, 2000). In contrast, the incidence of underachievement among controls was only 12 per cent, which is what would be expected based on a normal distribution of literacy skills. Retrospective analyses confirmed that at-risk children who showed delayed literacy development at 6 years did not differ from controls in non-verbal ability at 3 years 9 months. However, they gained lower scores on tests of receptive vocabulary and expressive language and they showed weaknesses in a variety of tasks considered to assess phonological processing, namely, nonword repetition, nursery-rhyme knowledge and verbal short-term memory. By contrast, the unimpaired at-risk children were indistinguishable from controls.

Of course, the interaction of genes and environment is taken for granted in development, and the higher rate of slow literacy development among at-risk children might have been a consequence of being raised in a 'dyslexic' household. Contrary to this expectation, our assessment of the literacy environment of the poor-reading children in the sample suggested it was very similar to that of children from the high-risk group who were developing literacy normally. Furthermore, questionnaire responses supplied by parents suggested that the at-risk children received more assistance with the development of early literacy skills, particularly letter knowledge, than the children from control families with no history of reading difficulties.

The evidence from the various prospective studies of children at genetic risk of dyslexia bolsters the view that such children come to the task of learning to read with poorly developed phonological skills. But it seems that the development of their other language skills is also delayed. As Scarborough's and our own study show, slow vocabulary development is a concomitant of dyslexia, and expressive grammatical difficulties can be associated. It could be argued that this is quite a different picture from the one that has been painted of a specific phonological deficit in dyslexia.

However, it needs to be borne in mind that studying children at genetic risk of dyslexia is a quite different enterprise from studying children classified as dyslexic because they are failing to learn to read at the expected rate, only some of whom will have positive family histories. Importantly, studies that have rigorous exclusionary criteria may have excluded dyslexic children with vocabulary impairments of the type uncovered by at risk studies. Moreover, it is likely to be the case that dyslexic children recruited following reading failure will have more severe deficits than those whose difficulties are identified early.

There is another caveat too, and that is that the core phonological deficit in dyslexia could affect the early acquisition of vocabulary (cf. Gathercole and Baddeley, 1990); in other words the vocabulary deficit may be a *consequence* later in development of the phonological processing impairment (Frith and Happé, 1998). Later, during the school years, when vocabulary development depends more upon the ability to infer the meanings of new words than the ability to acquire their phonological forms, the receptive vocabulary of dyslexic children may go through a period of 'catch-up', leaving only expressive vocabulary deficits to be observed.

Thus, the interpretation of the findings of studies of children at risk of dyslexia turns on whether the vocabulary and grammatical delays that are observed are causally linked to their literacy failure. An alternative worthy of exploration is that these resolve during the early school years. Notwithstanding these considerations, the evidence that dyslexic children come to the task of learning to read with poor phonological skills is strong, and as we have shown, this has a deleterious effect on their ability to learn to read.

Dyslexia and the Brain

An obvious question that follows from the genetic study of dyslexia is what brain systems mediate the phonological processing difficulties seen in dyslexia. A sophisticated understanding of brain mechanisms is beyond the scope of this book. However, at a very basic level, the human brain can be thought of as divided through the midline into two hemispheres connected by the corpus callosum, and it is generally accepted that in the majority of individuals, it is the left hemisphere that is specialized for language. Within each hemisphere there are broadly four regions (lobes) with different specializations (see figure 8.2a), and it has long been established that regions in the temporal lobe of the left hemisphere, on either side of the Sylvian fissure, are involved in language processing. In particular, Wernicke's area is involved in language comprehension and Broca's area in speech production (see figure 8.2b).

With respect to the reading process, a simple view would be that print is processed through the retina via pathways to visual cortex at the back of the brain (see figure 8.2b). From there, activation must

149

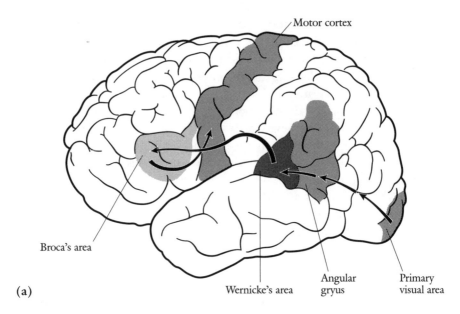

(a)

Motor cortex

Broca's area

Wernicke's area

Angular gryus

Primary visual area

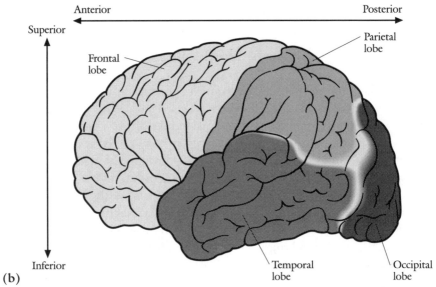

Anterior

Posterior

Superior

Parietal lobe

Frontal lobe

Inferior

Temporal lobe

Occipital lobe

(b)

Figure 8.2 (a) Figure showing the brain indicating the four lobes; (b) Figure showing the language areas of the brain and depicting the pathway used for reading aloud a printed word

Source: Posner and Raichle, 1997

pass to regions in the temporal lobe to make contact with the language processing resources required for phonological decoding and reading comprehension. It is believed that the normal human brain is asymmetric in these regions, such that the left side of the brain is larger than the homologous regions in the right hemisphere in about 65 per cent of cases (Geschwind and Levitsky, 1968).

The first kind of evidence about the brain structure and function of dyslexic individuals came from a series of post-mortem studies of dyslexic brains carried out by Galaburda and his colleagues (Galaburda, 1994; Galaburda and Kemper, 1978). These studies involved making two kinds of measurements, microscopic examinations throughout the perisylvian region of the left hemisphere, and measurements of the planum temporale, a posterior region of the Sylvian fissure (which usually shows asymmetry).

Microscopic examination of dyslexic brains conducted by Galaburda revealed several abnormalities in the brains involving ectopias and dysplasias (a kind of scarring) of the neurons. These cortical lesions were taken to suggest atypical patterns of neuronal circuitry. An associated finding was of symmetry of the planum temporale. Rather than finding the left planum to be larger than the right in these dyslexic brains, they were equivalent in size, with the right larger than normal. Taken together, these findings suggest that differences in brain structure in dyslexia date back to prenatal brain differentiation, a process that is under genetic control.

The first reports of these brain differences between dyslexic and normal readers were viewed sceptically, not least because there was little documentation about the dyslexics' difficulties prior to their demise. However, findings of symmetrical plana in dyslexia have now been replicated in a number of studies using non-invasive techniques such as magnetic resonance imaging (MRI), in which images of sections of the brain can be examined to make assessments of its structure. A common finding (see table 8.2) appears to be that, whilst asymmetry of the planum temporale is the case in the majority of normal readers, it is symmetrical in about the same proportion of dyslexics (Hynd and Hiemenz, 1997).

An important study by Larsen, Hoien, Lundberg and Odegaard (1990) made a direct link between planum symmetry and phonological deficiency based on MRI scans taken from 19 15-year-old dyslexic children matched individually to controls for age, gender, IQ,

Table 8.2 The planum temporale in reading disorders

Authors	Measurement	Finding	Lateralization
Galaburda (1993)	surface area	symmetry	larger right
Hynd et al. (1990)	length	right ≥ left	shorter left
Larsen et al. (1990)	length	symmetry	longer right
Leonard et al. (1993)	length	–	–
Rumsey et al. (1997)	surface area	left > right	normal pattern
Schultz et al. (1994)	convolutional surface area	left > right	normal pattern

Source: Filipek, 1999

socio-economic class and educational environment. Larsen et al. used these MRI data to reconstruct the size of the planum temporale from successive coronal sections of the lower bank of the Sylvian fissure. The dominant pattern found for the dyslexics was symmetry of the planum (70 per cent) with the right planum being larger. In contrast, 70 per cent of controls showed asymmetry. The dyslexic children were then classified on the basis of performance on tests of phonological and orthographic reading skills. Although this classification had short-comings and there was a degree of overlap between groups, all five of those with pure phonological problems showed symmetry of the planum, as did seven out of nine with mixed phonological-orthographic problems. One child with orthographic problems showed the normal pattern of asymmetry as did three of the four who were left unclassified.

Technological advances in recent years have made it possible to view not only the structure of the brain but also how it functions when engaged in cognitive processing. These brain imaging techniques, such as positron emission tomography (PET) or functional magnetic resonance imaging (fMRI), have been used increasingly to investigate developmental disorders, including dyslexia (Filipek, 1999). In one of the first of these, Rumsey et al. (1992) observed brain activity while 14 dyslexic adults participated in rhyme detection and auditory attention tasks. The rhyme detection task involved listening to pairs of one- to three-syllable words, half of which rhymed, presented to both ears at the rate of 16 per minute. The task was to press a button every time they heard a rhyming pair. The attention task involved listening to a series of tones of three different intensities, presented for 1 second with an interval of 2 seconds between pairs of tones. The task was to detect the tone that was lowest in volume. The dyslexic readers performed with as high a level of accuracy on these tasks as controls matched for age, IQ and educational level, and they showed normal levels of brain activity during resting periods and during the attention task. However, the dyslexics showed a different pattern of brain activation during rhyming. In this task, controls activated left temporoparietal regions but this activation was not seen among dyslexics.

Along similar lines, Paulesu et al. (1996) examined patters of brain activation in five well-compensated dyslexic adults with documented childhood histories of dyslexia whilst they carried out phonological processing tasks. Two tasks involving phonological processing and two control tasks involving visual processing were contrasted. The first phonological task involved deciding whether pairs of visually presented letters rhymed (for example BD rhyme but BW do not). The parallel visual tasks required the volunteers to make judgements about the shape similarity of pairs of unfamiliar letters from the Korean alphabet. The second phonological task required memory search for a target letter in a series of successively presented letters and therefore engaged verbal short-term memory, while the parallel search task for Korean letters engaged visual memory.

It is conventional when analysing brain activity during performance on a complex task to use what is known as the subtraction methodology. Basically this method involves taking away the activation involved in one facet of the task from that involved in the task as a whole. To take an example from the present experiment, making rhyme judgements about pairs of visually presented letters involves an appreciation of their visual attributes as well as their phonological codes. In contrast, making visual similarity judgements between pairs of Korean letters (given no knowledge of Korean) involves only the visual element of the more complex task. By subtracting the activation involved in the visual task from that involved in the phonological task, an attempt can be made to isolate the mental processes involved in the phonological comparison.

A summary of the brain activity during the completion of the phonological tasks when that involved in the completion of the control tasks has been removed is shown in figure 8.3. Although the

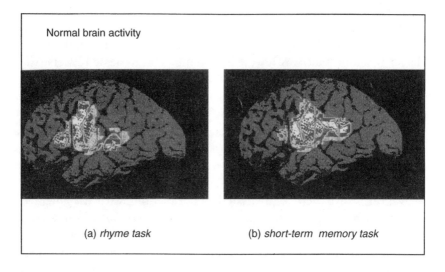

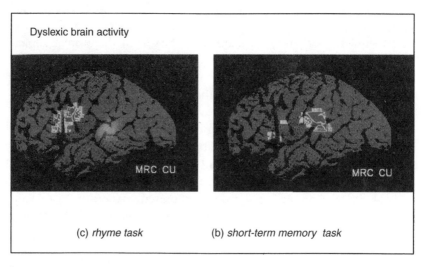

Figure 8.3 Patterns of activation across the left hemisphere during (a) rhyme and (b) verbal short-term memory tasks by normal and dyslexic readers. Light areas show activation. Dyslexic brains are shown in the lower part of the figure

Source: Paulesu et al., 1996

dyslexics and their controls performed as well as each other on the experimental tasks, there was less activation across the left hemisphere in the dyslexic brains than in those of the normal readers, both during rhyme processing and during the short-term memory task. Specifically, a region called the insula that connects Wernicke's and Broca's regions received less activation in dyslexics.

In a similar vein, Brunswick, McCrory, Price, Frith and Frith (1999) conducted PET scans of young dyslexic adults whilst reading aloud and when completing a graphic-feature detection task involving words and nonwords that required only implicit reading. Relative to a rest condition, dyslexics showed less activation than controls of similar age and IQ in the left posterior temporal cortex when completing both tasks (Brodmann area 37: BA 37). Interestingly, BA 37 has been implicated in previous studies of naming, and its limited activation in dyslexics is suggestive of a deficit in retrieving lexical codes. In the explicit reading tasks, compensatory activity was observed in a pre-motor region of Broca's area for dyslexics probably associated with the use of compensatory strategies when reading.

Similar findings were reported by Shaywitz et al. (1998) from a functional MRI study in which dyslexic adults carried out a series of tasks varying in phonological demands whilst undergoing functional MRI. Once again there was under-activation of left posterior regions of the cortex, especially Wernicke's area, angular gyrus and striate cortex. In addition, over-activation of left frontal and right posterior regions suggested anomalous brain function (possibly compensatory) in these dyslexic subjects.

Thus, a growing body of evidence suggests that the behavioural findings of phonological processing deficits may be the result of differences in left-hemisphere brain function between dyslexic and normal readers. In particular, the regions that link brain areas for speech perception and speech production seem to be affected. It is interesting to speculate that this could be the 'site' of the phono-logical representations critical to reading development.

Laterality, immune disorders and dyslexia

According to an influential theory proposed by Geschwind and his colleagues, differences in brain structure and function between dyslexic and normal readers originate early in development, possibly in the prenatal period (Geschwind and Galaburda, 1985). According to their hypothesis, a high level of prenatal testosterone acts independently on the developing brain and the thymus, a gland controlling the body's immunity. The effects on the brain lead to an increased likelihood of both left-handedness and dyslexia because of altered left-hemisphere development, while the effects on the thymus lead to an increased risk of immune disorders. It follows that there should be an association between left-handedness and immune disorders in learning disabilities.

As a way of testing Geschwind's theory, Pennington, Smith, Kimberling, Green and Haith (1987) examined the frequency of immune disorders and left-handedness in 87 dyslexics and 86 normal readers from 14 extended families. The sample included 136 adults and 37 children. Autoimmune disorders were reported in 10 per cent of the dyslexics, a figure similar to that mentioned by Geschwind and Galaburda. This frequency was significantly greater than that found for non-dyslexic family members. This difference could not be attributed to an over-reporting of symptoms by affected families because differences in the frequency of, for example, migraines was not reported. The dyslexics also showed an increased proportion of allergic disorders, such as hay fever and asthma, and of developmental disorders such as stuttering and hyperactivity, but not of major psychiatric disorders. However, there was no elevation of left- or mixed-handedness in the study sample, nor was there an association between handedness and immune disorders.

The association between reading skill and laterality has been studied by Marian Annett and her colleagues within the context of her 'right-shift' theory of handedness (Annett, 1985 and 1991). According to the right-shift theory, there is a genetic basis for a factor that induces both left-hemisphere speech and the associated displacement of hand skill towards the right. An important aspect of the approach taken by this group is that in addition to asking about hand preference, they use a peg-moving task to determine the relative skill of the two hands. The initial hypothesis explored by Annett was that strong left-handers, who are in the minority in the population, would be at high risk of speech difficulties and of difficulties in learning that depend on speech, such as dyslexia.

Annett and Kilshaw (1984) reported a raised incidence of strong left-handers and also children with mixed handedness in a clinical sample of dyslexic readers. However, the dyslexics did not differ from controls in overall mean performance, as measured by the difference in skill between right and left hands. In a study designed to follow up these findings, Annett and Manning (1990) tested the hand prefer-ence and peg-moving skill of 300 British children, as well as assessing their reading ability and non-verbal IQ. They found that poor readers tended to be more frequent at both the left and the right extremes of hand skill. Biases to dextrality (right-handedness) were strong in many poor readers but others tended to have poor right-hand skills. Thus, the association between handedness, hand-skill and reading ability is not straightforward and, perhaps contrary to prediction, only a small sub-group of dyslexics with high IQs have good left-hand skills. The possibility that poor readers at the extreme left and the extreme right of the hand-skill distribution might differ in their cognitive abilities and in the ways in which their reading problems are manifest deserves further research.

Understanding the biological bases of dyslexia is at a relatively early stage and significant questions remain both about its molecular genetic basis and the brain mechanisms that are involved. However, there seems little doubt, given existing knowledge, that the cognitive diffi-culties that characterize dyslexic readers stem from inherited differ-ences in speech processing mechanisms located in the left hemisphere of the brain. The analysis of these differences among children at genetic risk of dyslexia from infancy onwards has already begun. Indeed, Leppanen, Pihko, Eklund and Lyytinen (1999) reported pre-liminary evidence that already at birth, children at genetic risk of dyslexia show different patterns of brain activity from control infants in response to changes in speech stimuli. These very early differences in the processing of auditory-speech stimuli may well set the stage for delays in the development of phonological representations in dyslexic children.

Chapter 9

Dyslexia: A Sensory Impairment?

In the last chapter we showed that, some 30 years after the World Federation of Neurology suggested that dyslexia was of constitutional origin, there is a rapidly growing body of evidence concerning its biological bases. Furthermore, findings of differences in brain structure and function between dyslexic and normal readers raise the possibility that the problems of dyslexia might be traced to deficits in basic sensory processes. If this is the case, there is no reason why only reading should be affected in dyslexic individuals (Stein and Talcott, 1999). In this chapter we explore the evidence that dyslexia is associated with problems of basic auditory and visual processing before considering an alternative hypothesis, that dyslexic readers have deficits in the mechanisms subserving the temporal resolution of sensory information, a 'pan-modality' deficit.

Dyslexia as a Visual Processing Impairment

Although the consensus view is that dyslexia stems from a phonological processing deficit, the role of visual problems is a topic of continuing debate (Willows, Kruk and Corcos, 1993). Since reading requires processing of the spatial location of letters while the eyes move across text, it is reasonable to hypothesize, as many have done, that dyslexics might have problems with processes involved in visual analysis or in the temporal integration of visuo-spatial information over time.

An old idea was that dyslexia might stem from an inability to control the rapid eye movements that are necessary when reading text. This idea was popularized by Pavlides (1981), who claimed that dyslexic children, when compared to age-matched controls, showed a specific

158

difficulty in sequencing eye movements to follow successively illuminated lights. However, a number of subsequent studies failed to replicate this finding (Olson, Kliegel and Davidson, 1983; Stanley, Smith and Howell, 1983) and there is really no evidence that deficits in eye movement control are common in dyslexia (but see Pirrozolo and Rayner, 1978 for a highly unusual case of an adult in whom poor reading skills seemed linked to a severe problem in controlling eye movements).

A slightly different idea explored by Stein and his colleagues was that dyslexic readers lacked 'ocular motor dominance' (see Stein, 1989 for a review). According to this view, dyslexic children have difficulty in integrating information between the two eyes and this is detectable by an orthoptic test, the 'reference' eye test (Dunlop, Dunlop and Fenelon, 1973). Fowler (1991) suggested that because these children have poor visual localization, they find it difficult to identify or sequence letters, so that words appear blurred or run into one another and 'letters may jump about on the page'. In order to establish a reference eye, Stein and Fowler (1985) designed an intervention in which dyslexic children wore occluded spectacles for six months (one eye was effectively patched). At the end of the intervention, the reading skills of these children were compared with those of controls who had worn plain glasses. Those who had established better binocular control, as indicated by their having developed a fixed reference eye, had advanced in reading by 11.6 months. In contrast, children whose reference remained unfixed advanced by only 5.6 months.

A problem for this research was that there was no control over the amount of reading tuition the children received during the intervention period, and there were no checks regarding how often the children wore the spectacles. A further limitation was that the dyslexics were not allocated to treatment groups at random and that when appropriate statistical analyses were conducted, there was no support for the idea that occluding one eye produced beneficial effects on children's reading (Bishop, 1989).

Also refuting these results, Newman et al. (1985) reported data from an unselected sample of 328 8-year-old children in which rates of unstable ocular dominance did not differ between those with and without reading and spelling problems. Similarly, Goulandris, McIntyre, Snowling, Methel and Lee (1998) found that orthoptic difficulties were no more frequent in a group of dyslexic readers than controls (but see Stein, 1998 for a reply).

Impairments of the visual transient system

During the 1980s, Lovegrove and his colleagues proposed a different hypothesis, that dyslexic readers have low-level visual impairments affecting the transient visual system (Lovegrove, Martin and Slaghuis, 1986). In order to discuss the influential body of research that has stemmed from this hypothesis, it is important first to provide an outline description of the human visual system (see figure 9.1). A simple account of vision begins at the eye, where visual stimuli are first received at the retina. Nerve cells (retinal ganglion cells) that pick up information from the photoreceptors in the retina pass information on through the optic chiasma to the two hemispheres of the brain via the lateral geniculate nucleus (LGN). The LGN can be thought of as a kind of way station en route to primary visual cortex (also referred to as V1 or striate cortex). Area V1 is where the preliminary visual analysis of a stimulus takes place, prior to transfer of the signals through extra-striate cortex to the higher levels of the visual system including V5 (also known as area MT) in the temporal lobe.

An important aspect of brain organization is that separate functions are segregated. This is particularly clear in the visual system, where different aspects of the visual world, such as form, colour and motion, appear to be processed via different regions of extra-striate cortex. These different pathways through the human visual cortex have their origins in two types of nerve cell in the retina. P cells predominately project from the fovea or centre of the retina and terminate in the parvocellular (P) layers of the lateral geniculate nucleus (LGN). P cells are specialized for form and colour vision. M cells project from areas more evenly across the centre and periphery of the retina and terminate in the magnocellular (M) layers of LGN. M cells are specialized for detecting motion and rapidly changing stimuli.

Although there is likely to be substantial interconnectedness of the M and the P pathways (Zeki, 1993), the input from LGN to V5 is dominated by the magnocellular stream which then projects from V5 to temporal cortex and is concerned with analysing 'where' visual objects are to be located (the dorsal stream). In contrast, the P

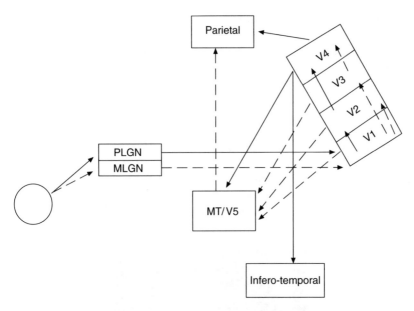

Figure 9.1 Schematic diagram of the visual system showing some of the main neural pathways. The solid lines represent parvocellular, the dashed lines represent magnocellular input; V1–V4 visual cortex, LGN lateral geniculate nucleus (M and P sections), MT/V5 middle temporal area

Source: adapted from Johnson, 1997

pathway projects to the inferior parietal lobe and is concerned with 'what' visual objects are (the ventral stream). In the literature on dyslexia, the distinction between the magnocellular and the parvo-cellular pathways (defined both histologically and physiologically) has often been aligned with the psychophysically defined transient and sustained systems. In fact, this may be an oversimplification but, for present purposes, we will use the terms interchangeably. The transient visual system is basically responsible for detecting moving stimuli and is fast-acting but with poor acuity, while the sustained system is of higher acuity but transmits information more slowly. Table 9.1 summarizes the properties of the transient and sustained systems.

A variety of psychophysical techniques have been used to assess functioning of the transient and sustained systems. These involve

Table 9.1 Properties of the sustained and transient visual systems

Sustained system	Transient system
Sensitive to high spatial frequencies	Sensitive to low spatial frequencies
Sensitive to low temporal frequencies	Sensitive to high temporal frequencies
Slow transmission	Fast transmission
Responds continuously throughout stimulus presentation	Responds at stimulus onset and offset
Predominates in central vision	Predominates in peripheral vision

Source: adapted from Lovegrove, 1991, p. 149

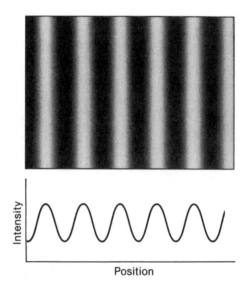

Position

Figure 9.2 Since wave grating such as commonly used in vision research with spatial frequency channels

Source: Goldstein, 1984

assessments of a viewer's thresholds for detecting particular stimulus properties. Two stimulus properties that have been particularly well investigated are spatial and temporal frequency.

Spatial frequency can be thought of in terms of stimulus size. Figure 9.2 shows a sine wave grating of medium spatial frequency. The grating consist of white and black stripes; the relative spacing between the dark stripes determines its spatial frequency. Contrast refers to the difference between the maximum and minimum luminances of the gratings. In a typical experiment, subjects are shown a stimulus like this one, flickering at different rates, and they have to set contrast levels so that they can see the flicker or the pattern. Dyslexics have been reported to be less sensitive to flicker, particularly as its rate or temporal frequency increases.

Visible persistence refers to the continued perception of a stimulus after it has been switched off, and typically, visible persistence increases with increasing spatial frequency. In line with the hypothesis that dyslexics have transient system impairments, the increase is much less in dyslexic readers than in controls (Slaghuis and Lovegrove, 1985). Dyslexic and normal readers also differ in their contrast sensitivity at low but not high spatial frequencies.

Taken together, these findings point to impairments in the transient visual system in dyslexia. In contrast, the functioning of the sustained system, as assessed for example by the ability to detect non-flickering high-spatial frequency gratings, appears to be normal. The importance of these findings for dyslexia is that, during reading, information has to be combined from peripheral and central vision. Low spatial frequency information is picked up from peripheral vision from an area about five to six letters to the right of fixation, while high-spatial frequency information is picked up from central vision during fixations. Transient system deficits that affect the extraction of forthcoming information to the right of fixation would naturally be expected to impair reading. Furthermore, if transient responses failed to inhibit sustained activity, as they are thought to do in the normal case, then the persistence of information extracted through foveal vision could obscure or mask information from later fixations (Breitmeyer, 1980).

Livingstone, Rosen, Drislane and Galaburda (1991) took these findings as the starting point for a study in which they examined the functioning of the magnocellular and parvocellular sub-divisions of the visual system using physiological measures, namely, evoked potentials. At high contrasts, visual evoked potentials were similar for dyslexic and normal subjects. However, at low contrasts, the dyslexics showed differences early in the sensory processing chain (though it should be noted that between-group statistical comparisons were not reported). In a second study they examined the lateral geniculate nucleus in autopsy specimens taken from five dyslexic and five normal brains. The parvocellular layers appeared similar in both groups, whereas the magnocellular layers were more disorganized in the dyslexic brains and the cell bodies appeared smaller. Thus, Livingstone and colleagues presented anatomical and physiological evidence for the transient system deficits reported in psychophysical experiments with dyslexic readers.

The view that magnocellular deficits underlie the reading problems of dyslexic children was first criticized by Hulme (1988), who questioned the causal significance of the findings. In particular, if there is a direct relationship between visual impairments and reading difficulties, then dyslexic children should have more problems in reading prose rather than single words. On the contrary, this is seldom the case (Frith and Snowling, 1983). A second difficulty for the view that magnocellular impairments cause reading problems is that there have been a number of failures to replicate the basic behavioural findings.

Cornelissen, Richardson, Mason, Fowler and Stein (1995) examined contrast sensitivity in a group of dyslexic and normal readers in luminance conditions that were similar to those required for reading. For static and flickering stimuli, there was negligible difference in threshold at any spatial frequency between dyslexics and controls. Similarly, Hayduk, Bruck and Cavanagh (1996) failed to demonstrate differences in contrast sensitivity thresholds for flickering gratings at low and high spatial frequencies between dyslexic and normal adults and between dyslexic and normal children using a modification of the adult paradigm.

An argument put forward to account for the disparate findings between studies is sampling differences. Borsting, and colleagues (Borsting et al., 1996) compared the contrast sensitivity at different spatial and temporal frequencies of a group of 'dyseidetic' dyslexic adults with a group of mixed dysphonetic-dyseidetic and control readers. Overall there were no group differences at low temporal frequencies but there were at high temporal frequencies. The group difference occurred because the dysphonetic-dyseidetic dyslexics showed reduced sensitivity to low spatial frequency gratings at high temporal frequency. This was an interesting finding. Contrary to what might have been predicted, however, it was the group who had additional phonological impairments that showed the magnocellular deficits, not those with specifically visual problems. The lack of inclusion of a group of dysphonetic dyslexics limits the interpretation of the authors' findings. A further problem with the study is that few details are provided of how the dyslexic group was classified, and in particular, how it differed from controls.

Motion discrimination in dyslexic and normal readers

Another paradigm that has been used to assess functioning of the magnocellular system in dyslexic readers is one requiring discrimination of either the direction or velocity of movement (Eden et al., 1996). Cornelissen, Richardson, Mason, Fowler and Stein (1995) assessed the performance of dyslexics on tasks requiring perception of motion coherence using visual arrays known as random dot kinematograms. Stimulus patterns comprised two rectangular patches of over 1,000 random square white dots on a darker background. Motion was generated by shifting the positions of the dots from screen to screen every 20 milliseconds. Perception of motion in these displays is related to the percentage of dots that move coherently. The subject's task is to view two adjacent panels and to decide in which they can see a stream of movement while the experimenter varies the proportion of dots moving until a threshold for perceiving motion is reached. It is important to note that this was a shearing motion display; in the target patch, an inner strip moved against the direction of motion of the two outer strips. This type of motion is detected fairly early on in the visual processing chain, in V1 rather than V5 (Reppas, Niyogi, Dale, Sereno and Tootell, 1997).

A group of 29 10-year-old dyslexic and 29 age-matched normal readers were compared in the first experiment. The mean threshold for motion coherence was higher for dyslexics initially. After the first block of trials, both groups improved, the dyslexics by more. The finding of higher thresholds for motion coherence was replicated in a further experiment involving dyslexic adults, but importantly, Cornelissen and colleagues noted that there was significant overlap between the groups. What this variability might relate to was explored in a later study that related thresholds for motion coherence to the propensity to make particular types of reading error in an unselected group of children (Cornelissen, Hansen, Hutton, Evangelinou and Stein, 1997).

In this later study there was a positive relationship between children's motion detection thresholds and the likelihood that they made errors containing letters not in the target stimulus (for example, *garden* → 'grandeen'; *suspect* → 'subpact'). This relationship held even when age, IQ, reading level and phonological awareness were controlled. In contrast, there was no correlation between motion detection threshold and performance on phonological tasks or with reading ability. However, a limitation of this study was that the error classification was subjective and reliability data were not reported.

A further problem for the interpretation of studies of dyslexic motion perception was raised by Raymond and Sorensen (1998). When long duration stimuli are used in such tasks, they elicit smooth pursuit eye movements that have typically not been taken into account. It is possible therefore that the reported deficits in motion perception are attributable to faulty mechanisms for the temporal integration of moving events across successive frames, rather than an insensitivity to movement per se.

In their first experiment, Raymond and Sorensen (1998) compared ten dyslexic and ten normal readers aged 9–10 years on a motion detection task using 4-frame random dot kinetograms (RDKs) with short duration stimuli. Although the dyslexic children performed with 95 per cent accuracy on simple versions of the task, indicating that they understood its demands, their thresholds were almost double those of the age-matched control group who performed like adults. Furthermore, six out of the ten dyslexic children had thresholds that fell outside of normal limits though there was nothing obvious that distinguished these children from the others and none had attentional deficits.

In a second experiment, they assessed motion perception thresholds in conditions that differed in the number and the duration of frames in the RDKs. There were no group differences with brief frame durations of 32 ms in a 2-frame condition. However, the dyslexics' thresholds were raised in a 7-frame condition. With longer durations of 112 ms, group mean thresholds for normals dropped from 25 to 10.5 per cent respectively for 2 frames to 7 frames. For dyslexics the improvement was only from 26.3 per cent to 19.9 per cent, suggesting that they show poorer integration over time. Since differences between groups for the two long frames were not significant, this suggests they have similar sensitivity to motion when a single displacement of dots is presented.

Raymond and Sorensen concluded that children with dyslexia show deficits in global motion detection, but that these do not reflect an inability to detect motion per se, but rather an abnormality in the perceptual integration of motion information. Thus, dyslexics may have abnormal co-operative mechanisms in the visual domain. The finding that dyslexic readers show a lack of V5 activation under functional MRI scan when perceiving moving stimuli (Eden et al., 1996) is consistent with this idea, but it is at odds with the findings of Cornelissen's group (1995 and 1997) that suggest an impairment at a lower level in V1.

Though inconclusive, the evidence that dyslexic readers have reduced sensitivity to movement is more consistent than that suggesting they have poorer contrast sensitivity than normal readers. As a consequence, motion tasks appear to have been adopted as more reliable indicators of magnocellular deficits (cf. Demb, Boynton, Best and Heeger, 1998). However, it remains important to emphasize that the significance of these findings still needs to be explained (Hogben, 1997). The magnocellular deficit is subtle and not serious enough to cause symptomatic complaint. Furthermore, it seems that it co-occurs with phonological processing impairments (Eden et al., 1996; Lovegrove, 1991). An obvious possibility is that magnocellular deficits are a biological marker for dyslexia but unrelated to it at the cognitive level (Frith and Frith, 1996); they may, in other words, be irrelevant to explaining dyslexic reading problems.

Temporal Processing Deficits in Dyslexia

As we saw earlier, there is some mixed evidence for speech perception deficits in dyslexic readers. A hypothesis that has gained popularity in recent years is that such difficulties might be traced to more basic auditory processing deficits, particularly in tasks that require temporal processing (Farmer and Klein, 1995). This idea stems from work by Tallal and her colleagues in the 1970s (Tallal and Piercy, 1973, 1975) which investigated the performance of children with specific language impairment (SLI) rather than dyslexia on auditory tasks. SLI is a condition

167

in which oral language skills are impaired while non-verbal ability is within the normal range (Bishop, 1997).

The SLI children who participated in these studies were first taught to discriminate a pair of tones by pressing one of two keys to indicate whether they heard the higher or the lower of the tones. Once the children had learned this discrimination, they listened to sequences of the tones (high–low; low–high, high–high or low–low) and they had to indicate the order in which they had been presented by pressing the keys representing the tones that they had heard successively. This temporal order judgement task is also referred to as the Repetition task.

When it had been established that the children could make temporal order judgements, the time between the tones (the inter-stimulus interval) was varied. Thus, the children made a series of temporal order judgements in response to pairs of tones with inter-stimulus intervals varying at random from short (at 50 ms) to long at 400 ms durations. The main claim made on the basis of these studies was that language impaired children have no difficulty in making the temporal order judgements when the inter-stimulus intervals are long. However, they have significantly more difficulty than age-matched controls when the inter-stimulus intervals are short. A specific prediction that followed from this work was that language impaired children should have particular difficulty with the discrimination of stop consonants since this would require the analysis of rapid changes or transitions. Tallal and Piercy (1974) went on to show that this was indeed the case in an experiment showing impairments in the discrimination of stop consonants but not steady state vowels.

The extension of the theory and its applications to children with developmental dyslexia began with a study by Tallal (1980), who related difficulty with temporal ordering to problems in phonological decoding. Later, Reed (1989) asked 7- to 10-year-old dyslexics to make temporal judgements regarding the order of presentation of pairs of verbal and non-verbal stimuli. The dyslexics had difficulty in judging the order of two stop consonants or two brief tones but their ability to make temporal judgements involving steady state vowels was normal. In line with the hypothesis that the perception of stop consonants requires the temporal resolution of rapidly changing acoustic information in the speech signal, the dyslexics also had more difficulty than controls on a task in which spoken words had to be matched with pictures differing by a single phoneme, for example, matching 'goal' to one of two pictures: *goal* versus *bowl*. Thus, Tallal proposed that dyslexic children, together with others who have language learning impairments, have difficulty with rapid auditory processing (see Tallal, Miller, Jenkins and Merzenich, 1997 for a review).

However, as Tallal's own study (1980) showed, only a minority of dyslexic children experience difficulty with auditory temporal processing. Similarly, Heath, Hogben and Clark (1999) reported that only children with reading difficulties that were accompanied by oral language impairments showed such deficits. In their study, it was the children with the poorest performance on phonological awareness tasks that tended to require long inter-stimulus intervals to perform well. In Tallal's (1980) study it was also those with more severe phonological difficulties as revealed by their poor nonword reading who had most difficulty on the auditory task.

In recent work from our laboratory, Catherine Marshall assessed 12-year-old dyslexic children on auditory discrimination and temporal order judgement tasks using the same stimulus characteristics as Tallal and Piercy (1973), as well as on tests of phonological awareness and nonword repetition. The dyslexic group performed less well than children of the same age when required to discriminate tone pairs and also when copying their order on the Repetition task. However, performance was in line with that of younger reading-age matched controls. Contrary to Tallal's theory, the group difference in temporal order judgement was significant at all inter-stimulus intervals, not only when successive tones were presented rapidly.

The relationship between temporal order judgment and phonological processing was significant among the dyslexics, and also across a large sample of normal readers, even when age and non-verbal IQ were controlled. Furthermore, a sub-group of four out of 18 dyslexic readers who performed particularly badly on the auditory tasks were among the most impaired readers in the sample. These children also had severe impairments of phonological awareness and nonword repetition. However, it is important to note that other dyslexics with equally severe phonological difficulties performed normally on the auditory processing tasks.

Overall, the relationship between the auditory and phonological tasks was stronger than the relationship between auditory processing and reading skill. In turn, reading ability was better predicted by phonological processing. The pattern of relationships among the measures makes interpretation of the findings less than straightforward. One possibility is that children who have better phonological skills are more likely to give the tones verbal labels when completing the temporal judgement task. This strategy would facilitate task performance but leave the causal significance of the auditory processing deficit unexplained. In similar vein, Bishop et al. (1999) found that deficits in nonword repetition were highly heritable in a twin study of language impairment. However the genetic contribution to individual differences in auditory temporal judgements was not significant, even though the two behavioural measures were inter-correlated.

More generally, Tallal's theory has proved controversial because of a challenge to its basic assumption that the processes involved in the processing of non-verbal sounds are similar to those involved in speech processing (Studdert-Kennedy and Mody, 1995). Pursuing this critique, Mody, Studdert-Kennedy and Brady (1997) tested the predictions of Tallal's theory for developmental dyslexia directly by comparing the performance of good and poor readers on discrimination tasks that involved either speech stimuli or non-verbal stimuli with identical acoustic characteristics (sine waves). The dyslexic children performed like normal readers on the non-verbal but not on the speech perception tasks. These findings suggest that they experience a deficit specific to the speech module and not in more basic auditory processes.

In a similar vein, Nittrouer (1999) compared the performance of 17 children with poor phonological processing, who scored more than one standard deviation below the mean in reading, with that of 93 normal readers with normal phonological processing, on tasks tapping speech perception and temporal processing. The temporal processing task was like the Repetition task of Tallal but used two sinusoidal waves of 75 ms duration. Following training, the children had to repeat tone sequences played at five inter-stimulus intervals between 20 ms (the shortest) and 320 ms. After completing the block containing two-tone sequences, the children were then instructed to repeat three-tone and finally four-tone sequences at each of the ISIs.

The speech perception tasks were designed to investigate the acoustic cues used by the children to differentiate between phonemes. If Tallal's theory is correct, then children with poor phonological processing (ppp) might be expected to have difficulty using brief auditory cues. For each task, a single stimulus was presented and the children had to assign one of two response labels to it. The children discriminated synthetic stimuli along the [dɑ] – [tɑ], [sɛɪ] – [stɛɪ] and [s] – [ʃ] continua in four different tests. Following training using the best exemplars on each continuum, they were presented with ten blocks of trials to determine the phoneme boundary in each case.

There was a main effect of ISI with performance being worse at short ISIs, and a main effect of list length in the temporal processing task. However, there was no group difference in performance although a small number of the children in the PPP group seemed to be impaired. Contrary to Tallal's theory, the group difference was not larger at shorter ISIs or at longer list lengths. Nor were there group differences on either the [dɑ] – [tɑ] or the [sɛɪ] – [stɛɪ] identification tasks, as would have been predicted by Tallal's theory. Rather, the children with poor phonological processing could make use of formant transitions as well as brief bursts in the acoustic signal to make decisions about the voicing of these consonants, and could detect a short gap in the signal to make decisions about a stop closure.

Despite the normal performance of the poor readers on these tests of temporal and speech processing, they differed from normal readers in their use of fricative-noise spectra, as revealed by the difference in the slopes of their identification functions for [sa] – [ʃa] and [su] – [ʃu] continua. Interestingly, the children with poor phonological processing skills performed more like younger children in these tasks and based their judgements more on the formant transitions than on the spectral changes associated with the noise burst.

To conclude, this study revealed subtle perceptual deficits in poor readers. However, the observed deficits were not specifically with the processing of rapidly presented stimuli and, importantly, they were not with the formant transitions of consonants, the locus of the putative difficulty in Tallal's theory.

Auditory Processing Impairments in Dyslexia

Despite its controversial status, Tallal's hypothesis has stimulated a great deal of research that now includes the investigation of auditory temporal resolution in adults with a developmental history of dyslexia.

McAnally and Stein (1996) carried out three experiments to investigate this issue, comparing adult dyslexics with age-matched controls using psychophysical methods. In the first experiment, subjects had to detect a short interruption in a white noise stimulus. Sets of three stimuli were presented with a 'gap' in one of these. The extent of the interruption varied in duration from short and imperceptible to reasonably long. The task of the listener was to detect the one with the gap. The second experiment used a similar oddity procedure to assess the ability of listeners to detect a tone varying minimally in frequency from a reference tone. Target tones were presented at frequencies varying above and below a standard tone of 1 kHz.

McAnally and Stein's third experiment assessed thresholds for detecting a 1 kHz tone in noise. Both tone and masking noise were presented to both ears, with the tone either in phase at the two ears (which would make it difficult to detect) or out of phase (which would make it easier to separate the tone from the noise). The relative ease of the 'out of phase' condition depends upon listeners being able to exploit differences in the time of arrival of the sounds at the two ears (inter-aural differences). A measure of this, the 'binaural masking level difference' (BMLD), is derived by assessing the facilitation provided by the inter-aural stimulus differences. If dyslexics have difficulty in temporal processing, they should find it difficult to detect these differences and their BMLDs should be smaller than those of controls.

In the gap detection test, the dyslexic listeners performed as well as controls, suggesting they could detect stimulus onset and offset normally. They also performed like controls when required to detect a low-frequency tone in noise when it arrived at both ears at the same time. However, the dyslexics displayed higher thresholds for frequency discrimination, and the BMLD required for detecting the tone in binaural masked noise was smaller for dyslexics, suggesting they were less able to exploit differences in the timing of auditory stimuli at the two ears.

McAnally and Stein (1997) also took physiological recordings of the brain's response to auditory stimulation in the dyslexic and normal readers. Frequency following responses (FFRs) were measured to sequences of tones varying in frequency, with silent intervals. In addition, recordings were taken from the auditory brain stem in response to clicks. In line with the behavioural findings, the dyslexics' auditory brain stem responses to clicks were normal but the average amplitude of their FFRs was smaller than in controls.

McAnally and Stein (1997) interpreted their results as showing that dyslexic listeners have deficits in either the production or detection of neural discharges early on in processing in the auditory system. Their hypothesis depends upon a theoretical framework in which temporal resolution reflects how precisely stimulus onsets and offsets are coded. Although the performance of the dyslexics in the gap detection task indicated that they could detect stimulus onsets and offsets, frequency discrimination is thought to be mediated by the timing intervals between neural discharges that are 'phase-locked' to the fine structure of auditory stimuli. Phase-locking is used in the processing of low frequency but not high frequency acoustic stimuli, where discrimination depends upon spectral cues. Phase-locking can also be used to enhance the binaural detection of a tone in noise. The dyslexic listeners' performance suggested that they were less able to exploit interaural phase differences between the tone and the masking noise, consistent with a difficulty in generating or decoding phase-locked discharges.

Following up this study, Baldeweg, Richardson, Watkins, Foale and Gruzelier (1999) took physiological measurements from a group of ten dyslexic and ten normal readers in response to the occurrence of deviant auditory stimuli embedded in an unattended sequence of standard stimuli. The recordings they made were of an event-related potential termed *mismatch negativity* (MMN). The authors hypothesized that, if McAnally and Stein's proposals were correct, there would be differences in dyslexics' MMNs to tones that deviated in frequency, but not to tones that deviated in duration. This was just what they found; the dyslexics and their controls were indistinguishable in their response to tones that differed in duration or by large differences in frequency. However, the dyslexics showed reduced and delayed MMN peaks to small deviations in the frequency of tones.

Overall then, the findings of this study supported the hypothesis that dyslexic readers may have a low-level impairment in the phase-locking mechanisms of the auditory system (see Dougherty, Cynader, Bjornson, Edgell and Giaschi, 1998 for similar findings with children). However, a failure to find evidence of deficits in frequency discrimination and in the detection of frequency modulation both at high and low frequencies in all but a small sub-set of adult dyslexics tested in our laboratory suggest that the interpretation of the findings as a 'phase-locking' deficit is in need of modification (Hill, Griffiths, Bailey and Snowling, 1999).

Evidence for a 'Pan-modal' Deficit

An obvious question that stems from the findings of low-level visual and auditory impairments in dyslexia is whether the deficits in the two modalities are associated. While Livingstone, Rosen, Drislane and Galaburda (1991) were the first to suggest that the types of abnormality found in the visual system may extend to the auditory system, only recently has evidence in support of this idea been reported.

Witton et al. (1998) examined how sensitivity to dynamic auditory and visual stimuli predicted nonword reading ability in a study examining the performance of 21 dyslexic adults and 23 controls of the same age on two psychophysical tasks. To assess auditory sensitivity, subjects were presented with pairs of two tones, one of which was frequency modulated. They were required to report verbally which tone was the target tone at 6 depths of frequency modulation (FM) spanning threshold in equal levels.

To assess sensitivity to coherent motion, the same subjects were presented with random dot kinograms (RDKs) with the percentage of coherently moving dots varied adaptively to threshold. Subjects viewed a fixation point and then pressed a left or right key according to their judgement of whether motion was present.

There were group differences in frequency modulation discrimination at low (2 and 40 Hz) but not at high (240 Hz) modulation frequencies, with the dyslexics showing higher thresholds. Similarly, dyslexics were less sensitive to coherent motion. Moreover, visual-motion thresholds correlated with auditory thresholds particularly for the low-frequency tones. An interesting finding of this study was that sensory thresholds also correlated with measures of nonword reading. Once again, this applied only to the auditory thresholds for the detection of modulated tones at low frequency.

In similar vein, Baldeweg, Richardson, Watkins, Foale and Gruzelier (1999) reported strong correlations between the auditory frequency discrimination deficit and visual motion detection performance of dyslexic readers but not among controls. They also found significant correlations between MMN latency and reading performance for sets of regular words and nonwords, but not irregular words, for the sample as a whole.

Thus, a growing body of evidence suggests that dyslexic readers as a group show elevated thresholds for the detection of stimulus dimensions in both the visual and auditory modalities, particularly those that involve temporal resolution. There is also some suggestion that the performance of dyslexic readers on these sensory processing tasks correlates with their reading skill. However, it is fair to state that the paradigms that have to be used to assess sensory thresholds reliably are both time-consuming and effortful. Uncontrolled group differences in attention control or even in general cognitive skills that may dictate the use of different strategies could well account for the subtle group differences that have been reported. In line with this conjecture, individual analyses suggest that it is only a minority (may be as few as 25 per cent) of the dyslexic group who show impairments. An important question for future research is how these affected individuals differ from those who show perfectly normal performance on sensory processing tasks.

A limitation of the studies reported in this chapter is that, in general, they include a paucity of data concerning the performance of the dyslexic and control groups on psychometric tests, and have seldom employed the range of tasks needed to assess phonological processing, independent of reading. While it seems likely that in dyslexic samples performance on sensory processing tasks is related to the severity of the reading impairments, care needs to be exercised in interpreting this correlation. Poor reading in adults with dyslexia is unlikely to be a direct reflection of poor phonological processing skills working alone. Rather, the effects of poor phonology may be moderated by speed of processing and other cognitive skills, not least IQ. It follows that the poorest readers are likely to be those with poor phonology as well as poor compensatory resources. Those with concomitant language impairments are especially likely to falter. Hence, the sensory processing impairment in dyslexia may be associated with poor reading skill via the operation of one or more cognitive skills. It is simply too early to argue that it is causally related to the core phonological deficit. However, the investigation of sensory processing skills both behaviorally and physiologically and of their relationship to what is known about the cognitive characteristics of dyslexia undoubtedly sets an important research agenda for the neuroscience of dyslexia.

Chapter 10

Helping to Overcome Dyslexia

In the last two chapters, we have reviewed evidence suggesting that dyslexia is the consequence of inherited brain-based differences in the cognitive mechanisms that subserve reading. If this is the case, it might be inferred that dyslexic children's problems are fixed and immutable. However, just because a disorder has a genetic basis, this does not mean it is not susceptible to environmental interventions. To take a simple and very well-known example, PKU involves a genetic deficit that prevents the proper metabolism of phenylalanine, a component of protein. This defect in metabolism leads inexorably to mental retardation. However, identification of the genetic disorder by a blood test soon after birth allows the individual to be given a specifically modified diet that prevents the development of mental retardation. Thus, a genetic defect can be prevented from manifesting itself by a specific environmental intervention.

Morton and Frith's (1995) framework for modelling developmental disorders highlights the fact that the manifestations of a biologically specified cognitive disorder depend upon a complex interaction between the deficient processes and the environment in which the child develops. Being at genetic risk of dyslexia need not lead to extreme underachievement provided that intervention can start early before the downward spiral of events associated with failure sets in. In this chapter, we discuss the teaching methods that have been found to be effective for dyslexic readers.

The importance of phonological skills to reading development is, on the face of it, good evidence for the inclusion of instruction in the alphabetic principle in the reading curriculum (Adams, 1990). As Tunmer (1994) and others have pointed out, children cannot learn effectively by associating graphic cues with meanings. Since some

35–40 per cent of the words used in beginning materials are used only once (Jorm and Share, 1983), and the strategy provides no means for decoding unfamiliar words apart from contextual guessing, an exclusive focus on whole words in teaching stands seriously to constrain children's ability to learn to read (Stanovich and Stanovich, 1995).

However, even if it is accepted that teaching approaches which explicitly encourage the development of orthography-to-phonology mappings are to be preferred, there are still pertinent issues to be resolved in relation to dyslexic children. It is reasonable to ask, for example, whether there are grounds for teaching dyslexic children differently from children not at risk of reading failure. A related issue is at what age reading intervention should begin and, if the teaching strategy aims to promote phonological awareness, what the optimal size of phonological unit to teach is, the rime or the phoneme (Bruck and Treiman, 1992). At present, there are not satisfactory answers to all of these questions. Before discussing current knowledge derived from the studies of the teaching of reading to normal and dyslexic children, let us begin by considering the criteria that should be used in evaluating such interventions.

What Makes a Good Training Study?

Over the years, there have been many treatments, if not 'cures', proffered for dyslexia. Many specialist teachers and teaching organizations use well-established techniques to help dyslexic children to learn orthographic principles. Most notable amongst these are multisensory approaches that use the senses of vision, hearing and kinaesthesis in combination. Well respected as these methods are, however, few have been properly evaluated. Although they may work, it is important to show that they make a significant difference over and above that which could be made by simply giving the child more attention. In Psychology, this is called controlling for the Hawthorne effect. The idea behind the Hawthorne effect is that people who are given more attention work better. It is important therefore to compare the relative efficacy of different interventions that are similar in duration and intensity, just as when trialling a drug it is important to test its effects in relation to a 'placebo' treatment.

In a comprehensive review of studies that had aimed to train phonological awareness, Troia (1999) evaluated 39 interventions according to criteria informed by the internal and external validity of the study. From 68 published studies that could be identified, the 39 studies were chosen as those that contained a control group and were of reasonable duration. In addition to including a control intervention to guard against Hawthorne effects, Troia regarded it as important that children be allocated at random to different forms of training, that the quality of delivery of the teaching was monitored and that objective and reliable measures were used to assess treatment gains.

Altogether, 18 studies met two-thirds of the criteria laid out by Troia, which included criteria specifying that the study should not only be well conducted, but also well documented. On the basis of an analysis of these studies, Troia (1999) concluded that 'metaphonological training can improve analytic and synthetic phonological awareness skills and literacy acquisition in as little as two months of small-group or individual instruction' (p. 49). This is indeed a positive conclusion, though it begs the question of how well dyslexic children will respond. One limitation of studies that take the group as their unit of analysis is that, if a majority of well-prepared learners respond very well to a treatment, then this may mask the slow progress of others. This is an issue to which we will return. Before we do that, let us discuss some of the studies that have aimed to prevent reading failure.

The Prevention of Reading Difficulties

Studies of children at risk of reading difficulties have fostered increasing interest in the role of intervention programmes to prevent reading problems. Relevant to this enterprise are the results of interventions with unselected samples of children in their pre-school years. In one such study, Byrne and Fielding-Barnsley (1991 and 1995) carried out a 12-week intervention in which kindergarteners were taught the principle of phoneme identity, namely that words can begin and end with the same sound. The children worked in small groups and the activities they used involved pictures and games. Children in a control group used the same materials but worked on activities involving semantic categorization.

At the end of the training period, the children from the experimental group outperformed those from the control group on a test of phoneme identity in which they had to indicate which of three pictured items (for example, *seal, key, book*) started or ended with the same sound as a pictured target (for example, *kite* or *sock*). They were also ahead on a decoding task, though not in word identification. Two years later, at the end of first grade, the experimental groups performed better than the control groups in nonword reading and they showed a marginal advantage when reading regular words. At the end of second grade, three years after the intervention, the experimental groups remained ahead of controls in decoding skills and they also did better in reading comprehension. However, there was no significant difference between the groups in the automaticity of their reading (Byrne and Fielding-Barnsley, 1995). A long-term follow-up of these children in fifth grade revealed that those who had been trained in phoneme identity were superior to controls on irregular word reading (Byrne, Fielding-Barnsley and Ashley, submitted). Although the gains were in some ways modest, they were impressive given the fact that the children had received just six or seven hours of training in phoneme identity prior to starting school.

Lundberg, Frost and Petersen (1988) designed a programme for groups of Danish pre-school children that included metalinguistic games involving rhymes and phonemes. At school entry a year later, the trained children gained higher scores than children in a control group on tests of phonemic awareness. Their reading performance was then monitored at approximately seven-monthly intervals over the first three grades in school. At each point in time, the group who had received pre-school training did better than the untrained group in reading. Moreover, children identified as 'at risk' of reading failure who had been trained in pre-school reached a normal level of attainment three years later (Lundberg, 1994). The results suggest that pre-school training in phonological awareness can have a long-term positive effect on reading development.

Cunningham (1990) compared the efficacy of two different forms of phonological awareness training with groups of kindergarten and first-grade children. A 'skill and drill' group received training in phonological awareness that included segmentation and blending activities. A 'metalevel' group also received training in phonological awareness skills but these were explicitly practised in the context of reading. The control group listened to stories and discussed them with a teacher. Over a period of ten weeks, the children given phonological training explicitly linked to reading activities made the most significant progress. Along similar lines, Ball and Blachman (1991) found that kindergarten children who were provided with training in phonological awareness and spelling–sound correspondences progressed better in reading than a group taught letter names and sounds in the context of more general language activities.

The results of these two studies suggest that the benefits of training phonological awareness are increased when children are taught to make explicit links between sounds and letters. Their results concur with those of Bradley and Bryant (1983) working with children who were identified as 'at risk' of reading failure by virtue of their poor performance on a test of sound categorization at 4 and 5 years of age. These children received two years of intervention, beginning when they were 6 years old. The training study had four conditions. The first experimental group received training in sound categorization (phonological awareness) throughout the two years; the second received a similar training protocol for the first year, followed by teaching of letter–sound correspondences during the second. There were two control groups; the first received training in semantic categorization, using the same materials as the sound categorization training, and the second was unseen.

At the end of the intervention, the experimental groups were ahead of the control groups; however, the gain of the group who had been given training in sound categorization alone was less impressive when considered in relation to the seen control group who had been given semantic categorization training. The experimental group that had made the most significant progress was the one that had been taught letter–sound correspondences in the context of phonological training; their reading scores were some eight to ten months ahead of those of the seen control group.

Taken together, the results of these intervention studies hint that phonological awareness training alone is not as effective in promoting reading as training which also emphasizes letter–sound correspondences (cf. Bond and Dykstra, 1967; Foorman, Francis, Novy and Liberman, 1991). There are at least two ways of thinking about this finding. Most simply, drawing children's attention to letters as well as speech sounds will facilitate the development of mappings between orthography and phonology when reading proper is introduced. An alternative worthy of consideration is that such techniques work at the level of the hypotheses that children have about print. According to Byrne, Fielding-Barnsley, Ashley and Larsen (1997), to become alphabetic readers children must learn to abandon the morphological principle that printed words map (exclusively) to units of meaning. It is possible that interventions that work at the phonological level in isolation do not encourage this reconceptualization of the reading process.

Early intervention for children at risk of reading failure

The studies discussed so far, with the exception of Bradley and Bryant (1983), have been concerned primarily with the promotion of reading skill in unselected populations of schoolchildren. It is important to consider if the findings also apply in the case of children at known risk of reading problems.

Borstrøm and Elbro (1997) were among the first to carry out an intervention study involving children at genetic risk of dyslexia. There were three groups of children in this Danish intervention study. Thirty-six high-risk children from dyslexic families received intervention in kindergarten focusing upon the promotion of phonological awareness at the level of phonemes; 52 high-risk children and 46 low-risk children served as controls and received no intervention. Owing to the recruitment methods used, the at-risk children were dispersed among many school districts. Therefore the children's own class teachers were trained to deliver the programme to their class. Thus, an interesting feature of this study was that the phonemic training was delivered to whole classes.

At the end of the kindergarten year, the experimental group were doing as well as the low-risk controls, and there was a trend for the high-risk children in the control group to lag behind. In first grade, the experimental group gained more in letter naming, word reading and phoneme deletion than the untrained group, and in second grade, they were similar to normal controls on all reading measures including a combined nonword reading and pseudohomophone detection measure. The authors also report that the prevalence of dyslexia, using a cut-off criterion based on poor phonological decoding, was reduced

182

to 17 per cent in the experimental group, compared with 40 per cent in the high-risk children who were not trained.

Byrne, Fielding-Barnsley, Ashley and Larsen (1997) reported less optimistic results from a study of 54 children at familial risk of dyslexia, studied from the age of $4\frac{1}{2}$ years. At the beginning of the study, the at-risk children were poorer than controls on tests of phonological awareness and alphabet knowledge, and they were less familiar with print and books. In pre-school, the children were trained in groups of from one to six for 40 minutes a week in which they received an intervention programme that had three main components. In addition to the phonemic awareness program discussed above (Byrne and Fielding-Barnsley 1991 and 1995), it included intensive training in letter–phoneme knowledge and shared book reading (Whitehurst et al., 1994).

After between 16 and 20 weeks of training, the children's phonemic and rhyme awareness, alphabetic knowledge and print awareness had increased significantly. However, when their performance was compared with that of a group of children from their earlier longitudinal study, the improvements were less impressive; whereas only 5 per cent of the normal sample showed no growth in phonological awareness across the period of instruction, 32 per cent of the at-risk group failed to improve and a substantial improvement occurred in only 48 per cent of the at-risk children (the figure for the comparison sample was 93 per cent).

A number of procedural differences could account for the difference between the results of this study and that of Borstrom and Elbro. A major difference was in the timing of the intervention; Danish children do not enter kindergarten until 6 years of age and therefore they received the training later in their development than those in the Australian study of Byrne and colleagues. Another methodological point is that the children who received the Danish intervention may have been given more attention than their controls. The way in which the intervention was implemented in the child's own classroom was such that teacher expectations across the curriculum could have brought additional benefits to the high-risk children in the experimental group. Thus, the impact of the intervention may have been magnified.

Byrne and colleagues concluded from their study that the resistance of at risk children to normal interventions is an example of 'the cognitive impenetrability...of modularity' (Byrne, Fielding-Barnsley, Ashley and Larsen, 1997: 279). A similar position is held by Torgesen, Wagner and Rashotte (1994), who reported that about 30 per cent of children at risk of reading disabilities failed to profit from an eight-week training programme that was effective with the majority of children. In a further study carried out to identify the predictors of progress in phonological awareness training, Torgesen and Davis (1996) reported that the children who fared less well were those who started out with a poor grasp of segmentation and sound–spelling translation skills, as evidenced by poor nonword spelling and slow naming speed. Their recommendation on the basis of these results was that training procedures that go beyond those typically found in the research literature, in terms both of explicitness and intensity, may be required in order to have a substantial impact on the phonological awareness of children at risk for serious learning difficulties.

Torgesen et al. (in press) used such procedures with kindergarten children who were considered to be at risk of reading failure because of their poor performance on tests of letter naming and phoneme identity. These 180 children, selected from 13 schools, were assigned to one of four groups, three of which received intensive instruction consisting of four 20-minute training sessions each week on a one-to-one basis for two and a half years, and the fourth forming a no-treatment control group.

The first intervention involved training in Phonological Awareness and Synthetic Phonics (PASP). The programme had a number of different components. First, it involved explicit instruction in phonological awareness leading children to discover and label articulatory gestures and phonemes (Lindamood and Lindamood, 1984). Second, it involved reading practice, both with high-frequency words and with stories in which children were encouraged to rely on their decoding skills and to ask themselves whether the words 'made sense' in the context of the story. Teachers also discussed the meanings of stories with the children.

In the second programme, Embedded Phonics (EP), children were taught to recognize a small group of whole words using drills ands word games. They also learned letter–sound correspondences in the context of these words and wrote then read them in sentences. In reading practice, they focused on acquiring word-level reading skills rather than on using context (extending their sight vocabulary and decoding single words), and once again, teachers discussed the meanings of the stories with them.

The third group of children received Regular Classroom Support (RCS), delivered on an individual basis. Because this intervention was based on what would have been taught in each child's regular classroom, its content varied between children and tended to include a wide range of activities, from phonics-based instruction through to approaches focusing on meaning. Teachers kept a log of the activities they used in teaching sessions and these were grouped into three general categories: phonological awareness training, direct instruction and sight vocabulary work and reading or writing instruction with connected text. The balance of the work in the RCS condition was more similar to that in the EP than in the PASP programme, with most time being spent on connected text activities (43 per cent), equal amounts on phonological awareness and direct instruction (24 per cent) and a smaller amount on spelling (9 per cent).

The programmes were delivered by nine specially trained tutors who had been selected for the excellence of their teaching, supported by teaching 'aides'. The tutors received three weeks of in-service training prior to the commencement of the programme and they met with the programme director once every two weeks. The tutors taught either in the PASP or the EP programmes and they all taught in the RCS programme, where the programme they delivered was under the direction of the classroom teacher. The aides taught between two and 15 children each; they were given two hours training, a training manual, and a further two hours in-service training by the programme director.

The delivery of the programmes was carefully monitored, as was the progress of the children over five semesters. At the end of the intervention, the children in the PASP showed the best overall outcome and the performance of this group was within the average range for their age. Children from the PASP group performed significantly above children from the other three groups in phonemic decoding skills, and similar to the EP group in word identification skills but better than the RCS and no-treatment control group. The results are similar to those of studies by Brown and Felton (1990) and Foorman Francis, Fletcher, Schatschneider and Mehta (1998), who showed that children given explicit instruction in phonemic decoding made the strongest gains in word reading skills.

Reading Intervention

The results of early intervention studies need to be considered along-side those that have investigated the best methods for teaching reading to children who have already failed. An influential approach to helping poor readers is 'reading recovery', a programme pioneered by Clay (1985) in New Zealand. The poorest readers in each school enter such programmes following screening at the age of 6 years, and leave around 20 weeks later when their reading attainment matches that of their peer group in the same schools. The success of the programme depends upon the availability of highly trained tutors who attend a specially designed training programme for a year before they begin to use the approach (Pinnell, Lyons, Deford, Bryk and Seltzer, 1994).

Clay's original work focused upon reading training and did not explicitly promote phonological awareness or instruction in alphabetic strategies (Clay, 1985). The aim of reading recovery was to encourage children to use all the strategies they have available and to monitor their own reading to promote independence and fluency. While the programme is generally regarded to be successful, there have been few systematic comparisons with other methods (see Snowling, 1996, for discussion). In one such study, Iversen and Tunmer (1993) compared the progress of 6-year-old children who either received a standard reading recovery programme, or who received a modified version of the programme that incorporated exercises linking phonology and reading, based on Bradley and Bryant's (1983) approach. A third group received standard small group remediation.

Children in both reading recovery groups made better progress than children in the control group. However, children in the modified reading recovery group learned more quickly than children who received the standard reading recovery programme. It is normal practice in 'reading recovery' to discharge children when they have reached their target outcome. It took children in the modified programme significantly fewer lessons to reach this point; the modified programme was some 37 per cent more efficient than the traditional programme that did not include exercises linking spellings and sounds (Tunmer, 1994).

Hatcher, Hulme and Ellis (1994) also compared a modified reading recovery programme with three other kinds of intervention in a study

186

of children from the bottom 25 per cent of 7-year-old readers in a county in northern England. The children were allocated to one of four training conditions, the children in each group being matched for age, sex, IQ and reading age at the start of the intervention. Three groups went on to receive individual training for 40 half-hour training sessions spread over 20 weeks; the fourth group acted as a control and received no specific help from the study, although they were receiving the normal compliment of remediation as offered by their schools.

The first experimental group received training in reading following a format outlined by Clay (1985), but without any reference to the sounds of words (reading alone). The children were each taught on an individualized programme that involved reading books at the instructional level emphasizing the use of context and meaning-based strategies, re-reading books that could be read with greater than 94 per cent accuracy and reading and writing words. The second group were given training in phonological awareness (phonology alone). This training consisted of nine types of phonological task, each graded in difficulty, and no reading was involved (see figure 10.1). The third group received both reading and phonological training as well as activities that explicitly linked reading with phonology. These linking activities included practising letter–sound associations, relating spellings to sounds using plastic letters and reading and writing words in context while paying attention to letter–sound relationships.

At the end of training, the group that received the integrated package linking reading with phonology had made significantly more progress in reading than the control group. In contrast, the progress made by the other two training groups was not significantly better than that of controls in receipt of standard remedial work. The beneficial effects of the 'reading with phonology' programme were specific to literacy and were not associated with more general improvements in educational attainment, as measured by arithmetic skills. Nine months later, the gains of the children who had received the reading with phonology package held up, but the differential effect on spelling progress, evidenced at the end of training, was no longer significant.

Thus, the practice of making explicit links between phonology and orthography appears not only to facilitate reading development in normal populations, but also to be responsible for the greatest gains

Figure 10.1 Example of a phonological training activity. In each row, 'which two pictures start with the same sound?'

Source: Hatcher, 1994

in literacy development in poor readers. Turning to controlled treatment studies of more severely impaired populations, namely dyslexic children, a persistent problem is the difficulty in transferring what has been taught to new situations (Lovett, Ransby and Barron, 1988; Lovett, Ransby, Hardwick, Johns and Donaldson, 1989).

Lovett, Warren-Chaplin, Ransby and Borden (1990) improved the word identification skills of dyslexic readers using a programme that specifically focused on the acquisition of word recognition at the single word level. Use of this technique led to a substantial increase in sight vocabulary. However, the children were unable to abstract

188

grapheme–phoneme correspondences and they could not use their newly acquired knowledge to read words on which they had not been trained (cf. Rack, Snowling and Olson, 1992).

Following on from this, Lovett et al. (1994) evaluated two different interventions that focused on promoting procedures for identifying unknown words and dealt with print at sub-word as well as word levels, with a view to improving generalization. The first programme involved a carefully graduated sequence of training in phonological analysis and blending in the context of printed words, and direct instruction in letter–sound correspondences. The second form of intervention involved training in word identification strategies. The strategies trained were reading by analogy, looking for the part of the word that is not known, attempting variable vowel pronunciations and peeling off prefixes and suffixes where appropriate. It concentrated on larger units than the phonological training and encouraged children to match the words they were trying to decode to their spoken vocabulary. A third intervention served as an alternative treatment control. Children in this group received instruction in a variety of study skills.

The dyslexic children in the study were taught in pairs for 35 one-hour sessions. At the end of the training period, gains in letter and word identification for specifically trained key words were significantly greater for children in the experimental groups than for those in the alternative treatment control. However, of central importance was a comparison of their success on tests of the transfer of learning. Both the experimental groups performed better than the group who received study skills training. They also showed transfer of learning to words derived from the trained items and to sets of regular words. There were, however, group differences on two further tests of transfer. The group who had received the phonological intervention did better than those trained in strategies for word identification in nonword reading; the latter group did better on a set of exception words.

These results are important because they show that the interventions were specifically affecting the targeted skills; training in phonological strategies was most effective for reading nonwords and least effective for reading exception words. In contrast, monitoring reading in relation to spoken vocabulary was most effective for reading words and least for reading nonwords. This finding is reminiscent of those of Byrne and Fielding-Barnsley (1991 and 1995), who found that early training in phoneme invariance led to substantial effects on regular and nonword learning but not on irregular word reading (see also Olson, Wise, Johnson and Ring, 1997). Training focusing on word identification, by contrast, promoted exception word reading, but generalization to nonwords was poor.

Another important set of studies that speak to the efficacy of remedial approaches with dyslexic children is the Colorado remediation project (see Olson and Wise, 1992 for a review). The teaching technique used in these studies involves children reading from books that are computer-presented, at the appropriate level of difficulty. Whenever the child encounters an unfamiliar word they highlight it and the computer provides feedback using synthesized speech. The feedback consists of either the pronunciation of the whole word or segmented feedback (at onset-rime or phonemic levels) which the children are encouraged to blend. Wise, Olson and Treiman (1990) showed that normal first-grade readers derived more benefit from speech-segmented feedback if segmentation was at the onset-rime boundary (*d/ish*, *b/oat*) than between the vowel–consonant group (*di/sh*, *boa/t*). The group proceeded to investigate the best ways of improving the reading skills of dyslexic children in a series of studies.

In the first of these, disabled readers received teaching on the computer coupled with a high level of experimenter monitoring and encouragement. All children receiving speech feedback read more words at post-test than children in a control group that was untrained, but there was no significant advantage of one form of feedback over another. The children who received segmented feedback demonstrated impressive gains in nonword reading, contrasting with small gains in the whole-word feedback condition. So, specific teaching targeted at the sub-word level encouraged the development of generalizable phonological decoding skills.

A second study produced poorer results. In this study, children were given substantially less pre-training and, as a consequence, they targeted fewer words during the training period. The segmented feedback conditions showed substantially reduced gains in nonword reading compared to the control condition. In fact, whole-word feedback led to the greatest gains and onset-rime feedback to the weakest gains in this phase of the research. These results highlight a problem inherent in the practical application of research findings: when reading independently, poor readers are likely to skip difficult words. Thus, if left to their own devices, they will have fewer opportunities than normal readers for learning mappings between orthography and phonology. It is important to invest effort to try to teach them to 'stick with' reading, even though it is difficult for them.

In the wider context, dyslexic children have less print exposure than proficient readers (Stanovich and West, 1989). Ironically, Byrne, Fielding-Barnsley, Ashley and Larsen (1997) showed that the relative contribution of print exposure to reading skill in disabled readers is greater than that of decoding ability. This finding is in line with the idea that dyslexic children can use context to support inefficient decoding skills. It is vital therefore that they have sufficient reading practice; yet it is just these children who tend to shun this.

Individual differences in children's response to intervention

This review of intervention studies has taken as its focus the impact of different training regimes, and, perhaps indirectly, different levels of print exposure, on children's reading achievement. However, it would be naive to ignore the role of individual differences in determining prognosis. Dyslexic children differ not only in the severity of their underlying phonological difficulties but also in the compensatory strategies that they bring to the task of learning to read, such as visual and semantic skills (Snowling, 1987). Thus, children who have different cognitive profiles may well respond differently to different kinds of intervention.

Data from the Colorado studies suggest there is an interaction between the severity of children's reading deficit and their response to treatment. Thus, Wise and Olson (1998) reported that more severely disabled readers responded best to syllable feedback and less well to onset-rime feedback during training. In contrast, less severely retarded readers responded best to onset-rime feedback and made only modest gains with syllable feedback. A similar pattern of results emerged when progress was analysed with respect to pre-test performance on tests of phonological awareness. Overall, children with lower phoneme awareness benefited less from reading instruction than children with higher levels of segmentation ability.

191

A logical next step was to design a program to promote phono-logical awareness and to use this in conjunction with reading re-mediation. Wise and Olson (1998) compared two kinds of reading intervention incorporated into the computer-reading routines. Forty-five 9-year-old dyslexic readers were assigned to a teaching condition in which they were instructed in metacognitive comprehension strate-gies (after Palincsar and Brown, 1984) and 48 children were assigned to a phonological awareness training condition. These children re-ceived training in speech-motor phoneme awareness using elements of an approach devised by Lindamood and Lindamood (1984). This approach placed emphasis on the development of concrete articula-tory (speech-motor) representations to distinguish and compare phonemic differences. The next stage of the phonological awareness programme involved printed/spoken nonword matching and spelling with speech feedback.

Both groups received sessions of small group teaching and indi-vidualized computer instruction. At the end of training, the group who had received phonological awareness training had made signifi-cantly greater gains in phonological awareness and in recognition of the words they had targeted. However, the group who had received metacognitive comprehension training had gained more in time-limited word recognition. Moreover, the groups did not differ in how well they read a set of untrained words.

IQ was a poor predictor of children's progress in this phonological teaching regime. A similar conclusion was reached by Hatcher and Hulme (1999) who assessed the responsiveness of the 124 7-year-old children in the Hatcher, Hulme and Ellis (1994) intervention study. It will be recalled that in this study, children were placed into one of four interventions at random and it was those who received a com-bination of phonological awareness training and systematic reading instruction who did best.

There were two unique predictors of improvements in children's reading accuracy. These were their performance on a test of phoneme manipulation together with the intervention they received. Neither verbal nor non-verbal IQ made a difference. In contrast, when it came to predicting outcome in terms of reading comprehension, verbal ability was a significant predictor, in addition to phoneme manipulation skill. The results were strikingly similar for the different groups. In fact, the only group for whom phoneme manipulation was not as good a predictor was the group who had received phonological awareness training. It can be assumed that the training these children received swamped the effects of initial differences in phonological skill.

Slightly different conclusions both from those of Hatcher and Hulme (1999) and from their own earlier studies were reported by Wise, Ring and Olson (1999) in a training studying involving 122 children with severe reading deficits from second to fifth grade. This study compared three different remediation programmes. Each programme involved 40 hours of intervention using computer reading with speech feedback and an emphasis on phonics. In one version, the children were also trained in both phonological awareness and articulatory awareness, a combination they had found effective previously (the phonological awareness training in this study included nonword reading exercises and spelling input). In two other versions, training involved either articulatory awareness or phonological awareness training. The amount of time spent in training was the same across experimental groups. Hence, the group given articulatory awareness training alone (who did not do the nonword reading or spelling exercises) spent longer reading on the computer with speech feedback.

At the end of the intervention period, there were highly significant differences between the performance of children in the three intervention conditions and that of children in a control condition that involved regular reading instruction. However, there were no group differences in mathematics. There were also some subtle differences in the outcome of children from the different training regimes. Primarily, these related to the nature of the interventions themselves. Performance in phoneme deletion following the interventions that involved phonological awareness training was better than that following articulatory awareness training. However, the children who had received articulatory awareness training and extra time reading did better in orthographic coding tests. Overall, there was rather little evidence that the type of phonological training mattered to the progress that the children made. Wise, Ring and Olson (1999) concluded that their findings 'lend support to the consensus that phonological awareness work prior to and melded within a well-structured approach to reading is helpful for children with specific reading difficulties' (p. 301). However, contrary to the results of other training studies, children with higher IQs gained more from training on nearly all of the reading measures, and the effects of the intervention generalized better for them.

Of primary interest were the predictors of children's responsiveness to training. These were IQ, grade and initial phoneme awareness. Contrary to the results of other training studies, IQ was positively correlated with growth in all reading measures and the effects of intervention generalized better for children of higher IQ. IQ did not, however, predict gains in phoneme awareness. Grade effects indicated that the youngest children gained the most and initial phoneme awareness was a good predictor of all outcome measures.

It is worth dwelling for a moment on these findings. Two facets of the results need to be stressed. First, the children in the present study were on average older than those in the studies of Hatcher and colleagues and of, Torgesen and colleagues. Second, IQ did not predict improvements in phonological awareness. Together with the finding that younger children benefited more from the interventions, these results suggest that analytic phonics instruction is more applicable at lower reading levels (few of the older children were reading below third-grade level). Among older children, it is likely that other resources, such as semantic skills, come into play to promote reading development. It seems to be the case that, among older children, it is those who have higher IQs that are better placed to use such skills to compensate for decoding difficulties.

Accepting that most poor readers have deficits in phonological awareness, Levy, Bourassa and Horn (1999) compared the benefits of segmentation and whole-word training for children who differed in naming speed on a rapid naming test. Following the double deficit hypothesis of Bowers and Wolf (1993), their hypothesis was that more repetitions of word patterns would be required to form the associations needed to learn new words for children with slow naming speed.

Their study included 128 children from second grade, classified into fast and slow RAN groups. The groups were matched in IQ, rhyme generation and phoneme counting and orthographic knowledge. Both groups had difficulty with decoding strategies; however, a significant advantage in word identification for the fast RAN group was taken into account statistically when analysing the results of the intervention.

Children were trained to read 48 words that included letter onset clusters. There were four instances of each of 12 rhyming families, for example *unch, ide, ain*. On the first day, the experimenter modeled the training condition. Subsequently, the child read each word through once and the experimenter gave corrective feedback. In a rime condition, all four words from same family were presented on the same card and feedback was given using coloured highlighting. This procedure was repeated daily for 15 days or until the child reached a criterion of perfect performance for two consecutive days. It was then replaced with training using black and white letters that lasted five days or until criterion was met. For the phoneme and whole-word conditions, four words were presented in random sets on each card. In the phoneme condition, each phonemic unit was printed in a different colour. Otherwise the training regime was identical.

The children in the fast RAN group were more successful in both phases of the training than the children in slow RAN group, and training in both segmentation methods was better than in the whole word condition. However, the two RAN sub-groups responded differently to the training. While the effects of segmentation were the same for both groups, whole-word training disadvantaged the slow RAN group. Moreover, there was poorer generalization of this training to nonword reading in the slow RAN groups.

In short, the results of this study suggest that, in addition to phonological awareness, rapid naming speed is a predictor of a child's ability to benefit from reading instruction. These findings are interesting in the light of those of Torgesen and Davis (1996), who found that RAN speed was a predictor of blending skill. Torgesen and Davis interpreted this finding as suggesting that RAN is a measure of lexical access. If, as we have suggested, successful reading depends upon the child being able to decode words and access their meanings to bootstrap the process, the findings make a good deal of sense. Children with slow RAN speed will be doubly disadvantaged if, in addition to being slow to access words in their vocabulary, they are not given the segmentation training that will enhance their decoding skills. In short, slow naming seems to mark a deficit in the rate of learning and this is exacerbated when word-level orthographic units are to be learned.

A cautionary note about generalization

As we have seen, there is now a good deal of evidence that the most effective teaching methods for dyslexic readers combine reading instruction and phonological awareness training. A word of caution is necessary, however. First, this type of intervention appears to be most helpful for children of lower levels of reading ability who still need to become proficient users of the alphabetic code. Indeed, there is a hint that interventions for both normally developing and reading disabled children that place an exclusive focus on training the mappings between orthography and phonology do not enhance exception word reading skill. Nor do they ensure the development of rapid word identification. Whilst further research is needed, the findings are highly suggestive of the fact that, in order to bring about long-lasting gains, training needs to highlight the relationships between letter strings and meaning-based units (morphemes) as well as between letters and their sounds (see Broom and Doctor, 1995 for one such technique). Indeed, the neglect of such training could unwittingly lead a child to develop the behavioural profile of surface dyslexia if their phonological skills are weak and they have slow speed of processing.

One of the most successful intervention studies to date, in terms of its effects on growth in both phonemic decoding and word identification skills, is the one we discussed earlier by Torgesen et al. (in press), in which children trained in Phonological Awareness and Synthetic Phonics made very positive progress. However, it is important to note that, even after this programme in which the intervention was both explicit and intensive, between 20 and 25 per cent of children remained poor readers (more than one standard deviation below average for their age). The predictors of responsiveness in this study were not IQ but rapid naming, a measure of phonological processing, and two non-cognitive variables: home background and classroom behaviour ratings. Arguably, future research needs to address how best to encourage reluctant readers who are disadvantaged in terms of their development of literacy not only by virtue of their poor phonological processing, but also by home and classroom variables. It appears to be vitally important that such children practise their reading skills in a wide variety of contexts, rather than solely during reading instruction.

From a practical perspective, it is important to reiterate that there is nothing incompatible about combining phonological and 'whole-language' approaches to reading (Adams, 1990). As well as training in phonological awareness, children require opportunities to read connected text, and they benefit from exposure to a range of literature for their reading practice (Juel, 1995). Indeed the use of such materials is crucial. As we shall see in the following chapter, poor readers, even more than good readers, use context to facilitate their decoding skills (Nation and Snowling, 1998a; Pring and Snowling, 1986; Rego and Bryant, 1993; Stanovich, 1984). If this prop is removed, their reading falters still further.

Chapter 11

Proficiency and Deficiency: The Role of Compensation

The strong version of the phonological deficit hypothesis of dyslexia adhered to throughout this book proposes that the cognitive basis of the problem is a difficulty in establishing phonological representations for words. The core difficulty is in one sense mild. Dyslexic children are often slow to start to talk, but speech problems have normally resolved by school age, particularly for words that are used frequently. On the other hand, the consequences of this representational deficit are not trivial for children learning to read in an alphabetic language. Although the symptoms of dyslexia change with age, phonological processing difficulties persist into adulthood, and verbal short-term memory problems are ubiquitous.

As we have seen, the clearest consequence of the phonological deficit in dyslexia is on reading and spelling development. Although the dyslexic person may laboriously learn to read familiar words, reading unfamiliar words typically remains very difficult and prone to error. In addition, spelling may be dysphonetic, especially in free writing when attentional resources are directed at composition rather than monitoring performance. Yet not all dyslexics fit this behavioural profile. It is this diversity among dyslexic readers that has led some researchers to doubt the universality of the phonological deficit hypothesis. In chapter 7 we suggested that the severity of an individual's phonological processing impairment has an influence on the reading and spelling skills they develop. In this chapter I will propose that the impact of the deficit can also be modified by the availability of compensatory resources working in interaction with the teaching that the child receives. Teaching covers a broad range of influences here. They include early interventions to remedy speech and language difficulties and interventions to promote metalinguistic awareness, as well as instruction in school. The argument is that it is the interplay of strengths and weaknesses that will determine the literacy outcome for a child with a susceptibility to dyslexia, and factors both intrinsic and extrinsic to the child need to be taken into account.

Achieving Literacy in Spite of a Phonological Deficit

The case of RE (Campbell and Butterworth, 1985), a dyslexic young woman with phonological difficulties, highlights the potential of compensatory factors in 'dyslexic-literacy'. RE was a student at university when she was assessed and, although dyslexic, she had learned to read and spell exceedingly well. On the surface, RE performed as well as her undergraduate peers, but her pattern of performance was such that she was deemed to have 'developmental phonological dyslexia'. RE's ability to perceive phonemic categories was normal but she performed well below expectation on tests of phoneme segmentation. She could not count the phonemes accurately in spoken words and her auditory rhyme judgements were impaired (RE stated that she couldn't hear the little sounds in words).

A central feature of RE's dyslexic condition was a marked verbal memory deficit. Her memory span was confined to four digits that she could repeat equally well backwards as forwards. Regardless of list length, her memory for visually presented material was far better than her auditory recall, and consequently she relied on her visual skills whenever it was feasible to do so. Campbell and Butterworth argued that RE had been unable to learn spelling–sound correspondences because the auditory component of short-term memory could not support phonemic parsing processes. Her decoding skills were very weak, as evidenced by a severe nonword reading deficit. Yet literacy had been achieved and it is probable that visual memory had supported its development.

Campbell and Butterworth went further to propose that RE had used lexical analogies to learn to read, using a mechanism proposed by Glushko (1979). According to this view, novel letter strings are segmented in all possible ways, each segment being matched to a segment stored in an orthographic lexicon. Within this mechanism, the pronunciations of new words are synthesized from the different pronunciations active throughout the network. Hence, knowledge of how to read *moth* would be brought to bear to read *froth* and *moss* by virtue of their orthographic similarity. While details of how the new pronunciations were synthesized were not clarified, it can be seen that the use of analogous mappings would not place such stringent demands on phonological skills as would the use of sequential spelling–sound rules. Therefore these could be used to provide an alternative means for learning to read. Consistent with this idea, Treiman, Goswami and Bruck (1990) showed that dyslexic readers could read nonwords that shared their rime segments with many lexical items (for example *tain*, *goach*) more easily than nonwords that had few orthographic neighbours (for example *goan*, *taich*).

Language Skills and Learning to Read

The case of RE raises the interesting possibility that some dyslexic children learn to read by following an atypical course of development. In her case, it was proposed that visual memory skills had supported the acquisition of a sight vocabulary. JM's case, as we saw in chapter 1, suggested that the mechanism can also involve a process of semantic 'bootstrapping' (Hulme and Snowling, 1992). Thus, contextual facilitation primed semantic knowledge which JM used to assess the plausibility of his partial decoding attempts. To speculate, once a word's pronunciation has been determined, its visual form may be committed to memory with a word-specific link to phonology (Share, 1995).

It is worth pausing at this point to consider an issue that has often been overlooked in the study of dyslexia, which is that reading almost always takes place in context. While it is clear that dyslexic children have problems at the level of single-word reading, this observation does not speak to their ability to read words in sentences that are embedded in texts. It might be argued that dyslexic readers have more opportunity to learn words during their everyday reading experience than their phonological skills predict because they can use higher-level language processes in this endeavour. It is crucial to be clear that phonological skills predict reading through decoding ability (Share, 1995). However, there is more to reading than decoding (Gough and Tunmer, 1986). The same decoding skills that allow children to pronounce letter strings such as *contented* or *tegwop* do not ensure that exception words like *yacht* or *beautiful* will be read correctly. Furthermore, decoding skills do not allow the accurate reading of ambiguous words such as the word *bow* in the sentence 'the magician took a *bow*'.

Stanovich (1980) argued that poor readers whose low-level decoding processes are slow make use of 'top-down' knowledge-based processes to compensate for their deficits. Dyslexic readers have much less difficulty with the semantic and pragmatic aspects of reading than with its phonological basis. Therefore they may be able to use sentence level contexts to promote their reading accuracy. To investigate this idea, Frith and Snowling (1983) carried out a study comparing dyslexic children's reading with that of normal as well as autistic readers. In this study, the children were asked to read sentences containing homographs such as 'they started to *row* across the river' or 'she waved her wand and the boat became *minute*'. Interestingly, the dyslexic readers performed *better* than their reading-age matched controls who could read nonwords better. The finding that dyslexic readers could read the homographs more accurately despite their decoding difficulty highlighted their ability to use context in a compensatory manner.

Following on from this, Nation and Snowling (1998a) assessed the performance of dyslexic readers in an experiment in which the children were presented with a printed word, either in isolation or in a sentence context. Target words such as *aunt* and *hymn* were presented on a computer screen, and in the context condition, they were preceded by a spoken sentence frame (for example 'I went shopping with my mother and my——'; 'We end our assembly with a——'). The speed with which the children read the target words in isolation and in the spoken context was measured and their accuracy recorded. Their performance was compared with that of reading-age matched normal readers and also children with specific comprehension difficulties.

There was a significant facilitation effect of context for all children, such that their reading was both more accurate and faster when the printed words occurred following the sentence context. Importantly, however, the groups performed differently. While the poor comprehenders benefited less from context than controls, the dyslexic readers reaped the greatest advantage.

The findings of this experiment confirmed that dyslexic readers could use information from the sentence frame to bring their pronunciations of target words in line with context. Indeed, they benefited more from the availability of semantic and syntactic constraints than other children whose word-level reading skills were equivalent. A follow-up study involving over 90 children found that the size of the contextual facilitation effect was related to the children's semantic processing skills. Children, including dyslexic readers, who were good at judging whether pairs of words had the same meaning, and generating lists of semantically related words, benefited most from context. Thus, semantic skills can act as a compensatory resource for poor readers whose phonological skills are weak.

A few years ago, Olson and his colleagues developed a similar argument to the one proposed here but on rather different grounds (Olson, Kleigel, Davidson and Foltz, 1985). The basic tenet of the argument was that dyslexic readers are developmentally delayed in the acquisition of phonological codes. In the absence of these types of code at stages in development when they are critical, compensatory strategies are developed. Consequently, they use different coding strategies in verbal memory tasks (Olson, Davidson, Kliegel and Davies, 1984; Rack, 1985), and to a large extent, it is compensatory strategies that dictate individual differences in reading and spelling skill.

Taking this argument a stage further, Olson et al. (1985) monitored the eye movements that dyslexics made during prose reading. An important dimension of reading style emerged. At one pole were children who fixated each word sequentially and made a high proportion of regressive eye movements to look back at words they had already read. These children were described as 'plodders'. At the other end of the scale were 'explorers'. These children read with a higher proportion of forward movements, often skipping words altogether. The dimension had a normal distribution and the majority of the sample fell between the two extremes.

It turned out that the position of a dyslexic child on this dimension was predictable from their cognitive characteristics. For younger children, those who had poor orthographic skills and therefore used phonology tended to be 'plodders', whereas those with good orthographic skills were more likely to be 'explorers'. For older children, it was verbal IQ that predicted reading style. Children with higher verbal skills were the explorers, while children with poor verbal abilities were towards the 'plodder' end of the spectrum.

There is a chicken-and-egg problem here. It is not clear whether the explorer reading style was conducive to the development of orthographic skills or rather, whether children who were poorer at phonology were more likely to rely on context and therefore looked like 'explorers'. The study of poor comprehenders provides a lead on this. Such children have normal phonological skills but weak syntactic and semantic processing abilities. Although their use of phonological decoding strategies is normal, they have poor orthographic skills (Nation and Snowling, 1998b). We have argued elsewhere that their ability to set up an orthographic system is constrained by a problem activating semantic knowledge (Nation and Snowling, 1999). They also show reduced context effects. Taken together, these findings suggest that it is strengths and weaknesses in basic language processes that drive the development of orthographic skills. These verbal abilities (indexed by verbal IQ) are also likely to influence the style of text exploration these children will adopt.

Our proposal aligns well with the way Olson, Kliegel, Davidson and Foltz (1985) summarized their view: '. . . an interaction between basic phonological coding skills and higher level verbal skills [determines] subjects' ability to recognize words. The more verbally intelligent can supplement their weak phonological skills and can reach a level which the less verbally intelligent would have to use phonological skills to reach' (p. 52).

The Interaction of Phonological and Semantic Skills in Learning to Read

In order to consider more formally how dyslexic children might compensate for their phonological difficulties when learning to read, let us return to the framework of reading proposed by Seidenberg and McClelland (1989). It will be recalled that within this framework, learning to read is conceptualized as a process of setting up mappings between the orthographic forms of printed words and their phonological forms. This process is supported by semantic knowledge and an appreciation of context.

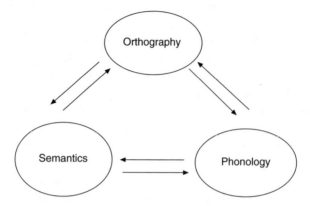

Figure 11.1 Schematic representation of Plaut, McClelland, Seidenberg, and Patterson's (1996) semantic and phonological pathways

As noted in chapter 4, although Seidenberg and McClelland's model, SM89, did not deal with meaning, a version implemented by Plaut, McClelland, Seidenberg and Patterson (1996) attempted to do so in a preliminary way. This model, depicted in figure 11.1, contains two pathways by which orthographic information can influence phonological information: a phonological pathway and a semantic pathway. It is this model that is important for considering the ways in which decoding difficulties might be compensated for in dyslexic children who have proficient semantic skills.

In essence, the simulation of Plaut et al. involved training a network in which a semantic pathway provided additional input to the phoneme units. An effect of combining semantic and phonological influences in the model was to increase the rate of learning, particularly of exception words. In the later stages of training, Plaut et al. (1996) showed that the two pathways became highly specialized, so that the semantic pathway dealt primarily with the pronunciation of exception words while the phonological pathway continued to be involved in the pronunciation of words with consistent pronunciations.

As already discussed, dyslexic children have problems in establishing the orthography–phonology mappings that comprise the phonological pathway (Snowling, Hulme and Goulandris, 1994). However, their exception word reading is in line with reading age, suggesting that they can establish orthography–semantic mappings better. Indeed, we have suggested that the extent to which dyslexic children can use semantic support to bootstrap word recognition processes is an important variable predicting the qualitative nature of the reading strategies they adopt. When broader language impairments affecting semantic skills preclude this, the ability of children to compensate for their reading deficits is reduced; the pervasive reading problems that affect both word recognition and reading comprehension, often seen in cases of children with specific language impairment, illustrate the consequences of such broader language deficits (Snowling, Bishop and Stothard, in press).

In connectionist terms, a reading disorder such as dyslexia can be modeled by constraining the mappings that are established between orthography and phonology during acquisition. As we saw in chapter 6, different ways of doing this mimic differences in the severity of the deficit at the level of phonological representations. Likewise, the reading problems of children with broader language impairments that extend beyond phonology can be simulated by reducing the semantic knowledge they can draw upon. Another way of doing this would be to reduce the activation of semantic units by context.

The Role of Environmental Factors

The discussion so far makes clear that, although phonology is central to the acquisition of decoding skills, its influence on reading development is modified by other language skills. In fact, arguments have been made for the role of within-child factors such as semantic, syntactic and even pragmatic skills in learning to read (Whitehurst and Lonigan, 1998). Differences in reading skill between children also depend upon extrinsic factors including the environments in which they learn. Indeed, one of the most important environmental predictors of reading acquisition is maternal educational level, a factor that is likely to be mediated not only through child-rearing practices but also via the linguistic milieu in the home.

Another very important environmental influence on children's reading acquisition is the teaching they receive. As was discussed in the previous chapter, there is now considerable evidence showing that children who have reading difficulties benefit from interventions that combine explicit training in phonological awareness with highly structured reading programmes emphasizing both meaning and the links between spellings and sounds. However, to some extent teaching approaches reflect the nature of the task to be learned, and there is increasing evidence that the demands of learning to read differ between languages. Our discussion has thus far been remarkably 'Anglocentric', and this reflects the fact that most of the research on dyslexia has been conducted on English-speaking children. However, it is now known that there are differences in the ease with which children acquire literacy skills in different languages. As we shall see, this has usually been attributed to inherent differences in the way in which they represent spoken words at the level of phonology.

Cross-linguistic factors

Languages differ in the inherent difficulty they pose to young readers who are trying to 'crack the code' because they differ in the regularity or transparency of their orthographies. German and Italian are two of the more transparent European orthographies, and in these languages, letters and groups of letters (graphemes) correspond to single phonemes. The same is true for Greek though the alphabetic script is different. In contrast, the English writing system is much more opaque, and very frequently a grapheme may correspond to more than one phoneme. For example, the grapheme *e* may correspond to [ɛ] as in 'bed', to [i] as in 'eve' and to [ə] as in 'believe'. In particular, there are many inconsistencies in the way in which vowels are represented.

It turns out that normally developing children learn to read and spell more quickly in relatively transparent writing systems than in opaque systems such as English. In a comparative study of French- and English-speaking children, Bruck, Genesee, and Caravolas (1997) found that French-Canadian children, who showed no signs of superior phonological awareness in kindergarten, were better word and nonword readers than a group of English peers by the end of first grade. The French language has a less transparent orthography than German or Italian, but it is more consistent in terms of its grapheme–phoneme correspondence than English, particularly for reading. A faster rate of reading acquisition has also been observed among readers of Italian (Cossu, Shankweiler, Liberman, Katz and Tola, 1988), German (Frith, Wimmen and Landerl, 1998) and Greek (Nikolopoulos, 1999). Similarly, children learning to spell in transparent orthographies are at an advantage relative to English-speaking children in the first years of schooling. In Czech, which has a highly transparent writing system, first-grade children were better able to spell nonwords than English-speaking children of the same age (Caravolas and Bruck, 1993); German-speaking children in second, third and fourth grades performed better on a word spelling task than English children of the same age (Wimmer and Landerl, 1998).

Another finding that is important for our present discussion is that phonological awareness also develops quickly in readers of transparent orthographies (Cossu, 1999). The corollary of this is that the core phonological deficits of dyslexia are harder to detect in children who have learned to read in a regular orthography where phonological awareness is not a sensitive predictor of reading skill (Bruck, Genesee and Caravolas, 1997). In these languages, difficulties can be identified most clearly on tasks that require implicit phonological processing, such as verbal short-term memory, rapid naming and visual–verbal paired associate learning tasks (Wimmer, Mayringer and Landerl, 1998).

The reading and spelling symptoms of dyslexia are also different in regular orthographies as compared to English, and in particular, nonword reading is relatively easy. Wimmer and his colleagues have conducted several studies showing that German-speaking dyslexic children can read long unfamiliar words and also nonwords as well as their peers (Frith, Wimmer and Landerl, 1998). However, the fluency of their reading is affected; they read single words more slowly than controls and sometimes, reading comprehension difficulties follow as the consequence of a 'bottleneck' in the reading process (Wimmer, Mayringer and Landerl, 1998). In similar vein, Nikolopoulos (1999) found that Greek-speaking dyslexic readers were accomplished in their use of alphabetic skills but their reading rate was impaired.

Studies of this type remind us that, although the main symptom of dyslexia is often a reading problem, the reading deficit is more properly considered one of several possible behavioural manifestations of an underlying cognitive deficit (Frith, 1997). Clearly, an important source of variation in this behavioural manifestation is the nature of the orthography in which the dyslexic child is learning. It is of further interest that experience in reading appears to have consequences for the development of other surface manifestations. Thus, neither German nor Greek dyslexic children have marked deficits in phonological awareness. It seems that feedback to the phonological system from the consistent orthography–phonology connections may be sufficient to sharpen the segmental organization of phonological representations (cf. Harm and Seidenberg, 1999). Evidently this does not happen in English, where dyslexic readers show persistent deficits on phonemic awareness tasks into adulthood (Bruck, 1990). Access to phonological representations, as evidenced for example by rapid naming tasks, is nonetheless predictive of individual differences in reading of German and Greek as well as English, and poor paired-associate learning has been observed to discriminate dyslexic from normal readers in German (Wimmer, Mayringer and Landerl, 1998), Dutch (de Jong, Seveke and Van Veen, in press) and English (Wind-fuhr and Snowling, submitted).

The cross-linguistic study of dyslexia offers a stringent test of the phonological representations hypothesis. The findings of studies of children learning a range of European languages are now consistent with this view. The different manifestations of dyslexia in regular orthographies highlight the importance of separating the core cognitive deficit in dyslexia from its behavioural manifestations.

Reading practice

From the standpoint of cognitive psychology, it is easy to overlook a final factor that determines the rate of children's reading development, and that is practice. Reading practice is particularly important for ensuring progress in an opaque reading system such as English where there are many words that cannot be decoded using spelling–sound rules. Though it is quite clear to the lay person that children create literacy environments for themselves, fuelled by their interest in reading, motivation is just beginning to feature in the science of reading development (Guthrie and Wigfield, 1999).

While the sensitivity of measures of print exposure has been questioned, print exposure accounts for variance in reading skills when other critical variables such as IQ and phonological awareness have been controlled (Stanovich and West, 1989). It is quite probable that one source of individual differences between dyslexic children is in the time they spend reading. Dyslexic children who read a lot quite obviously have more chance of developing a sight vocabulary than children who shy away from literacy activities. Arguing along these lines,

Stanovich, Siegel and Gottardo (1997) suggested that lack of print exposure may contribute to the reading pattern of surface dyslexia in children who rely too heavily on word attack skills. Put in connectionist terms, such children can establish basic mappings between orthography and phonology but have not had sufficient 'training' on exception words for the orthographic system to function normally.

The Issue of Co-morbidity

It is the case in the field of children's developmental disorders that two different conditions frequently occur together in the same individual. The term 'co-morbidity' describes this tendency (See Angold, Costello and Erkanli, 1999, for a review). In fact, the probability of two disorders co-occurring is greater than expected from the population incidence of either disorder alone (Caron and Rutter, 1991). The issue of co-morbidity needs to be raised here because when other difficulties are present in combination with dyslexia, there will be a change in its behavioural manifestations.

Children with dyslexia often have problems with attention control and it is frequent for parents and teachers to complain about their lack of concentration. It is therefore reasonable to ask whether problems of attention and organization are direct consequences of dyslexia or whether they reflect a co-morbid difficulty. There has, in fact, been little research investigating this question. In a recent study of our own in which we screened the entire population of a large UK primary school (Adams, Snowling, Hennessy and Kind, 1999), we found that 12.5 per cent of poor readers were rated by their teachers as having a significant problem with attention. The rate was 15.6 per cent among children from that school identified with specific reading difficulties (dyslexia). However, to be clinically diagnosed as having attention deficit/hyperactivity syndrome (ADHD) (DSM-IV, 1994), attentional problems must be pervasive, affecting behaviour both at home and at school. Dyslexic children who display poor attention only during school lessons are more likely to be failing to concentrate as a consequence of their reading or writing difficulties rather than because of a true attentional deficit.

An important study that looked at this issue directly was conducted by Pennington, Grossier and Welsh (1993). This study involved three groups of children: a group of dyslexic readers who did not have attentional problems, a group of children diagnosed with ADHD and a co-morbid group who had dyslexia and ADHD. The children were given two sets of tasks to complete. These were phonological tasks designed to tap the core deficit in dyslexia, and executive function tasks, to tap the core deficit in ADHD. Tests of executive function require sustained attention, organization and planning for their completion. The critical question was, how would the co-morbid group who showed both dyslexia and ADHD perform?

In line with expectation, the group who had reading difficulties performed poorly on tests of phonological processing. However, they had no difficulty with the executive function tasks. In contrast, the ADHD group showed executive deficits while their phonological processing was normal. The co-morbid group performed like the dyslexics, showing phonological but not executive deficits. These findings are important. The resemblance of the co-morbid group to the dyslexic group suggested that these were dyslexic children who had developed attention problems as a secondary consequence of their learning difficulties. The fact that they did not show executive deficits set them out as distinct from children with ADHD. It might be argued, therefore, that the co-occurrence of ADHD and dyslexia did not reflect true co-morbidity in this case, but rather the development of one disorder as the consequence of another.

In contrast, some years ago Nicolson and Fawcett (1990) proposed that dyslexic children have a general automatization deficit. Their evidence came from the finding that dyslexic children showed deficits in a dual task where they had to balance whilst performing a secondary task, though they had no difficulty with single task balancing. However, more recent research suggests that their results may have been the result of co-morbid problems in attention control. Thus, Wimmer, Mayringer and Raberger (1999) found that poor dual-task balancing only characterized children with high ADHD ratings, and that those with low ratings for attention problems performed just like normal children. In this example, it can be assumed that the presence of ADHD with dyslexia was an instance of true co-morbidity, and as the study shows, this combination can change the behavioural manifestations of dyslexia.

Another problem that frequently co-occurs with dyslexia is poor motor skills. Indeed, the first clinical case reports of dyslexic children mentioned 'poor penmanship' as a classic feature of the syndrome. However, as with ADHD, it remains unclear whether the handwriting problems of dyslexic children follow as a consequence of problems with spelling or whether they stem from a distinct problem of motor incoordination.

The term 'dyspraxia' is sometimes used to describe the motor difficulties of dyslexic children. Dyspraxia, or developmental coordination disorder (DCD) (DSM-IV, 1994) is characterized by a difficulty with gross and fine motor movements that is out of line with age and stage of development. In addition, speech development may be affected. It is therefore not surprising that the condition can be confused with dyslexia, especially in young children. However, empirical evidence suggests that the two disorders are distinct. Lord and Hulme (1987) showed that children with DCD have normal reading and spelling skills, though writing difficulties are frequently associated with the condition.

The two developmental disorders chosen here to illustrate the problem of co-morbidity are by no means exclusive. However, there has also been speculation that dyslexia co-occurs with conduct disorders leading to patterns of offending behaviour (Fergusson and Lynsky, 1997). While empirical evidence for these associations is weak, the implication is that the manifestations of dyslexia will be modified when there is a co-morbid difficulty affecting another aspect of development.

Finally, it can sometimes be difficult to decide where the borders of dyslexia lie. Commonly people speak of the continuum of language disorder of which dyslexia is a part. As we saw from studies of preschool children at risk of dyslexia, broader language impairments than phonological may be part of the dyslexia spectrum. From another angle, we recently assessed the literacy outcomes of 71 adolescents who had a pre-school history of language impairments (Snowling, Bishop and Stothard, in press). By and large, these children had made a normal start with reading and spelling (Bishop and Adams, 1990) but at 15, the incidence of specific reading difficulties in the group had increased markedly to around 48 per cent, and nonword reading skills were poor. Had these children been referred for the first time as teenagers, many of them would certainly have been diagnosed as dyslexic. From a cognitive perspective, however, these young people had followed a different developmental pathway from classically defined dyslexics. Indeed, when they were 8 years old, their decoding skills had been indistinguishable from those of controls matched for age and IQ. Our suggestion is that these children's reading skills had not kept pace with development because their relatively poor general language skills had limited the use of semantic resources needed to support the development of word recognition and advanced phonological decoding skills.

The educational needs of children with specific language impairments differ from those of children with specific reading difficulties, even though the core of their reading problems may be similar. It does them no service to include them under the umbrella of dyslexia unless the specific nature of their difficulties, and their associated deficits, are taken into account when planning intervention.

Thus, it is crucial for both theory-building and for clinical diagnosis to be clear about the symptoms that are causally related to the core deficit in dyslexia, and those that are linked with the co-occurring conditions. If this is not done, then interventions may be misplaced. To put this plainly, dyslexic children benefit from training in phonological skills; their reading difficulties will not improve if they are medicated for ADHD or given motor co-ordination exercises.

Towards a Definition of Dyslexia

Dyslexia has, throughout its history, defied definition. As recommended by Tønnesen (1995), the hypothesis that dyslexia is a specific cognitive deficit affecting phonological processing and compromising the acquisition of literacy has been taken as a working definition. But is it really necessary to be so cautious? There is an empirically well-supported theory regarding the cognitive basis of dyslexia, and a growing consensus regarding its biological basis. Furthermore, if the argument developed in this book is accepted, heterogeneity in the behavioural profile of dyslexia need not challenge the fundamental assumption that dyslexia reflects a phonological deficit. Rather, individual differences in dyslexia can be attributed to variations in the severity of the underlying phonological deficit, modified by other language and cognitive skills intrinsic to the child, in interaction with environmental factors.

What about the role of IQ? There are cogent arguments for removing IQ from the definition of reading disability (Siegel, 1988). However, there are also strong counterarguments. Our example of the different course of reading development followed by children of lower verbal ability is one such example. As Torgesen (1989) stated, 'saying that phonological processing deficits are the key [to understanding dyslexia] does not necessarily deny that low IQ can be a cause of poor reading skill' (p. 485). In fact, about 16 per cent of the variance in reading is accounted for by IQ, and language processes tapped by verbal IQ measures, particularly vocabulary, are crucial for reading comprehension. Moreover, as Nation and Snowling (1998a) have shown, semantic skills are an important compensatory device for dyslexic readers. Taking this argument a step further, because of lower levels of verbal IQ, generally poor readers may not read in the same way as those with more specific difficulties. Although there is some evidence that the two groups do not differ in prognosis (Shaywitz, Escobar, Shaywitz, Metcher and Makugh, 1992), there is other evidence to the contrary (Olson, Forsberg, Gayan and DeFries, in press), and Hatcher (in press) found that dyslexic children benefited more from an intervention linking reading with phonology than children with moderate learning difficulties in an IQ range of 55–75. There is a danger that by grouping all poor readers under the term 'dyslexia', the weak language skills of some children will be overlooked. In the longer term, this can result in a decline in reading accuracy relative to age (Snowling, Bishop and Stothard, in press; Snowling, Nation and Muter, 1999).

A further source of evidence in support of the discrepancy definition of dyslexia comes from behaviour-genetic analyses. Thus, Olson and colleagues (1999) reported a higher genetic susceptibility for discrepancy-defined dyslexia than for 'garden variety' poor reading skill. A proviso is that the increased environmental contribution to generally poor reading may come through shared variance with vocabulary. As we have also argued, vocabulary skills can modify an inherited susceptibility to dyslexia.

To conclude, dyslexia need not be a definition by exclusion. There are positive signs of dyslexia that persist throughout the life-span. Dyslexia is a specific form of language impairment that affects the way in which the brain encodes the phonological features of spoken words. The core deficit is in phonological processing and stems from poorly specified phonological representations. Dyslexia specifically affects the development of reading and spelling skills but its effects can be modified through development leading to a variety of behavioural manifestations.

It is important to recognize that the impairment in dyslexia does not affect reading directly but affects the development of the spoken language substrate that is critical for learning to read. It is for this reason that dyslexia has a different manifestation in transparent than in opaque orthographies, and similarly the reading deficit might be almost hidden in children learning to read in logographic scripts. The fact that it has its origins in early spoken language skills holds out great hope for early intervention to circumvent what otherwise can be a downward spiral of literacy impairment and educational underachievement.

Chapter 12

Conclusions and Future Prospects

In the past decade, there has been a major growth in research on dyslexia moving the field away from the statistical definitions of the 1970s and 1980s towards a more positive definition of the disorder that takes account of its key characteristic, a phonological deficit that persists across the life-span. This, in turn, has led to a clearer specification of the nature of the phonological impairment that we now know encompasses problems of both phonological awareness and phonological retrieval mechanisms. These measurable problems have been conceptualized theoretically as a deficit at the level of phonological representations; one way of thinking about this is that the images of the sounds of words stored in a dyslexic brain are fuzzy or blurred. At the same time, the development of connectionist models of reading have led to a re-framing of the effects that the phonological deficit has on learning to read and also on how semantic processes can facilitate decoding. Perhaps most importantly, our greater understanding of the nature of the cognitive deficit in dyslexia has led to the implementation of theoretically motivated interventions to promote reading skills in children at risk of reading failure. The evaluation of these interventions has given birth to a scientific approach to practice that for too long was divorced from theory.

To add to this body of knowledge, biological research has identified gene markers for dyslexia in affected families leading to a growth in interest in the precursors of dyslexia during the pre-school years in children at genetic risk. Scientists have begun to look for behavioural markers of dyslexia in sensory systems, and the advent of brain imaging has indicated that many of the impairments observed in dyslexia are associated with abnormalities of brain function, primarily in the left temporal regions of the brain.

So what will the next decade bring? Undoubtedly, theoretical developments in neuroscience will have a major impact on the field of dyslexia and lead to computationally explicit theories of its nature and development. The neuroscientific study of brain mechanisms should begin to tell us more about how the connections between different brain regions are different in dyslexic people, and perhaps begin to explain their much reported abilities as well as their difficulties. The developing area of cross-linguistic research will allow us better insights into how the behavioural manifestations of dyslexia depend upon the language in which a child is learning, and there will be a second generation of studies of children at risk of dyslexia from infancy to childhood. A major issue that such studies raise is the nature of the relationship between the development of language and phonology. Much more empirical work is needed to refine understanding of this key issue. My prediction is that once this work has been done, the use of the term 'dyslexia' may be replaced, at least clinically, by the concept of a dyslexia-spectrum. Should this be the case, it will fall to molecular geneticists to show how the genes that code for dyslexia interact with other genes to bring about individual differences on this continuum, and for brain scientists to look for differences in brain circuitry that underlie these variations.

Finally, to intervention: while it is now clear that dyslexic children need much more than the usual diet of classroom support if they are to overcome their difficulties, we are a long way from catering for their needs. The research agenda for the next decade must certainly be directed to the 'treatment resisters', the term used by Torgesen (in press) to refer to those poor readers who do not respond well to current intervention programmes. One hope that we might entertain is that brain imaging studies could guide the way ahead for such children by utilizing intact rather than deficient systems.

References

Adams, J. W., Snowling, M. J., Hennessy, S. M. and Kind, P. 1999: Problems of behaviour, reading and arithmetic: Assessments of co-morbidity using the Strengths and Difficulties Questionnaire. *British Journal of Educational Psychology*, 69, 571–85.

Adams, M. J. 1990: *Beginning to Read – Thinking and Learning about Print*. Cambridge, MA: MIT Press.

Adlard, A. and Hazan, V. 1997: Speech perception in children with specific reading difficulties (dyslexia). *Quarterly Journal of Experimental Psychology*, 51, 153–77.

Aguiar, L. and Brady, S. 1991: Vocabulary acquisition and reading ability. *Reading and Writing*, 3, 413–25.

Angold, A., Costello, E. J. and Erkanli, A. 1999: Comorbidity. *Journal of Child Psychology and Psychiatry*, 40, 57–87.

Annett, M. 1985: *Left, Right, Hand and Brain: The Right Shift Theory*. Hove: Lawrence Erlbaum.

Annett, M. 1991: Speech lateralization and phonological skill. *Cortex*, 27, 583–93.

Annett, M. and Kilshaw, D. 1984: Lateral preference and skill in dyslexics: Implications of the right shift theory. *Journal of Child Psychology and Psychiatry*, 25, 357–77.

Annett, M. and Manning, M. 1990: Reading and a balanced polymorphism for laterality and ability. *Journal of Child Psychology and Psychiatry*, 31, 511–29.

Backman, J. E., Bruck, M., Hèbert, M. and Seidenberg, M. S. 1984: Acquisition and use of spelling-sound information in reading. *Journal of Experimental Child Psychology*, 38, 114–33.

Backman, J. E., Mamen, M. and Ferguson, H. G. 1984: Reading level design: Conceptual and methodological issues in reading research. *Psychological Bulletin*, 96, 560–8.

Baddeley, A. D. 1986: *Working Memory*. Oxford: Oxford University Press.

Baddeley, A. D., Thomson, N. and Buchanan, M. 1975: Word length and the structure of short-term memory. *Journal of Verbal Learning and Verbal Behaviour*, 14, 575–89.

Baldeweg, T., Richardson, A., Watkins, S., Foale, C. and Gruzelier, J. 1999: Impaired auditory frequency discrimination in dyslexia detected with mismatch evoked potentials. *Annals of Neurology*, 45, 495–503.

Ball, E. W. and Blachman, B. A. 1991: Does phoneme awareness training in kindergarten make a difference in early word recognition and developmental spelling? *Reading Research Quarterly*, 26, 49–66.

Baron, J. and Treiman, R. 1980: Some problems in the study of differences in cognitive processes. *Memory and Cognition*, 8, 313–21.

Beech, J. R. and Harding, L. M. 1984: Phonemic processing and the poor reader from a developmental lag viewpoint. *Reading Research Quarterly*, 19, 357–66.

Behan, P. and Geschwind, N. 1985: Dyslexia, congenital anomalies, and immune disorders: The role of the foetal environment. *Annals of the New York Academy of Sciences*, 457, 13–18.

Besner, D., Twilley, L., McCann, R. S. and Seergobin, K. 1990: On the association between connectionism and data: Are a few words necessary? *Psychological Review*, 97, 432–46.

Bird, J., Bishop, D. V. M. and Freeman, N. H. 1995: Phonological awareness and literacy development in children with expressive phonological impairments. *Journal of Speech and Hearing Research*, 38, 446–62.

Bishop, D. V. M. 1989: Unstable vergence control and dyslexia – a critique. *British Journal of Ophthalmology*, 73, 223–35.

Bishop, D. V. M. 1997: *Uncommon Understanding*. Hove: Psychology Press.

Bishop, D. V. M. and Adams, C. 1990: A prospective study of the relationship between specific language impairment, phonological disorders and reading retardation. *Journal of Child Psychology and Psychiatry*, 31, 1027–50.

Bishop, D. V. M., Bishop, S. J., Bright, P., James, C., Delaney, T. and Tallal, P. 1999: Different origin of auditory and phonological processing problems in children with language impairment: Evidence from a twin study. *Journal of Speech, Language and Hearing Research*, 42, 155–68.

Bishop, D. V. M. and Butterworth, G. E. 1980: Verbal-performance discrepancies: Relationship to birth risk and specific reading retardation. *Cortex*, 16, 375–90.

Bissex, G. L. 1980: *GNYS at Work: A Child Learns to Write and Read*. Cambridge, MA: Harvard University Press.

Blachman, B. (ed.) 1997: *Foundations of Reading Acquisition and Dyslexia: Implications for Early Intervention*. Mahwah, NJ: Lawrence Erlbaum Associates.

References

Boder, E. 1971: Developmental dyslexia: Prevailing diagnostic concepts. In H. R. Mykelbust (ed.), *Progress in Learning Disabilities and a New Diagnostic Approach*, New York: Grune and Stratton, 293–321.

Boder, E. 1973: Developmental dyslexia: A diagnostic approach based on three atypical reading-spelling patterns. *Developmental Medicine and Child Neurology*, 15, 663–87.

Bond, G. L. and Dykstra, R. 1967: The co-operative research programme in first grade reading instruction. *Reading Research Quarterly*, 2, 5–142.

Borsting, E., Ridder, W. H., Dudeck, K., Kelley, C., Matsui, L. and Motoyama, J. 1996: The presence of magnocellular defect depends on the type of dyslexia. *Vision Research*, 36, 1047–53.

Borstrøm, I. and Elbro, C. 1997: Prevention of dyslexia in kindergarten: Effects of phoneme awareness training with children of dyslexic parents. In C. Hulme and M. J. Snowling (eds), *Dyslexia: Biology, Cognition and Intervention*, London: Whurr, 235–53.

Bowers, P. G. 1993: Text reading and rereading – determinants of fluency beyond word recognition. *Journal of Reading Behaviour*, 25, 133–53.

Bowers, P. G. 1995: Tracing symbol naming speed's unique contributions to reading disabilities over time. *Reading and Writing*, 7, 189–216.

Bowers, P. G. and Swanson, L. B. 1991: Naming speed deficits in reading disability: Multiple measures of a singular process. *Journal of Experimental Child Psychology*, 51, 195–219.

Bowers, P. G. and Wolf, M. 1993: Theoretical links among naming speed, precise timing mechanisms and orthographic skill in dyslexia. *Reading and Writing*, 5, 69–85.

Bowey, J. A. 1996: On the association between phonological memory and receptive vocabulary in five-year olds. *Journal of Child Psychology*, 63, 44–78.

Bowey, J. A. 1999: The limitations of orthographic rime analogies in beginners' word reading: A reply to Goswami (1999). *Journal of Experimental Child Psychology*, 72, 220–31.

Bowey, J. A. and Underwood, N. 1996: Further evidence that orthographic rime usage in nonword reading increases with word-level reading proficiency. *Journal of Experimental Child Psychology*, 63, 526–62.

Bowey, J. A., Vaughan, L. and Hansen, J. 1998: Beginning reader's use of orthographic analogies in word reading. *Journal of Experimental Child Psychology*, 68, 108–33.

Bradley, L. and Bryant, P. E. 1978: Difficulties in auditory organisation as a possible cause of reading backwardness. *Nature*, 271, 746–7.

Bradley, L. and Bryant, P. E. 1983: Categorising sounds and learning to read – a causal connection. *Nature*, 301, 419–21.

References

Brady, S. A. 1997: Ability to encode phonological representations: An underlying difficulty for poor readers. In B. Blachman (ed.), *Foundations of Reading Acquisition and Dyslexia: Implications for Early Intervention*, Mahwah, NJ: Lawrence Erlbaum Associates, 21–48.

Brady, S. A., Shankweiler, D. and Mann, V. 1983: Speech perception and memory coding in relation to reading ability. *Journal of Experimental Child Psychology*, 35, 345–67.

Brandt, J. J. and Rosen, J. 1980: Auditory-phonemic perception in dyslexia: categorised identification and discrimination of stop consonants. *Brain and Language*, 9, 324–37.

Breitmeyer, B. G. 1980: Unmasking visual masking: A look at the 'why' behind the veil of 'how'. *Psychological Review*, 87, 52–69.

Broom, Y. M. and Doctor, E. A. 1995: Developmental surface dyslexia: A case study of the efficacy of a remediation programme. *Cognitive Neuropsychology*, 12, 69–110.

Brown, G. D. A. 1997: Connectionism, phonology, reading, and regularity in developmental dyslexia. *Brain and Language*, 59, 207–35.

Brown, G. D. A. and Deavers, R. 1999: Units of analysis in nonword reading: Evidence from children and adults. *Journal of Experimental Child Psychology*, 73, 208–42.

Brown, G. D. A. and Watson, F. 1991: Reading development in dyslexia: A connectionist approach. In M. J. Snowling and M. Thomson (eds), *Dyslexia: Integrating Theory and Practice*, London: Whurr, 165–83.

Brown, I. S. and Felton, R. H. 1990: Effects of instruction in beginning reading skills in children at risk for reading disability. *Reading and Writing*, 2, 223–41.

Bruck, M. 1988: The word recognition and spelling of dyslexic children. *Reading Research Quarterly*, 23, 51–69.

Bruck, M. 1990: Word recognition skills of adults with childhood diagnoses of dyslexia. *Developmental Psychology*, 26, 439–54.

Bruck, M., Genesee, F. and Caravolas, M. 1997: A cross-linguistic study of early literacy acquisition. In B. Blachman (ed.), *Foundations of Reading Acquisition and Dyslexia: Implications for Early Intervention*, Mahwah, NJ: Lawrence Erlbaum Associates.

Bruck, M. and Treiman, R. 1990: Phonological awareness and spelling in normal children and dyslexics – the case of initial consonant clusters. *Journal of Experimental Child Psychology*, 50, 156–78.

Bruck, M. and Treiman, R. 1992: Learning to pronounce words: The limitations of analogies. *Reading Research Quarterly*, 27, 375–88.

Brunswick, N., McCrory, E., Price, C. J., Frith, C. D. and Frith, U. 1999: Explicit and implicit processing of words and pseudowords by adult developmental dyslexics: A search for Wernicke's Wortschatz? *Brain*, 122, 1901–17.

Byrne, B. 1996: The learnability of the alphabetic system: Children's initial hypotheses about how print represents spoken language. *Applied Psycholinguistics*, 17, 401–26.

Byrne, B. 1998: *The Foundation of Literacy: The Child's Acquisition of the Alphabetic Principle.* Hove: Psychology Press.

Byrne, B. and Fielding-Barnsley, R. 1989: Phonemic awareness and letter knowledge in the child's acquisition of the alphabetic principle. *Journal of Educational Psychology*, 81, 805–12.

Byrne, B. and Fielding-Barnsley, R. 1991: Evaluation of a program to teach phonemic awareness to young children. *Journal of Educational Psychology*, 83, 451–5.

Byrne, B. and Fielding-Barnsley, R. 1995: Evaluation of a program to teach phonemic awareness to young children: A 2- and 3-year follow-up and a new pre-school trial. *Journal of Educational Psychology*, 87, 488–503.

Byrne, B., Fielding-Barnsley, R. and Ashley, L. (submitted): Effects of pre-school phoneme identity training after six years: Average benefits but no vaccination effect.

Byrne, B., Fielding-Barnsley, R., Ashley, L. and Larsen, K. 1997: Assessing the child's and the environment's contribution to reading acquisition: What we know and what we don't know. In B. Blachman (ed.), *Foundations of Reading Acquisition and Dyslexia: Implications for Early Intervention.* Mahwah, NJ: Lawrence Erlbaum Associates, 265–86.

Campbell, R. and Butterworth, B. 1985: Phonological dyslexia and dysgraphia in a highly literate subject: A developmental case with associated deficits of phonemic processing and awareness. *Quarterly Journal of Experimental Psychology*, 37A, 435–75.

Caravolas, M. and Bruck, M. 1993: The effect of oral and written language input on children's phonological awareness: A cross-linguistic study. *Journal of Experimental Child Psychology*, 55, 1–30.

Caravolas, M. and Bruck, M. (in press): Similarities and differences between English- and French-speaking poor spellers. In N. Goulandris (ed.), *Dyslexia: A Cross-linguistic Comparison*, London: Whurr.

Cardon, L. R., Smith, S. D., Fulker, D. W., Kimberling, W. J., Pennington, B. F. and DeFries, J. C. 1994: Quantitative trait locus for reading disability on chromosome 6. *Science*, 266, 276–9.

Caron, C. and Rutter, M. 1991: Comorbidity in child psychopathology: Concepts, issues and research strategies. *Journal of Child Psychology and Psychiatry*, 32, 1063–80.

Castles, A. and Coltheart, M. 1993: Varieties of developmental dyslexia. *Cognition*, 47, 149–80.

References

Castles, A., Datta, H., Gayan, J. and Olson, R. K. 1999: Varieties of developmental reading disorder: Genetic and environmental influences. *Journal of Experimental Child Psychology*, 72, 73.

Cataldo, S. and Ellis, N. 1988: Interactions in the development of spelling, reading and phonological skills. *Journal of Research in Reading*, 11, 86–109.

Catts, H. W. 1993: The relationship between speech-language and reading disabilities. *Journal of Speech and Hearing Research*, 36, 948–58.

Chall, J. S. 1967: *Learning to Read: The Great Debate*. New York: McGraw-Hill.

Clay, M. 1985: *The Early Detection of Reading Difficulties*, 3rd edn. Tadworth, Surrey: Heinemann.

Coltheart, M. 1978: Lexical access in simple reading tasks. In G. Underwood (ed.), *Strategies of Information Processing*, London: Academic Press, 151–216.

Coltheart, M., Masterson, J., Byng, S., Prior, M. and Riddoch, J. 1983: Surface dyslexia. *Quarterly Journal of Experimental Psychology*, 35, 469–95.

Coltheart, M., Patterson, K. and Marshall, J. C. 1980: *Deep Dyslexia*. London: Routledge and Kegan Paul.

Coltheart, V. and Leahy, J. 1992: Children's and adult's reading of nonwords: Effects of regularity and consistency. *Journal of Experimental Psychology: Learning, Memory and Cognition*, 18, 718–29.

Conrad, R. 1964: Acoustic confusions in immediate memory. *British Journal of Psychology*, 55, 75–84.

Cornelissen, P. L., Hansen, P. C., Hutton, J. L., Evangelinou, V. and Stein, J. F. 1997: Magnocellular visual function and children's single word reading. *Vision Research*, 38, 471–82.

Cornelissen, P. L., Richardson, A., Mason, A., Fowler, S. and Stein, J. 1995: Contrast sensitivity and coherent motion detection measured at phototopic luminance levels in dyslexics and controls. *Vision Research*, 35, 1483–94.

Cossu, G. 1999: Biological constraints on literacy acquisition. *Reading and Writing*, 11, 213–37.

Cossu, G., Shankweiler, D., Liberman, I., Katz, L. and Tola, G. 1988: Awareness of phonological segments and reading ability in Italian children. *Applied Psycholinguistics*, 9, 1–16.

Critchley, M. 1970: *The Dyslexic Child*. London: Heinemann Medical Books.

Critchley, M. and Critchley, E. A. 1978: *Dyslexia Defined*. London: Acford.

Cunningham, A. 1990: Explicit versus implicit instruction in phonemic awareness. *Journal of Experimental Child Psychology*, 50, 429–44.

Cunningham, A. and Stanovich, K. 1991: Tracking the unique effects of print exposure in children – associations with vocabulary, general knowledge, and spelling. *Journal of Educational Psychology*, 83, 264–74.

References

DeFries, J. C. 1991: Genetics and dyslexia: An overview. In M. J. Snowling and M. Thomson (eds), *Dyslexia: Integrating Theory and Practice*, London: Whurr, 3–20.

DeFries, J. C., Alarcon, M. and Olson, R. K. 1997: Genetic etiologies of reading and spelling deficits: developmental differences. In C. Hulme and M. J. Snowling (eds), *Dyslexia: Biology, Cognition and Intervention*. London: Whurr, 20–37.

DeFries, J. C. and Fulker, D. W. 1985: Multiple regression analysis of twin data. *Behaviour Genetics*, 15, 467–73.

DeFries, J. C., Fulker, D. W. and LaBuda, M. C. 1987: Reading disability in twins: Evidence for a genetic etiology. *Nature*, 329, 537–9.

DeJong, P. F., Seveke, M. J. and VanVeen, M. (in press): Phonological sensitivity and the acquisition of new words in children. *Journal of Experimental Child Psychology*.

Demb, J. B., Boynton, G. M., Best, M. and Heeger, D. J. 1998: Psychophysical evidence for a magnocellular pathway deficit in dyslexia. *Vision Research*, 38, 1555–9.

Denckla, M. B. and Rudel, R. G. 1976a: Naming of object-drawings by dyslexic and other learning disabled children. *Brain and Language*, 3, 1–15.

Denckla, M. B. and Rudel, R. G. 1976b: Rapid automatised naming: Dyslexia differentiated from other learning disabilities. *Neuropsychologia*, 14, 471–9.

Doehring, D. G. and Hashko, I. M. 1977: Classification of reading problems by the Q technique of factor analysis. *Cortex*, 13, 281–94.

Dougherty, R. F., Cynader, M. S., Bjornson, B. H., Edgell, D. and Giaschi, D. E. 1998: Dichotic pitch: A new stimulus distinguishes normal and dyslexic auditory function. *Neuroreport*, 9, 3001–5.

DSM-IV 1994: *Diagnostic and Statistical Manual*. Washington, DC: American Psychiatric Association.

Duncan, L. G., Seymour, P. H. K. and Hill, S. 1997: How important are rhyme and analogy in beginning reading? *Cognition*, 63, 171–208.

Dunlop, D. B., Dunlop, P. and Fenelon, B. 1973: Vision-laterality analysis in children with reading disability: The results of new techniques of analysis. *Cortex*, 9, 227–36.

Eden, G. F., VanMeter, J. W., Rumsey, J. M., Maisog, J. M., Woods, R. P. and Zeffiro, T. A. 1996: Abnormal processing of visual motion in dyslexia revealed by functional brain imaging. *Nature*, 382, 66–9.

Ehri, L. C. 1985: Sources of difficulty in learning to spell and read. In M. L. Wolraich and D. Routh (eds), *Advances in Developmental and Behavioural Paediatrics*, Greenwich, CT: Jai Press Inc.

Ehri, L. C. 1992: Reconceptualising the development of sight word reading and its relationship to recoding. In P. B. Gough, L. C. Ehri and R. Treiman (eds), *Reading Acquisition*, Hillsdale, NJ: Lawrence Erlbaum Associates, 107–43.

Ehri, L. C. 1995: Phases of development in learning to read words by sight. *Journal of Research in Reading*, 18, 116–25.

Ehri, L. C. and Wilce, L. S. 1980: The influence of orthography on readers' conceptualisation of the phonemic structure of words. *Applied Psycholinguistics*, 1, 371–85.

Ehri, L. C. and Wilce, L. S. 1985: Movement into reading: Is the first stage of printed word learning visual or phonetic? *Reading Research Quarterly*, 20, 163–79.

Elbro, C. 1997: Early linguistic abilities and reading development: A review and a hypothesis about underlying differences in distinctiveness of phonological representations of lexical items. *Reading and Writing*, 8, 453–85.

Elbro, C., Borstrøm, I. and Petersen, D. K. 1998: Predicting dyslexia from kindergarten: The importance of distinctness of phonological representations of lexical items. *Reading Research Quarterly*, 33, 36–60.

Elliot, L. L., Scholl, M. E., Grant, J. O. and Hammer, M. A. 1990: Perception of gated, highly familiar spoken monosyllabic nouns by children with and without learning disabilities. *Journal of Learning Disabilities*, 23, 248–53.

Ellis, A. W. 1994: *Reading, Writing and Dyslexia: A Cognitive Analysis*, 2nd edn. Hove: Lawrence Erlbaum Associates.

Ellis, N. and Large, B. 1987: The development of reading: As you seek so shall you find. *British Journal of Psychology*, 78, 1–28.

Farmer, M. E. and Klein, R. M. 1995: The evidence for a temporal processing deficit linked to dyslexia: A review. *Psychonomic Bulletin and Review*, 2, 460–93.

Felton, R. H. and Wood, P. B. 1989: Cognitive deficits in reading disability and attention deficit disorder. *Journal of Learning Disabilities*, 22, 3–22.

Ferguson, D. M. and Lynsky, M. T. 1997: Early reading difficulties and later conduct problems. *Journal of Child Psychology and Psychiatry*, 38, 899–907.

Filipek, P. A. 1999: Neuroimaging in the developmental disorders: The state of the science. *Journal of Child Psychology and Psychiatry*, 40, 113–28.

Fisher, S. E., Marlow, A. J., Lamb, J., Maestrini, E., Williams, D. F., Richardson, A. J., Weeks, D. E., Stein, J. F. and Monaco, A. P. 1999: A quantitative-trait locus on chromosome 6p influences different aspects of developmental dyslexia. *American Journal of Human Genetics*, 64, 146–56.

Foorman, B. R., Rancis, D. J., Novy, D. M. and Liberman, D. 1991: How letter-sound instruction mediates progress in first-grade reading and spelling. *Journal of Educational Psychology*, 83, 456–69.

Foorman, B. R., Francis, D. J., Fletcher, J. M., Schatschneider, C. and Mehta, P. 1998: The role of instruction in learning to read: Preventing reading failure in at-risk children. *Journal of Educational Psychology*, 90, 37–55.

Fowler, A. 1991: How early phonological development might set the stage for phoneme awareness. In S. A. Brady and D. P. Shankweiler (eds), *Phonological Processes in Literacy: A Tribute to Isabelle Liberman*, Hillsdale, NJ: Lawrence Erlbaum Associates, 97–117.

Frith, C. and Frith, U. 1996: A biological marker for dyslexia. *Nature*, 382, 19–20.

Frith, U. 1978: Spelling difficulties. *Journal of Child Psychology and Child Psychiatry*, 19, 279–85.

Frith, U. 1980: *Cognitive Processes in Spelling*. London: Academic Press.

Frith, U. 1984: Specific spelling problems. In R. N. Malatesha and H. A. Whitaker (eds), *Dyslexia: A Global Issue*, The Hague: Martinus Nijhoff, 83–104.

Frith, U. 1985: Beneath the surface of developmental dyslexia. In K. Patterson, M. Coltheart and J. Marshall (eds), *Surface Dyslexia: Neuropsychological and Cognitive Studies of Phonological Reading*, Hove: Lawrence Erlbaum, 301–30.

Frith, U. 1997: Brain, mind and behaviour in dyslexia. In C. Hulme and M. J. Snowling (eds), *Dyslexia: Biology, Cognition and Intervention*, London: Whurr, 1–19.

Frith, U. and Frith, C. D. 1980: Relationships between reading and spelling. In J. F. Kavanagh and R. L. Venezky (eds), *Orthography, Reading and Dyslexia*, Baltimore, MD: University Park Press, 289–96.

Frith, U. and Happé, F. 1998: Why specific developmental disorders are not specific: On-line and developmental effects in autism and dyslexia. *Developmental Science*, 1, 267–72.

Frith, U. and Snowling, M. J. 1983: Reading for meaning and reading for sound in autistic and dyslexic children. *British Journal of Developmental Psychology*, 1, 329–42.

Frith, U., Wimmer, H. and Landerl, K. 1998: Differences in phonological recoding in German and English speaking children. *Scientific Studies of Reading*, 2, 31–54.

Funnell, E. and Davison, M. 1989: Lexical capture: A developmental disorder of reading and spelling. *Quarterly Journal of Experimental Psychology*, 41A, 471–88.

Galaburda, A. M. 1993: Neuroanatomic basis of developmental dyslexia. *Neurology Clinics*, 11, 161–73.

Galaburda, A. M. 1994: Developmental dyslexia and animal studies: At the interface between cognition and neurology. *Cognition*, 50, 133–49.

Galaburda, A. M. and Kemper, T. L. 1978: Cytoarchitectonic abnormalities in developmental dyslexia: A case study. *Annals of Neurology*, 6, 94–100.

Gallagher, A., Frith, U. and Snowling, M. J. 2000: Precursors of literacy-delay among children at genetic risk of dyslexia. *Journal of Child Psychology and Psychiatry*, 41, 203–13.

Gathercole, S. E. and Baddeley, A. D. 1989: Evaluation of the role of phonological short-term memory in the development of vocabulary in children: A longitudinal study. *Journal of Memory and Language*, 28, 200–13.

Gathercole, S. E. and Baddeley, A. D. 1990: Phonological memory deficits in language disordered children: Is there a causal connection? *Journal of Memory and Language*, 29, 336–60.

Gathercole, S. E., Hitch, G. J., Service, E. and Martin, A. J. 1997: Phonological short term memory and new word learning in children. *Developmental Psychology*, 33, 966–79.

Gayan, J., Olson, R. K., Cardon, L. R., Smith, S. D., Fulker, D. W., Kimberling, W. J., Pennington, B. F. and DeFries, J. C. 1995: Quantitative trait locus for different measures of reading disability. *Behaviour Genetics*, 25, 266.

German, D. J. 1979: Word finding skills in children with learning disabilities. *Journal of Learning Disabilities*, 12, 176–81.

Geschwind, N. and Galaburda, A. M. 1985: Cerebral lateralization. Biological mechanisms, associations and pathology. I. A hypothesis and a program for research. *Archives of Neurology*, 42, 428–59.

Geschwind, N. and Levitsky, W. 1968: Human brain: Left–right asymmetries in temporal speech region. *Science*, 161, 186–7.

Gilger, J. W., Pennington, B. F. and DeFries, J. C. 1991: Risk for reading disability as a function of parental history in three family studies. *Reading and Writing*, 3, 205–18.

Glushko, R. J. 1979: The organisation and activation of orthographic knowledge in reading aloud. *Journal of Experimental Psychology: Human Perception and Performance*, 5, 674–91.

Godfrey, J. J., Syrdal-Lasky, A. K., Millay, A. K. and Knox, C. M. 1981: Performance of dyslexic children on speech perception tests. *Journal of Experimental Child Psychology*, 32, 401–24.

Goldstein, E. B. 1984: *Sensation and Perception*, 2nd edn. Belmont, CA: Wadsworth Publishing Co.

Gombert, J. E. 1992: *Metalinguistic Development*. London: Harvester-Wheatsheaf.

Goswami, U. 1986: Children's use of analogy in learning to read: A developmental study. *Journal of Experimental Child Psychology*, 42, 73–83.

Goswami, U. 1988: Orthographic analogies and reading development. *Quarterly Journal of Experimental Psychology*, 40A, 239–68.

Goswami, U. 1990: A special link between rhyming skill and the use of orthographic analogies by beginning readers. *Journal of Child Psychology and Psychiatry*, 31, 301–11.

Goswami, U. 1993: Towards an interactive model of reading development: Decoding vowel graphemes in beginning reading. *Journal of Experimental Child Psychology*, 56, 443–75.

Goswami, U. 1999: Orthographic analogies and phonological priming: A comment on Bowey, Vaughan and Hansen 1998. *Journal of Experimental Child Psychology*, 72, 210–19.

Goswami, U. and Bryant, P. E. 1990: *Phonological Skills and Learning to Read*. Hove: Lawrence Erlbaum.

Goswami, U. and Mead, F. 1992: Onset and rime awareness and analogies in reading. *Reading Research Quarterly*, 27, 153–62.

Gough, P. B. and Hillinger, M. 1980: Learning to read: An unnatural act. *Bulletin of the Orton Society*, 30, 179–96.

Gough, P. B. and Tunmer, W. E. 1986: Decoding, reading and reading disability. *Remedial and Special Education*, 7, 6–10.

Goulandris, N., McIntyre, A., Snowling, M. J., Bethel, J. M. and Lee, J. P. 1998: A comparison of dyslexic and normal readers using orthoptic assessment procedures. *Dyslexia*, 4, 30–48.

Goulandris, N. and Snowling, M. J. 1991: Visual memory deficits: A plausible cause of developmental dyslexia? Evidence from a single case study. *Cognitive Neuropsychology*, 8, 127–54.

Griffiths, Y. M. 1999: *Individual Differences in Developmental Dyslexia*. Unpublished D.Phil. thesis, University of York.

Griffiths, Y. M. and Snowling, M. J. (submitted): Predictors of nonword reading in dyslexic children.

Grigorenko, E. L., Wood, F. B., Meyer, M. S., Hart, L. A., Speed, W. C., Shuster, A. and Pauls, D. L. 1997: Susceptibility loci for distinct components of developmental dyslexia on chromosomes 6 and 15. *American Journal of Human Genetics*, 60, 27–39.

Grosjean, F. 1980: Spoken word recognition processes and the gating paradigm. *Perception and Psychophysics*, 28, 267–83.

Guthrie, J. T. and Wigfield, A. 1999: How motivation fits into a science of reading. *Scientific Studies of Reading*, 3, 199–205.

Hall, J. W., Ewing, A., Tinzmann, M. B. and Wilson, K. P. 1981: Phonetic coding in dyslexic and normal readers. *Bulletin of the Psychonomic Society*, 17, 177–8.

Harm, M. W. and Seidenberg, M. S. 1999: Phonology, reading acquisition, and dyslexia: Insights from connectionist models. *Psychological Review*, 106, 491–528.

Hatcher, P. J. 1994: *Sound Linkage*. London: Whurr.

References

Hatcher, P. J. (in press): Sound links in reading and spelling with discrepancy-defined dyslexics and children with moderate learning difficulties. *Reading and Writing*.

Hatcher, P. J. and Hulme, C. 1999: Phonemes, rhymes and intelligence as predictors of children's responsiveness to remedial reading instruction: Evidence from a longitudinal intervention study. *Journal of Experimental Child Psychology*, 72, 130–53.

Hatcher, P. J., Hulme, C. and Ellis, A. W. 1994: Ameliorating early reading failure by integrating the teaching of reading and phonological skills: The phonological linkage hypothesis. *Child Development*, 65, 41–57.

Hayduk, S., Bruck, M. and Cavanagh, P. 1996: Low-level visual processing skills of adults and children with dyslexia. *Cognitive Neuropsychology*, 13, 975–1015.

Heath, S. M., Hogben, J. H. and Clark, C. D. 1999: Auditory temporary processing in disabled readers with and without oral language delay. *Journal of Child Psychology and Psychiatry*, 40, 637–47.

Hill, N., Griffiths, Y. M., Bailey, P. J. and Snowling, M. J. 1999: Frequency acvity and binaural masking release in dyslexic listeners. *Journal of the Acoustical Society of America*, 106, L53–8.

Hinshelwood, J. 1917: *Congenital Word-blindness*. London: Lewis.

Ho, C. S. H. and Bryant, P. E. 1997: Phonological skills are important in learning to read Chinese. *Developmental Psychology*, 33, 946–51.

Hogben, J. 1997: How does a visual transient deficit affect reading? In C. Hulme and M. J. Snowling (eds), *Dyslexia: Biology, Cognition and Intervention*, London: Whurr, 59–71.

Hoien, T., Lundberg, I., Stanovich, K. E. and Bjaalid, I.-K. 1995: Components of phonological awareness. *Reading and Writing*, 7, 171–88.

Hulme, C. 1981: *Reading Retardation and Multi-sensory Teaching*. London: Routledge and Kegan Paul.

Hulme, C. 1984: Developmental differences in the effects of acoustic similarity on memory span. *Developmental Psychology*, 20, 650–2.

Hulme, C. 1988: The implausibility of low-level visual deficits as a cause of children's reading difficulties. *Cognitive Neuropsychology*, 5, 369–74.

Hulme, C., Maughan, S. and Brown, G. D. A. 1991: Memory for familiar and unfamiliar words: Evidence for a long-term memory contribution to short-term memory span. *Journal of Memory and Language*, 30, 685–701.

Hulme, C., Newton, P., Cowan, N., Stuart, G. and Brown, G. D. A. 1999: Think before you speak: pauses, memory search and trace redintegration processes in verbal memory span. *Journal of Experimental Psychology: Learning, Memory and Cognition*, 25, 447–63.

Hulme, C. and Roodenrys, S. 1995: Practitioner review: Verbal working memory development and its disorders. *Journal of Child Psychology and Psychiatry*, 36, 373–98.

Hulme, C., Roodenrys, S., Schweickert, R., Brown, G. D. A., Martin, S. and Stuart, G. 1997: Word-frequency effects on short term memory tasks: Evidence for a redintegration process in immediate serial recall. *Journal of Experimental Psychology: Learning, Memory and Cognition*, 23, 1217–32.

Hulme, C. and Snowling, M. J. 1992: Deficits in output phonology: An explanation of reading failure? *Cognitive Neuropsychology*, 9, 47–72.

Hulme, C. and Snowling, M. J. (eds) 1994: *Reading Development and Dyslexia*. London: Whurr.

Hulme, C. and Snowling, M. J. (eds) 1997: *Dyslexia: Biology, Cognition and Intervention*. London: Whurr.

Hulme, C., Snowling, M. J. and Quinlan, P. 1991: Connectionism and learning to read: Steps towards a psychologically plausible model. *Reading and Writing*, 3, 159–68.

Hulme, C., Thomson, N., Muir, C. and Lawrence, A. 1984: Speech rate and the development of short-term memory. *Journal of Experimental Child Psychology*, 38, 241–53.

Hurford, D. P. and Sanders, R. F. 1990: Assessment and remediation of a phoneme discrimination deficit in reading disabled second and fourth graders. *Journal of Experimental Child Psychology*, 50, 396–415.

Hynd, G. W. and Hiemenz, J. R. 1997: Dyslexia and gyral morphology variation. In C. Hulme and M. J. Snowling (eds), *Dyslexia: Biology, Cognition and Intervention*, London: Whurr, 38–58.

Hynd, G. W., Semrud-Clikeman, M., Lorys, A., Novey, E. A. and Eliopulus, D. 1990: Brain morphology in developmental dyslexia and attention deficit disorder/hyperactivity. *Archives of Neurology*, 47, 919–26.

Iverson, S. and Tunmer, W. E. 1993: Phonological processing skills and the reading recovery programme. *Journal of Educational Psychology*, 85, 112–26.

Johnson, D. J. and Mykelbust, H. R. 1967: *Learning Disabilities: Educational Principles and Practice*. New York: Grune and Stratton.

Johnson, M. H. 1997: *Developmental Cognitive Neuroscience*. Oxford: Blackwell.

Johnston, R. S. 1982: Phonological coding in dyslexic readers. *British Journal of Psychology*, 73, 455–60.

Johnston, R. S. 1983: Developmental deep dyslexia? *Cortex*, 19, 133–9.

Johnston, R. S., Rugg, M. and Scott, T. 1987: Phonological similarity effects, memory span and developmental reading disorders: The nature of the relationship. *British Journal of Psychology*, 78, 205–11.

Johnston, R. S. and Thompson, G. B. 1989: Is dependence on phonological information in children's reading a product of instructional approach? *Journal of Experimental Child Psychology*, 40, 131–45.

Jorm, A. F. and Share, D. L. 1983: Phonological reading and reading acquisition. *Applied Psycholinguistics*, 4, 103–47.

Juel, C. 1995: The messenger may be wrong, but the message may be right. *Journal of Research in Reading*, 18, 146–53.

Karmiloff-Smith, A. 1998: Is atypical development necessarily a window on the normal mind/brain? The case of Williams Syndrome. *Developmental Science*, 1, 273–7.

Katz, R. 1986: Phonological deficiencies in children with reading disability: Evidence from an object naming task. *Cognition*, 22, 225–57.

Kibel, M. and Miles, T. R. 1994: Phonological errors in the spelling of taught dyslexic children. In C. Hulme and M. J. Snowling (eds), *Reading Development and Dyslexia*, London: Whurr, 105–27.

Kinsbourne, M. and Warrington, E. K. 1963: Developmental factors in reading and writing backwardness. *British Journal of Psychology*, 54, 145–56.

LaBerge, D. and Samuels, S. J. 1974: Toward a theory of automatic information processing in reading. *Cognitive Psychology*, 6, 293–323.

Laing, E. and Hulme, C. 1999: Phonological and semantic processes influence beginning readers' ability to learn to read words. *Journal of Experimental Child Psychology*, 73, 183–207.

Larsen, J. P., Hoien, T., Lundberg, I. and Odegaard, H. 1990: MRI evaluation of the size and symmetry of the planum temporale in adolescents with developmental dyslexia. *Brain and Language*, 39, 289–301.

Laxon, V., Masterson, J. and Coltheart, V. 1991: Some bodies are easier to read: The effect of consistency and regularity on children's reading. *Quarterly Journal of Experimental Psychology*, 43A, 793–824.

Laxon, V., Masterson, J. and Moran, R. 1994: Are children's representations of words distributed? Effects of orthographic neighbourhood size, consistency and regularity of naming. *Language and Cognitive Processes*, 9, 1–27.

Lefly, D. L. and Pennington, B. F. 1996: Longitudinal study of children at high family risk for dyslexia: The first two years. In M. L. Rice (ed.), *Toward a Genetics of Language*, Mahwah, NJ: Lawrence Erlbaum Associates, 49–76.

Leonard, C. M., Voeller, K. K. S., Lombardino, L. J., Morris, M. K., Hund, G. W., Alexander, A. W., Andersen, H. G., Garofalakis, M., Honeyman, J. C., Mao, J., Agee, O. F. and Staab, E. V. 1993: Anomalous cerebral structure in dyslexia revealed with magnetic resonance imaging. *Archives of Neurology*, 50, 461–9.

Leppanen, P. H., Pihko, E., Eklund, K. M. and Lyytinen, H. 1999: Cortical responses of infants with and without a genetic risk for dyslexia. II: Group effects. *Neuroreport*, 10, 969–73.

Levy, B. A., Bourassa, D. C. and Horn, C. 1999: Fast and slow namers: Benefits of segmentation and whole word training. *Journal of Experimental Child Psychology*, 73, 115–38.

Liberman, I. Y. and Shankweiler, D. 1979: Speech, the alphabet and teaching to read. In L. Resnick and P. Weaver (eds), *Theory and Practice of Early Reading*, Hillsdale, NJ: Lawrence Erlbaum Associates.

Liberman, I. Y., Shankweiler, D., Liberman, A. M., Fowler, C. and Fischer, F. W. 1977: Phonetic segmentation and recoding in the beginning reader. In A. S. Reber and D. Scarborough (eds), *Toward a Psychology of Reading*. Hillsdale, NJ: Lawrence Erlbaum Associates, 207–26.

Liberman, I. Y., Shankweiler, D., Orlando, C., Harris, K. and Bell-Berti, F. 1971: Letter confusions and reversals of sequence in the beginning reader: Implications for Orton's theory of developmental dyslexia. *Cortex*, 7, 127–42.

Lindamood, C. H. and Lindamood, P. C. 1984: *Auditory Discrimination in Depth*. Austin, TX: PRO-ED, Inc.

Livingstone, M. S., Rosen, G. D., Drislane, F. W. and Galaburda, A. M. 1991: Physiological and anatomical evidence for magnocellular defect in developmental dyslexia. *Proceedings of the National Academic of Sciences, USA*, 88, 7943–7.

Locke, J. L., Hodgson, J., Macaruso, P., Roberts, J., Lambrecht-Smith, S. and Guttentag, C. 1997: The development of developmental dyslexia. In C. Hulme and M. J. Snowling (eds), *Dyslexia: Biology, Cognition and Intervention*, London: Whurr, 72–96.

Lord, R. and Hulme, C. 1987: Kinaesthetic sensitivity of normal and clumsy children. *Developmental Medicine and Child Neurology*, 29, 720–5.

Lovegrove, W. 1991: Spatial frequency processing in dyslexic and normal readers. In J. F. Stein (ed.), *Vision and Visual Dyslexia*, Basingstoke: Macmillan Press Ltd.

Lovegrove, W., Martin, F. and Slaghuis, W. 1986: The theoretical and experimental case for a visual deficit in specific reading disability. *Cognitive Neuropsychology*, 3, 225–67.

Lovett, M. W., Borden, S. L., DeLuca, T., Lacrerenza, L., Benson, N. J. and Brackstone, D. 1994: Treating the core deficits of developmental dyslexia: Evidence of transfer of learning after phonologically and strategy based reading training programs. *Developmental Psychology*, 30, 805–22.

Lovett, M. W., Ransby, M. J. and Barron, R. W. 1988: Treatment, subtype and word-type effects in dyslexic children's response to remediation. *Brain and Language*, 34, 328–49.

Lovett, M. W., Ransby, M. J., Hardwick, N., Johns, M. S. and Donaldson,

References

S. A. 1989: Can dyslexia be treated? Treatment-specific and generalised treatment effects in dyslexic children's response to remediation. *Brain and Language*, 37, 90–121.

Lovett, M. W., Warren-Chaplin, P. M., Ransby, M. J. and Borden, S. L. 1990: Training the word recognition skills of dyslexic children: Treatment and transfer effects. *Journal of Educational Psychology*, 82, 769–80.

Lundberg, I. 1994: Reading difficulties can be predicted and prevented: A Scandinavian perspective on phonological awareness and reading. In C. Hulme and M. J. Snowling (eds), *Reading Development and Dyslexia*, London: Whurr, 180–99.

Lundberg, I., Frost, J. and Petersen, O. 1988: Effects of an extensive program for stimulating phonological awareness in pre-school children. *Reading Research Quarterly*, 23, 263–84.

Lundberg, I., Olofsson, A. and Wall, S. 1980: Reading and spelling skills in the first school years predicted from phonemic awareness skills in kindergarten. *Scandinavian Journal of Psychology*, 121, 159–73.

Lyytinen, H. 1997: In search of the precursors of dyslexia: A prospective study of children at risk for reading problems. In C. Hulme and M. J. Snowling (eds), *Dyslexia: Biology, Cognition and Intervention*, London: Whurr, 97–107.

Manis, F. R., Custodio, R. and Szeszulski, P. A. 1993: Development of phonological and orthographic skill: A 2-year longitudinal study of dyslexic children. *Journal of Experimental Child Psychology*, 56, 64–86.

Manis, F. R., McBride-Chang, C., Seidenberg, M. S., Keating, P., Doi, L. M., Munson, B. and Petersen, A. 1997: Are speech perception deficits associated with developmental dyslexia? *Journal of Experimental Child Psychology*, 66, 211–35.

Manis, F. R., Seidenberg, M. S., Doi, L. M., McBride-Chang, C. and Petersen, A. 1996: On the bases of two subtypes of developmental dyslexia. *Cognition*, 58, 157–95.

Mann, V. A., Liberman, I. Y. and Shankweiler, D. 1980: Children's memory for sentences and word strings in relation to reading ability. *Memory and Cognition*, 8, 329–35.

Marsh, G. and Desberg, P. 1983: The development of strategies in the acquisition of symbolic skills. In D. A. Rogers and J. A. Sloboda (eds), *The Acquisition of Symbolic Skills*, New York: Plenum Press, 149–54.

Marsh, G., Friedman, M., Welch, V. and Desberg, P. 1980: The development of strategies in spelling. In U. Frith (ed.), *Cognitive Processes in Spelling*, London: Academic Press, 339–54.

Marsh, G., Friedman, M., Welch, V. and Desberg, P. 1981: A cognitive development theory of reading acquisition. In G. E. MacKinnon and T. G.

References

Waller (eds), *Reading Research: Advances in Theory and Practice*, Vol. 3, New York: Academic Press, 199–221.

Masonheimer, P. E., Drum, P. A. and Ehri, L. C. 1984: Does environmental print identification lead children into word reading? *Journal of Reading Behaviour*, 16, 257–71.

Mattis, S., French, J. M. and Rapin, I. 1975: Dyslexia in children and young adults: Three independent neuropsychological syndromes. *Developmental Medicine and Child Neurology*, 17, 150–63.

McAnally, K. I. and Stein, J. F. 1996: Auditory temporal coding in dyslexia. *Proceedings of the Royal Society London B*, 263, 961–5.

McAnally, K. I. and Stein, J. F. 1997: Scalp potentials evoked by amplitude modulated tones in dyslexia. *Journal of Speech, Language and Hearing Research*, 40, 939–45.

McBride-Chang, C. 1995: What is phonological awareness? *Journal of Educational Psychology*, 87, 179–92.

McBride-Chang, C. 1996: Models of speech perception and phonological processing in reading. *Child Development*, 67, 1836–56.

McBride-Chang, C., Wagner, R. K. and Chang, L. 1997: Growth modelling of phonological awareness. *Journal of Educational Psychology*, 89, 621–30.

McClelland, J. L. 1988: Connectionist models and psychological evidence. *Journal of Memory and Language*, 27, 107–23.

McDougall, S., Hulme, C., Ellis, A. W. and Monk, A. 1994: Learning to read: The role of short-term memory and phonological skills. *Journal of Experimental Child Psychology*, 58, 112–23.

McGee, R., Williams, S., Share, D. L., Anderson, J. and Silva, P. A. 1986: The relationships between specific reading retardation, general reading backwardness and behavioural problems in a large sample of Dunedin boys. *Journal of Child Psychology and Psychiatry*, 27, 597–610.

Metsala, J. L. 1997: Spoken word recognition in reading disabled children. *Journal of Educational Psychology*, 89, 159–69.

Metsala, J. L., Stanovich, K. E. and Brown, G. D. A. 1998: Regularity effects and the phonological deficit model of reading disabilities: A meta-analytic review. *Journal of Experimental Psychology*, 90, 279–93.

Miles, T. R. 1983: *Dyslexia: The Pattern of Difficulties*. London: Granada.

Mody, M., Studdert-Kennedy, M. and Brady, S. 1997: Speech perception deficits in poor readers: Auditory processing or phonological coding? *Journal of Experimental Child Psychology*, 58, 112–23.

Morais, J. 1991: Metaphonological abilities and literacy. In M. J. Snowling and M. Thomson (eds), *Dyslexia: Integrating Theory and Practice*, London: Whurr, 95–107.

References

Morais, J., Cary, L., Alegria, J. and Bertelson, P. 1979: Does awareness of speech as a sequence of phones arise spontaneously? *Cognition*, 7, 323–31.

Morton, J. 1989: An information processing account of reading acquisition. In A. M. Galaburda (ed.), *From Reading to Neurons*, Cambridge, MA: MIT Press, 43–6.

Morton, J. and Frith, U. 1995: Causal modelling: A structural approach to developmental psychopathology. In D. Cicchetti and D. J. Cohen (eds), *Manual of Developmental Psychopathology*, New York: John Wiley and Sons, 357–90.

Murphy, L. and Pollatsek, A. 1994: Developmental dyslexia – heterogeneity without discrete subgroups. *Annals of Dyslexia*, 6, 26–32.

Muter, V., Hulme, C., Snowling, M. and Taylor, S. 1998: Segmentation, not rhyming, predicts early progress in learning to read. *Journal of Experimental Child Psychology*, 71, 3–27.

Muter, V. and Snowing, M. J. 1998a: Concurrent and longitudinal predictors of reading: The role of metalinguistic and short-term memory skills. *Reading Research Quarterly*, 33, 320–37.

Muter, V. and Snowling, M. J. 1998b: Grammar and phonology predict spelling in middle childhood. *Reading and Writing*, 9, 407–25.

Muter, V., Snowling, M. J. and Taylor, S. 1994: Orthographic analogies and phonological awareness: Their role and significance in early reading development. *Journal of Child Psychology and Psychiatry*, 35, 293–310.

Mykelbust, H. R. and Johnson, D. J. 1962: Dyslexia in children. *Exceptional Children*, 29, 14–25.

Naidoo, S. 1972: *Specific Dyslexia*. London: Pitman Publishing.

Nation, K., Marshall, C. M. and Snowling, M. J. (in press): Phonological and semantic contributions to children's picture naming skill: Evidence from children with developmental reading disorders. *Language and Cognitive Processes*.

Nation, K. and Snowling, M. J. 1998a: Individual differences in contextual facilitation: Evidence from dyslexia and poor reading comprehension. *Child Development*, 69, 996–1011.

Nation, K. and Snowling, M. J. 1998b: Semantic processing and the development of word recognition skills: Evidence from children with reading comprehension difficulties. *Journal of Memory and Language*, 39, 85–101.

Nation, K. and Snowling, M. J. 1999: Developmental differences in sensitivity to semantic relations among good and poor comprehenders: Evidence from semantic priming. *Cognition*, 70, B1–13.

Nelson, H. E. and Warrington, E. K. 1974: Developmental spelling retardation and its relation to other cognitive abilities. *British Journal of Psychology*, 65, 265–74.

References

Nelson, H. E. and Warrington, E. K. 1980: An investigation of memory functions in dyslexic children. *British Journal of Psychology*, 71, 487–503.

Newman, S. P., Karle, H., Wadsworth, J. F., Archer, R., Hockly, R. and Rogers, P. 1985: Ocular dominance, reading and spelling: A reassessment of a measure associated with specific reading difficulties. *Journal of Research in Reading*, 8, 127–38.

Nicolson, R. I. and Fawcett, A. J. 1990: Automaticity: A new framework for dyslexia research. *Cognition*, 35, 159–82.

Nikolopoulos, D. S. 1999: *Cognitive and Linguistic Predictors of Literacy Skills in the Greek Language. The Manifestation of Reading and Spelling Difficulties in a Regular Orthography.* Unpublished Ph.D. thesis, University College London.

Nittrouer, S. 1999: Do temporal processing deficits cause phonological processing problems? *Journal of Speech, Language and Hearing Research*, 42, 925–42.

Nunes, T., Bryant, P. E. and Bindman, M. 1997a: Morphological spelling strategies: Developmental stages and processes. *Developmental Psychology*, 33, 637–49.

Nunes, T., Bryant, P. E. and Bindman, M. 1997b: Spelling and grammar. The necsed move. In C. A. Perfetti, L. Rieben and M. Fayol (eds), *Learning to Spell: Research, Theory and Practice Across Languages.* Mahwah, NJ: Lawrence Erlbaum Associates, 151–70.

O'Connor, N. and Hermelin, B. 1963: *Speech and Thought in Severe Subnormality.* London: Pergamon Press.

Olson, R. K., Datta, H., Gayan, J. and DeFries, J. C. 1999: A behavioural-genetic analysis of reading disabilities and component processes. In R. Klein and P. Macmullan (eds), *Converging Methods for Understanding Reading and Dyslexia*, Cambridge, MA: MIT Press, 133–52.

Olson, R. K., Davidson, B. J., Kliegel, R. and Davies, S. E. 1984: Development of phonetic memory in disabled and normal readers. *Journal of Experimental Child Psychology*, 37, 187–206.

Olson, R. K., Forsberg, H., Wise, B. and Rack, J. 1994: Measurement of word recognition, orthographic, and phonological skills. In G. R. Lyon (ed.), *Frames of Reference for the Assessment of Learning Disabilities: New Views on Measurement Issues*, Baltimore, MD: Paul H. Brookes Publishing Co., 243–77.

Olson, R. K., Kliegel, R. and Davidson, B. J. 1983: Dyslexic and normal children's tracking eye movements. *Journal of Experimental Psychology (Human Perception and Performance)*, 9, 816–25.

Olson, R. K., Kliegel, R., Davidson, B. J. and Foltz, G. 1985: Individual and developmental differences in reading disability. In G. E. MacKinnon and

T. G. Waller (eds), *Reading Research: Advances in Theory and Practice*, Vol. 4, New York: Academic Press, 1–64.

Olson, R. K. and Wise, B. W. 1992: Reading on the computer with orthographic and speech feedback. *Reading and Writing*, 4, 107–44.

Olson, R. K., Wise, B., Connors, F., Rack, J. and Fulker, D. 1989: Specific deficits in component reading and language skills: Genetic and environmental influences. *Journal of Learning Disabilities*, 22, 339–49.

Olson, R. K., Wise, B., Johnson, M. and Ring, J. 1997: The etiology and remediation of phonologically-based word recognition and spelling disabilities: Are phonological deficits the 'Hole' story? In B. Blachman (ed.), *Foundations of Reading Acquisition and Dyslexia: Implications for Early Intervention*, Mahwah, NJ: Lawrence Erlbaum Associates, 305–26.

Orton Dyslexia Society 1994: A new definition of dyslexia. *Bulletin of the Orton Dyslexia Society*, Fall.

Orton, S. T. 1925: 'Word blindness' in schoolchildren. *Archives of Neurology and Psychiatry*, 14, 581–615.

Palincsar, A. S. and Brown, A. L. 1984: Reciprocal teaching of comprehension-fostering and comprehension-monitoring activity. *Cognition and Instruction*, 2, 117–75.

Paulesu, E., Frith, U., Snowling, M., Gallagher, A., Morton, J., Frackowiak, F. S. J. and Frith, C. D. 1996: Is developmental dyslexia a disconnection syndrome? Evidence from PET scanning. *Brain*, 119, 143–57.

Pavlides, G. Th. 1981: Do eye movements hold the key to dyslexia? *Neuropsychologia*, 19, 57–64.

Pennington, B. F., Grossier, D. and Welsh, M. C. 1993: Contrasting cognitive defects in attention deficit hyperactivity disorder vs. reading disability. *Developmental Psychology*, 29, 511–23.

Pennington, B. F., Orden, G. C. V., Smith, S. D., Green, P. A. and Haith, M. M. 1990: Phonological processing skills and deficits in adult dyslexics. *Child Development*, 61, 1753–78.

Pennington, B. F., Smith, S. D., Kimberling, W. J., Green, P. A. and Haith, M. M. 1987: Left-handedness and immune disorders in familial dyslexics. *Archives of Neurology*, 44, 634–9.

Perfetti, C., Beck, I., Bell, L. and Hughes, C. 1987: Phonemic knowledge and learning to read are reciprocal: A longitudinal study of first grade children. *Merrill-Palmer Quarterly*, 33, 283–319.

Perin, D. 1983: Phonemic segmentation and spelling. *British Journal of Psychology*, 74, 129–44.

Petrauskas, R. J. and Rourke, B. P. 1979: Identification of subtype of retarded readers: A neuropsychological, multivariate approach. *Journal of Clinical Neuropsychology*, 1, 17–37.

References

Pinker, S. 1994: *The Language Instinct*. London: Penguin Press.

Pinnell, G. S., Lyons, C. A., Deford, D. D., Bryk, A. S. and Seltzer, M. 1994: Comparing instructional models for the literacy education of high-risk first graders. *Reading Research Quarterly*, 29, 8–39.

Pirrozolo, F. J. and Rayner, K. 1978: The normal control of eye movements in acquired and developmental disorders. In H. Avakian-Whitaker and A. H. Whitaker (eds), *Advances in Neurolinguistics and Psycholinguistics*. New York: Academic Press.

Plaut, D. C., McClelland, J. L., Seidenberg, M. S. and Patterson, K. 1996: Understanding normal and impaired word reading: Computational principles in quasi-regular domains. *Psychological Review*, 103, 56–115.

Plunkett, K., Karmiloff-Smith, A., Bates, E., Elman, J. L. and Johnson, M. H. 1997: Connectionism and developmental psychology. *Journal of Child Psychology and Psychiatry*, 38, 53–80.

Posner, M. I. and Raichle, M. E. 1997: *Images of the Mind*. New York: Scientific American Library.

Pring, L. and Snowling, M. J. 1986: Developmental changes in children's use of context in word recognition – an information processing analysis. *Quarterly Journal of Experimental Psychology*, 38A, 395–418.

Pringle-Morgan, W. 1896: A case of congenital word blindness. *British Medical Journal*, 2, 1378.

Prior, M. and McCorriston, M. 1984: Acquired and developmental spelling dyslexia. *Brain and Language*, 20, 263–85.

Rabin, M., Wen, X. L., Hepburn, M., Lubs, H. A., Feldman, E. and Duara, R. 1993: Suggestive linkage of developmental dyslexia to chromosone 1. *Lancet*, 342, 178.

Rack, J. P. 1985: Orthographic and phonetic coding in normal and dyslexic reading. *British Journal of Psychology*, 76, 325–40.

Rack, J. P., Hulme, C., Snowling, M. J. and Wightman, J. 1994: The role of phonology in young children learning to read words: The direct mapping hypothesis. *Journal of Experimental Child Psychology*, 57, 42–71.

Rack, J. P., Snowling, M. J. and Olson, R. K. 1992: The nonword reading deficit in developmental dyslexia: A review. *Reading Research Quarterly*, 27, 29–53.

Raymond, J. E. and Sorensen, R. E. 1998: Visual motion perception in children with dyslexia: Normal detection but abnormal integration. *Visual Cognition*, 5, 389–404.

Read, C. 1971: Pre-school children's knowledge of English phonology. *Harvard Educational Review*, 41, 1–34.

Read, M. A. 1989: Speech perception and the discrimination of brief auditory cues in reading disabled children. *Journal of Experimental Child Psychology*, 48, 270–92.

Rego, L. L. and Bryant, P. E. 1993: The connection between phonological, syntactic and semantic skills and children's reading and spelling. *European Journal of Psychology of Education*, 8, 235–46.

Reppas, J. B., Niyogi, S., Dale, A. M., Sereno, M. I. and Tootell, R. B. H. 1997: Representation of motion boundaries in retinotopic human visual cortical areas. *Nature*, 388, 175–9.

Rodgers, B. 1983: The identification and prevalence of specific reading retardation. *British Journal of Educational Psychology*, 53, 369–73.

Romani, C., Ward, J. and Olson, A. 1999: Developmental Surface Dysgraphia: What is the underlying cognitive impairment? *Quarterly Journal of Experimental Psychology, section A*, 52, 97–128.

Rumsey, J. M., Andreason, P., Zametkin, A. J., Aquino, T., King, A. C., Hamburger, S. D., Pikus, A., Rapoport, J. L. and Cohen, R. M. 1992: Failure to activate the left temporoparietal cortex in dyslexia. An oxygen 15 positron emission topographic study. *Archives of Neurology*, 49, 527–34.

Rumsey, J. M., Donohue, B. C., Brady, D. R., Nae, K., Giedd, N. J. and Andreason, P. 1997: A magnetic resonance imaging study of planum temporale assymmetry in men with developmental dyslexia. *Archives of Neurology*, 54, 1481–9.

Rutter, M. and Yule, W. 1975: The concept of specific reading retardation. *Journal of Child Psychology and Psychiatry*, 16, 181–97.

Salasoo, A. and Pisoni, D. B. 1985: Interaction of knowledge sources in spoken word identification. *Journal of Memory and Language*, 24, 210–31.

Savage, R. S. 1997: Do children need concurrent prompts in order to use lexical analogies in reading? *Journal of Child Psychology and Psychiatry*, 38, 235–46.

Scarborough, H. S. 1990: Very early language deficits in dyslexic children. *Child Development*, 61, 1728–43.

Scarborough, H. S. 1991: Antecedents to reading disability: Pre-school language development and literacy experiences of children from dyslexic families. *Reading and Writing*, 3, 219–33.

Schulke-Korne, G., Grimm, T., Nothen, M. M., MullerMyhsok, B., Propping, P. and Remschmidt, H. 1997: Evidence for linkage of spelling disability to chromosome 15. *American Journal of Medical Genetics*, 74, 661.

Schultz, R. T., Cho, N. K., Staib, L. H., Kier, L. E., Fletcher, J. M., Shaywitz, S. E., Shankweiler, D. P., Katz, L., Gore, J. C., Duncan, J. S. and Shaywitz, B. A. 1994: Brain morphology in normal and dyslexic children: The influence of sex and age. *Annals of Neurology*, 35, 732–42.

Seidenberg, M. S. and McClelland, J. 1989: A distributed, developmental model of word recognition. *Psychological Review*, 96, 523–68.

Seidenberg, M. S. and Tannenhaus, M. K. 1979: Orthographic effects on rhyme monitoring. *Journal of Experimental Psychology*, 5, 546–54.

Service, E. 1992: Phonology, working memory and foreign-language learning. *Quarterly Journal of Experimental Psychology*, 45A, 21–50.

Seymour, P. H. K. 1986: *A Cognitive Analysis of Dyslexia*. London: Routledge and Kegan Paul.

Seymour, P. H. K. 1990: Developmental dyslexia. In M. W. Eysenck (ed.), *Cognitive Psychology: An International Review*, Chichester: John Wiley and Sons, 135–95.

Seymour, P. H. K. and Bunce, F. 1992: Application of cognitive models to remediation in cases of developmental dyslexia. In M. J. Riddoch and G. W. Humphreys (eds), *Cognitive Neuropsychology and Cognitive Rehabilitation*. Hove: Lawrence Erlbaum.

Seymour, P. H. K., Duncan, L. G. and Bolik, F. M. 1999: Rhymes and phonemes in the common unit task: Replications and implications for beginning reading. *Journal of Research in Reading*, 22, 113–30.

Seymour, P. H. K. and Elder, L. 1986: Beginning reading without phonology. *Cognitive Neuropsychology*, 3, 1–36.

Seymour, P. H. K. and Evans, H. M. 1994: Levels of phonological awareness and learning to read. *Reading and Writing*, 6, 221–50.

Seymour, P. H. K. and MacGregor, C. J. 1984: Developmental dyslexia: A cognitive experimental analysis of phonological, morphemic and visual impairments. *Cognitive Neuropsychology*, 1, 43–82.

Shankweiler, D., Liberman, I. Y., Mark, L. S., Fowler, C. A. and Fischer, F. W. 1979: The speech code and learning to read. *Journal of Experimental Psychology: Human Learning and Memory*, 5, 531–45.

Share, D. L. 1995: Phonological recoding and self-teaching: Sine qua non of reading acquisition. *Cognition*, 55, 151–218.

Share, D. L., Jorm, A. F., Maclean, R. and Matthews, R. 1984: Sources of individual differences in reading acquisition. *Journal of Educational Psychology*, 76, 1309–24.

Share, D. L., McGee, R., McKenzie, D., Williams, S. and Silva, P. A. 1987: Further evidence relating to the distinction between specific reading retardation and general reading backwardness. *British Journal of Developmental Psychology*, 5, 35–44.

Shaywitz, B. A., Fletcher, J. M., Holahan, J. M. and Shaywitz, S. E. 1992: Discrepancy compared to low achievement definitions of reading disability: Results from the Connecticut longitudinal study. *Journal of Learning Disabilities*, 25, 639–48.

Shaywitz, S. E., Escobar, M. D., Shaywitz, B. A., Fletcher, J. M. and Makugh,

R. 1992: Evidence that dyslexia may represent the lower tail of a normal distribution of reading ability. *New England Journal of Medicine*, 326, 145–50.

Shaywitz, S. E., Shaywitz, B. A., Pugh, K. R., Fulbright, R. K., Constable, R. T., Mencl, W. E., Shankweiler, D. P., Liberman, A. M., Skudlarski, P., Fletcher, J. M., Katz, L., Marchione, K. E., Lacadie, C., Gatenby, C. and Gore, J. C. 1998: Functional disruption in the organisation of the brain for reading in dyslexia. *Proceedings of the National Academy of Sciences, USA*, 95, 2636–41.

Siegel, L. S. 1985: Deep dyslexia in childhood? *Brain and Language*, 26, 16–27.

Siegel, L. S. 1988: Evidence that IQ scores are irrelevant to the definition and analysis of reading disability. *Canadian Journal of Psychology*, 42, 201–15.

Silva, P. A., McGee, R. and Williams, S. 1985: Some characteristics of 9-year-old boys with general reading backwardness or specific reading retardation. *Journal of Child Psychology and Psychiatry*, 26, 407–21.

Slaghuis, W. and Lovegrove, W. 1985: Spatial frequency dependent visual persistence and specific reading disability. *Brain and Cognition*, 4, 219–40.

Smith, S. D., Kimberling, W. J., Pennington, B. F. and Lubs, H. A. 1983: Specific reading disability. Identification of an inherited form through linkage analysis. *Science*, 219, 1345–7.

Snowling, M. J. 1980: The development of grapheme–phoneme correspondence in normal and dyslexic readers. *Journal of Experimental Child Psychology*, 29, 294–305.

Snowling, M. J. 1981: Phonemic deficits in developmental dyslexia. *Psychological Research*, 43, 219–34.

Snowling, M. J. 1982: The spelling of nasal clusters by dyslexic and normal children. *Spelling Progress Bulletin*, 22, 13–18.

Snowling, M. J. 1987: *Dyslexia: A Cognitive Developmental Perspective*. Oxford: Blackwell.

Snowling, M. J. 1994: Towards a model of spelling acquisition: The development of some component skills. In G. D. A. Brown and N. C. Ellis (eds), *Handbook of Spelling: Theory, Process and Intervention*. Chichester: John Wiley and Sons, 111–28.

Snowling, M. J. 1996: Annotation: Contemporary approaches to the teaching of reading. *Journal of Child Psychology and Psychiatry*, 37, 139–48.

Snowling, M. J., Bishop, D. V. M. and Stothard, S. E. (in press): Is preschool language-impairment a risk factor for dyslexia? *Journal of Child Psychology and Psychiatry*.

Snowling, M. J., Bryant, P. E. and Hulme, C. 1996: Theoretical and methodological pitfalls in making comparisons between developmental and acquired dyslexia: Some comments on A. Castles and M. Coltheart 1993. *Reading and Writing*, 8, 443–51.

Snowling, M. J., Goulandris, N., Bowlby, M. and Howell, P. 1986: Segmentation and speech perception in relation to reading skill: A developmental analysis. *Journal of Experimental Child Psychology*, 41, 489–507.

Snowling, M. J., Goulandris, N. and Defty, N. 1996: A longitudinal study of reading development in dyslexic children. *Journal of Educational Psychology*, 88, 653–69.

Snowling, M. J., Goulandris, N. and Defty, N. 1998: Development and variation in developmental dyslexia. In C. Hulme and R. M. Joshi (eds), *Reading and Spelling: Development and Disorders*, Mahwah, NJ: Lawrence Erlbaum Associates, 201–17.

Snowling, M. J., Goulandris, N. and Stackhouse, J. 1994: Phonological constraints on learning to read: Evidence from single-case studies of reading difficulty. In C. Hulme and M. J. Snowling (eds), *Reading Development and Dyslexia*, London: Whurr, 86–104.

Snowling, M. J. and Griffiths, Y. M. (in press): Individual differences in dyslexia. In T. Nunes and R. E. Bryant (eds), *Handbook of Literacy*, Dordrecht, The Netherlands: Kluwer Academic Publishers.

Snowling, M. J. and Hulme, C. 1989: A longitudinal case study of developmental phonological dyslexia. *Cognitive Neuropsychology*, 6, 379–403.

Snowling, M. J. and Hulme, C. 1994: The development of phonological skills. *Philosophical Transactions of the Royal Society B*, 346, 21–8.

Snowling, M. J., Hulme, C. and Goulandris, N. 1994: Word recognition in developmental dyslexia: A connectionist interpretation. *Quarterly Journal of Experimental Psychology*, 47A, 895–916.

Snowling, M. J., Hulme, C., Wells, B. and Goulandris, N. 1992: Continuities between speech and spelling in a case of developmental dyslexia. *Reading and Writing*, 4, 19–31.

Snowling, M. J. and Nation, K. 1997: Phonology, language and learning to read. In C. Hulme and M. J. Snowling (eds), *Dyslexia: Biology, Cognition and Intervention*, London: Whurr, 153–66.

Snowling, M. J., Nation, K., Moxham, P., Gallagher, A. and Frith, U. 1997: Phonological processing deficits in dyslexic students: A preliminary account. *Journal of Research in Reading*, 20, 31–4.

Snowling, M., Nation, K. and Muter, V. 1999: The role of semantic and phonological skills in learning to read: Implications for assessment and teaching. In T. Nunes (ed.), *Learning to Read: An Integrated View from Research and Practice*, Dordrecht, The Netherlands: Kluwer Academic Publishers, 195–210.

Snowling, M. J., Stackhouse, J. and Rack, J. 1986: Phonological dyslexia and dysgraphia: A developmental analysis. *Cognitive Neuropsychology*, 3, 309–39.

Snowling, M. J., Wagtendonk, B. van and Stafford, C. 1988: Object-naming deficits in developmental dyslexia. *Journal of Research in Reading*, 11, 67–85.

Stackhouse, J. 2000: Barriers to literary development in children with speech and language difficulties, in D. Bishop and L. Leonard (eds), *Speech and Language Impairments in Children: Causes, Characteristics, Intevention and Outcome*, Hove: Psychology Press.

Stackhouse, J. and Snowling, M. J. 1992: Barriers to literacy development in two cases of developmental verbal dyspraxia. *Cognitive Neuropsychology*, 9, 273–99.

Stackhouse, J. and Wells, B. 1997: *Children's Speech and Literacy Difficulties: A Psycholinguistic Framework*. London: Whurr.

Stanley, G., Smith, G. A. and Howell, E. A. 1983: Eye movements and sequential tracking in dyslexic and control children. *British Journal of Psychology*, 74, 181–7.

Stanovich, K. E. 1980: Toward an interactive-compensatory model of individual differences in the acquisition of literacy. *Reading Research Quarterly*, 16, 32–71.

Stanovich, K. E. 1984: The interactive-compensatory model of reading: A confluence of developmental, experimental and educational psychology. *Remedial and Special Education*, 5, 11–19.

Stanovich, K. E. 1986: Matthew effects in reading: Some consequences of individual differences in the acquisition of literacy. *Reading Research Quarterly*, 21, 360–4.

Stanovich, K. E. 1991: Discrepancy definitions of reading disability: Has intelligence led us astray? *Reading Research Quarterly*, 26, 7–29.

Stanovich, K. E., Cunningham, A. E. and Cramer, B. B. 1984: Assessing phonological awareness in kindergarten children: Issues of task comparability. *Journal of Experimental Child Psychology*, 38, 175–90.

Stanovich, K. E., Feeman, D. J. and Cunningham, A. E. 1983: The development of the relation between letter naming speed and reading ability. *Bulletin of the Psychonomic Society*, 21, 199–202.

Stanovich, K. E. and Siegel, L. S. 1994: The phenotypic performance profile of reading-disabled children: A regression-based test of the phonological-core variable-difference model. *Journal of Educational Psychology*, 86, 24–53.

Stanovich, K. E., Siegel, L. S. and Gottardo, A. 1997: Progress in the search for dyslexia subtypes. In C. Hulme and M. J. Snowling (eds), *Dyslexia: Biology, Cognition and Intervention*, London: Whurr, 108–30.

Stanovich, K. E. and Stanovich, P. J. 1995: How research might inform the debate about early reading acquisition. *Journal of Research in Reading*, 18, 87–105.

Stanovich, K. E. and West, R. F. 1989: Exposure to print and orthographic processing. *Reading Research Quarterly*, 24, 402–33.

Stein, J. F. 1989: Visuospatial perception and reading problems. *Irish Journal of Psychology*, 10, 534–41.

Stein, J. F. 1998: The physiology of reading: The use of feedforward programmes. *International Journal of Psychophysiology*, 30, 110.

Stein, J. F. and Fowler, S. 1985: Effect of monocular occlusion on visuomotor perception and reading in dyslexic children. *Lancet*, 1985 2(8446), 69–73.

Stein, J. F. and Talcott, J. 1999: Impaired neuronal timing in developmental dyslexia – the magnocellular hypothesis. *Dyslexia*, 5, 59–77.

Stevenson, J., Graham, P., Fredman, G. and McLoughlin, V. 1987: A twin study of genetic influences of reading and spelling ability and disability. *Journal of Child Psychology and Psychiatry*, 28, 229–47.

Stone, B. and Brady, S. 1995: Evidence for phonological processing deficits in less-skilled readers. *Annals of Dyslexia*, 45, 51–78.

Stothard, S. E., Snowling, M. J. and Hulme, C. 1996: Deficits in phonology but not dyslexic? *Cognitive Neuropsychology*, 13, 641–72.

Stuart, M. and Coltheart, M. 1988: Does reading develop in a sequence of stages? *Cognition*, 30, 139–81.

Stuart, M. and Howard, D. 1995: KJ: A developmental deep dyslexic. *Cognitive Neuropsychology*, 12, 793–824.

Stuart, M., Masterson, J., Dixon, M. and Quinlan, P. 1999: Inferring sublexical correspondences from sight vocabulary: Evidence from 6- and 7-year-olds. *Quarterly Journal of Experimental Psychology*, 52A, 353–66.

Studdert-Kennedy, M. and Mody, M. 1995: Auditory temporal perception deficits in the reading-impaired: A critical review of the evidence. *Psychonomic Bulletin and Review*, 2, 508–14.

Swan, D. and Goswami, U. 1997: Phonological awareness deficits in developmental dyslexia and the phonological representations hypothesis. *Journal of Experimental Child Psychology*, 60, 334–53.

Taft, M. 1982: An alternative to grapheme–phoneme conversion rules? *Memory and Cognition*, 10, 465–74.

Tallal, P. 1980: Auditory-temporal perception, phonics and reading disabilities in children. *Brain and Language*, 9, 182–98.

Tallal, P., Miller, S. L., Jenkins, W. M. and Merzenich, M. M. 1997: The role of temporal processing in developmental language-based learning disorders: Research and clinical implications. In B. A. Blachman (ed.), *Foundations of Reading Acquisition and Dyslexia: Implications for Early Intervention*, Mahwah, NJ: Lawrence Erlbaum Associates, 49–66.

Tallal, P. and Piercy, M. 1973: Developmental aphasia: Impaired rate of non-verbal processing as a function of sensory modality. *Neuropsychologia*, 11, 389–98.

Tallal, P. and Piercy, M. 1974: Developmental aphasia: Rate of auditory processing and selective impairment of consonant perception. *Neuropsychologia*, 12, 83–93.

Tallal, P. and Piercy, M. 1975: Developmental aphasia: The perception of brief vowels and extended stop consonants. *Neuropsychologia*, 13, 69–74.

Temple, C. and Marshall, J. 1983: A case study of developmental phonological dyslexia. *British Journal of Psychology*, 74, 517–33.

Tønnesen, F. E. 1995: On defining 'Dyslexia'. *Scandinavian Journal of Educational Research*, 39, 139–56.

Torgesen, J. K. 1989: Why IQ is relevant to the definition of learning disabilities. *Journal of Learning Disabilities*, 22, 484–6.

Torgesen, J. K. (in press): Individual differences in response to early interventions in reading: The lingering problem of treatment resisters. *Learning Disabilities Research and Practice*.

Torgesen, J. K. and Davis, C. 1996: Individual difference variables that predict response to training in phonological awareness. *Journal of Experimental Child Psychology*, 63, 1–21.

Torgesen, J. K., Wagner, R. K., Balthazar, M., Davis, C., Morgan, S., Simmons, K., Stage, S. and Zirps, F. 1989: Developmental and individual differences in performance on phonological synthesis tasks. *Journal of Experimental Child Psychology*, 47, 491–505.

Torgesen, J. K., Wagner, R. K. and Rashotte, C. A. 1994: Longitudinal studies of phonological processing and reading. *Journal of Learning Disabilities*, 27, 276–86.

Torgesen, J. K., Wagner, R. K., Rashotte, C. A., Burgess, S. and Hecht, S. 1997: Contributions of phonological awareness and rapid automatic naming ability to the growth of word-reading skills in second- to fifth-grade children. *Scientific Studies of Reading*, 1, 161–85.

Torgesen, J. K., Wagner, R. K., Rashotte, C. A., Rose, E., Lindamood, P., Conway, T. and Garvan, C. (in press): Preventing reading failure in young children with phonological processing disabilities: Group and individual responses to instruction. *Journal of Educational Psychology*.

Treiman, R. 1993: *Beginning to Spell: A Study of First-grade Children*. New York: Oxford University Press.

Treiman, R. 1997: Spelling in normal children and dyslexics. In B. Blachman (ed.), *Foundations of Reading Acquisition and Dyslexia: Implications for Early Intervention*, Mahwah, NJ: Lawrence Erlbaum Associates, 191–218.

References

Treiman, R. and Breaux, A. M. 1982: Common phoneme and overall similarity relations among spoken syllables: Their use by children and adults. *Journal of Psycholinguistic Research*, 11, 569–98.

Treiman, R., Cassar, M. and Zukowski, A. 1994: What types of linguistic information do children use in spelling? The case of flaps. *Child Development*, 65, 1310–29.

Treiman, R., Goswami, U. and Bruck, M. 1990: Not all nonwords are alike: Implications for reading development and theory. *Memory and Cognition*, 18, 559–67.

Treiman, R. and Hirsh-Pasek, K. 1985: Are there qualitative differences in reading behaviour between dyslexics and normal readers? *Memory and Cognition*, 13, 357–64.

Treiman, R., Mullenix, J., Bijeljac-Babic, R. and Richmond-Welty, D. 1995: The special role of rimes in the description, use and acquisition of English orthography. *Journal of Experimental Psychology: General*, 124, 107–36.

Troia, G. A. 1999: Phonological awareness intervention research: A critical review of the experimental methodology. *Reading Research Quarterly*, 34, 28–52.

Tunmer, W. E. 1994: Phonological processing and reading remediation. In C. Hulme and M. J. Snowling (eds), *Reading Development and Dyslexia*, London: Whurr, 147–62.

Tunmer, W. E. and Nesdale, A. R. 1985: Phonemic segmentation skill and beginning reading. *Journal of Educational Psychology*, 77, 417–27.

Van der Wissel, A. and Zegers, F. E. 1985: Reading retardation revisited. *British Journal of Developmental Psychology*, 3, 3–19.

Van Ijzendoorn, M. H. and Bus, A. G. 1994: Meta-analytic confirmation of the nonword reading deficit in developmental dyslexia. *Reading Research Quarterly*, 29, 267–75.

Vellutino, F. R. 1979: *Dyslexia: Research and Theory*. Cambridge, MA: MIT Press.

Vellutino, F. R., Pruzek, R., Steger, J. A. and Meshoulam, U. 1973: Immediate visual recall in poor readers as a function of orthographic-linguistic familiarity. *Cortex*, 9, 368–84.

Vellutino, F. R. and Scanlon, D. M. 1991: The pre-eminence of phonologically based skills in learning to read. In S. A. Brady and D. P. Shankweiler (eds), *Phonological Processes in Literacy: A Tribute to Isabelle Liberman*, Hillsdale, NJ: Lawrence Erlbaum Associates, 237–52.

Vellutino, F. R., Scanlon, D. M., Sipay, E., Small, S., Pratt, A., Chen, R. and Denckla, M. 1996: Cognitive profiles of difficult to remediate and readily remediated poor readers: Towards distinguishing between constitutionally and experientially based causes of reading disability. *Journal of Educational Psychology* 88, 601–38.

Vellutino, F. R., Scanlon, D. M. and Spearing, D. 1995: Semantic and phonological coding in poor and normal readers. *Journal of Experimental Child Psychology*, 59, 76–123.

Vellutino, F. R., Steger, J. A., Harding, C. J. and Spearing, D. 1975: Verbal versus non-verbal paired associate learning in poor and normal readers. *Neuropsychologica*, 13, 75–82.

Vihmann, M. 1996: *Phonological Development*. Oxford: Blackwell.

Wagner, R. K. and Torgesen, J. K. 1987: The nature of phonological processing and its causal role in the acquisition of reading skills. *Psychological Bulletin*, 101, 192–212.

Wagner, R. K., Torgesen, J. K., Laughan, P., Simmons, K. and Rashotte, C. A. 1993: The development of young readers' phonological processing abilities. *Journal of Educational Psychology*, 85, 1–20.

Wagner, R. K., Torgesen, J. K. and Rashotte, C. A. 1994: Development of reading-related phonological processing abilities: Evidence of bi-directional causality from a latent variable longitudinal study. *Developmental Psychology*, 30, 73–87.

Walley, A. C., Michela, V. L. and Wood, D. R. 1995: The gating paradigm – effects of presentation format on spoken word recognition by children and adults. *Perception and Psychophysics*, 57, 343–51.

Wechsler, D. 1974: *The Wechsler Intelligence Scale for Children – Revised*. London: The Psychological Corporation.

Wechsler, D. 1992: *The Wechsler Intelligence Scale for Children*, 3rd edn. London: The Psychological Corporation.

Whitehurst, G. J., Epstein, J. N., Angell, A. L., Payne, A. C., Crone, D. A. and Fischel, J. E. 1994: Outcomes of an emergent literacy intervention in head start. *Journal of Educational Psychology*, 86, 542–55.

Whitehurst, G. J. and Lonigan, C. J. 1998: Child development and emergent literacy. *Child Development*, 69, 848–72.

Willows, D. M., Kruk, R. S. and Corcos, E. (eds) 1993: *Visual Processes in Reading and Reading Disabilities*. Hillsdale, NJ: Lawrence Erlbaum Associates.

Wimmer, H. 1996: The early manifestation of developmental dyslexia: Evidence from German children. *Reading and Writing*, 8, 171–88.

Wimmer, H. and Hummer, P. 1990: How German speaking first graders read and spell: Doubts on the importance of the logographic stage. *Applied Psycholinguistics*, 11, 349–68.

Wimmer, H. and Landerl, K. 1998: How learning to spell German differs from learning to spell English. In C. A. Perfetti, L. Rieben and M. Fayol

References

(eds), *Learning to Spell: Research, Theory and Practice Across Languages,* Mahwah, NJ: Lawrence Erlbaum Associates, 81–96.

Wimmer, H., Mayringer, H. and Landerl, K. 1998: Poor reading: A deficit in skill-automatization or a phonological deficit? *Scientific Studies of Reading,* 2, 321–40.

Wimmer, H., Mayringer, H. and Raberger, T. 1999: Reading and dual-task balancing: Evidence against the automatization deficit explanation of developmental dyslexia. *Journal of Learning Disabilities,* 32, 473–8.

Windfuhr, K. L. 1998: *Verbal Learning, Phonological Processing and Reading Skills in Normal and Dyslexic Readers.* Unpublished D. Phil. thesis, University of York.

Windfuhr, K. L. and Snowling, M. J. (submitted): The relationship between paired associate learning and phonological skills in normal and dyslexic readers.

Wise, B. W. and Olson, R. K. 1998: Studies of computer-aided remediation for reading disabilities, in C. Hulme and R. M. Joshi (eds), *Reading and Spelling: Development and Disorders,* Mahwah, NJ: Lawrence Erlbaum Associates, 473–87.

Wise, B. W., Olson, R. K. and Treiman, R. 1990: Sub-syllabic units as aids in beginning readers' word learning: onset-rime versus post-vowel segmentation. *Journal of Experimental Child Psychology,* 49, 1–19.

Wise, B. W., Ring, J. and Olson, R. 1999: Training phonological awareness with and without explicit attention to articulation. *Journal of Experimental Child Psychology,* 72, 271–304.

Witton, C., Talcott, J. B., Hansen, P. C., Richardson, A. J., Griffiths, T. D., Rees, A., Stein, J. F. and Green, G. G. R. 1998: Sensitivity to dynamic auditory and visual stimuli predicts nonword reading ability in both dyslexic and normal readers. *Current Biology,* 8, 791–7.

Wolf, M. 1986: Rapid alternating stimulus naming in the developmental dyslexias. *Brain and Language,* 27, 360–79.

Wolf, M. 1991: Naming speed and reading: The contribution of the cognitive neurosciences. *Reading Research Quarterly,* 26, 123–41.

Wolf, M. 1997: A provisional, integrative account of phonological and naming-speed deficits in dyslexia: Implications for diagnosis and intervention. In B. A. Blachman (ed.), *Foundations of Reading Acquisition and Dyslexia: Implications for Early Intervention,* Mahwah, NJ: Lawrence Erlbaum Associates, 67–92.

Wolf, M. and Bowers, P. G. 1999: The double deficit hypothesis for the developmental dyslexias. *Journal of Educational Psychology,* 91, 415–38.

Wolf, M. and Goodglass, H. 1986: Dyslexia, dysnomia and lexical retrieval: A longitudinal investigation. *Brain and Language* 28, 154–68.

Wolf, M. and Obregon, M. 1992: Early naming deficits, developmental dyslexia, and a specific deficit hypothesis. *Brain and Language*, 42, 219–47.

Yap, R. and Van der Leij, A. 1994: Automaticity deficits in word reading. In A. Fawcett and R. Nicolson (eds), *Dyslexia in Children: Multidisciplinary Perspectives*, Hemel Hempstead, UK: Harvester-Wheatsheaf, 660–5.

Yopp, H. K. 1988: The validity and reliability of phonemic awareness tests. *Reading Research Quarterly*, 23, 159–77.

Yule, W. 1973: Differential prognosis of reading backwardness and specific reading retardation. *British Journal of Educational Psychology*, 43, 244–8.

Yule, W., Rutter, M., Berger, M. and Thompson, J. 1974: Over and under achievement in reading: distribution in the general population. *British Journal of Educational Psychology*, 44, 1–12.

Zeki, S. 1993: *A Vision of the Brain*. Oxford: Blackwell Scientific Publications.

Index

acquired dyslexia *see* acquired
reading disorders
acquired reading disorders 108–9
ADHD (attention
deficit/hyperactivity syndrome)
209–11
adults with dyslexia 36, 44, 56, 60,
96, 164–5, 171–6, 199–200,
208
adult literacy 54–5
allergic disorders 156
alliteration 56, 77
alphabetic orthographies 1, 59, 65,
114
alphabetic principle 67–9, 87–8,
106, 177–8
analogies 64, 70–2, 199
articulation 147, 184–5, 192–3
at-risk studies 146–9
attention 198, 209–10
auditory discrimination 45, 168–
9
auditory processing 167–76
autoimmune disease 146, 155–6
automaticity 11, 210

back propagation 84
behavioural level 26, 196, 207, 209
binaural masking level difference *see*
BMLD
binocular control 159

biological bases of dyslexia 26,
138–57
BMLD (binaural masking level
difference) 172
brain 149–55
brain imaging 152–5
Broca's area 149, 155

case series approach 111–14
chromosomes 145–6
classification of dyslexia *see* sub-types
clumsiness *see* motor impairment
clusters *see* consonant clusters
cognitive level 26–7, 167
co-morbidity 209–12
comparison groups 30
compensation *see* compensatory
strategies
compensatory strategies 8–9, 56,
60, 74, 95, 103, 118, 122,
198–214
comprehension 142, 192, 201, 213
concordance rates 139
connectionist models 80–6, 121,
203–5, 209
consonant clusters 74–5, 91, 97
context, use of 94, 200–2
contrast sensitivity 164
cross-linguistic studies 58, 66, 77,
81–2, 206–8
cross-modal deficit 174–6

DCD (developmental coordination disorder) *see* dyspraxia
decoding 63
deep dyslexia 110
definitions of dyslexia 14–28, 29, 212–14
developmental coordination disorder *see* dyspraxia
developmental disorder 26, 32
developmentally contingent model of dyslexia 26
discrepancy definition 16–18, 111
double deficit hypothesis 44
Dunlop test 159
dyseidetic dyslexia 107, 164
dysphonetic dyslexia 107, 164
dyspraxia 211

early intervention 19, 179–80, 182–5
environmental factors 18, 26–7, 139–45, 148, 177, 205–9, 213
environmental print 62
epidemiology 16–23
evoked potentials 163–4, 172–3
exclusionary criteria 148
executive function 210
eye movements 158–9, 166, 202–3

familial risk 138
foreign language learning 48
frequency discrimination 172
future research 215–16

garden-variety poor readers *see* generally backward readers
gating task 52–3
gender 21–2
generalization of learning 196
generally backward readers 16, 21–3, 42

genetics 138–46, 170, 215
Gerstmann syndrome 105
grammatical skills 76, 147–9

heritability 138–45
home background 148, 196
hyperactivity 156, 209–10

immune disorders 155–6
individual differences in dyslexia 105–37
infancy 157
intelligence 16, 24
intervention 159, 177–97
IQ 192–4

JM, case study of 2–13, 60–1, 99–100, 122, 126–8

language impairment 211–12
language skills 146–8, 200–3
lateral geniculate nucleus 160
laterality 155–7
learning, phonological 57–8, 195, 207–8
left-handedness 156
left hemisphere 151
letter knowledge 68–9, 72–5, 80, 114, 147, 181
letter-by-letter reading 109–10
LGN *see* lateral geniculate nucleus
literacy development 62–86
logographic reading 64–5, 87–8, 114, 125
longitudinal studies 76–8

magnetic resonance imaging 151–5, 167
magnocellular system 160–4
mathematics 21, 77, 193
medical model of dyslexia 14–15
memory, long-term 38, 202

memory, short-term 35–43, 128, 148, 153–5, 199, 207

memory, working 79

mental-age match 30–1

meta-analysis 91–2, 94, 179

metacognitive strategies 192

metaphonological awareness *see* phonological awareness

methodology 30, 79, 106–7, 115–16, 153, 175, 178–9

models 14–15, 26–9, 59, 80, 93, 112, 207, 213; *see also* connectionist models

morphemes 67–8, 75–6, 122, 196

morphemic dyslexia 113; *see also* surface dyslexia

morphological awareness *see* morphemes

motion perception 160–7

motivation 208

motor impairment *see* dyspraxia

movement perception *see* motion perception

MRI *see* magnetic resonance imaging

multisensory approach 178

naming 39 *see also* RAN

naming speed 194–5

nonword reading deficit 32–3, 85, 88–92, 109, 119, 169, 174, 199

nonword repetition 44–7, 148, 169–70

ocular (motor) dominance 159

oddity tasks 55, 71

onset 70

orthographic development 9–13, 65–6, 73, 136–7

orthographic skills 56, 69, 141, 202–3

Orton Dyslexia Society (International Dyslexia Association) 24–5

paired associate learning 57–8, 195, 207–8

pan-modal deficit 174–6

parvocellular system 160

perceptual processing 46–7, 133–5

PET scans 152–5

phonemic awareness 50, 52, 54–7, 68–9, 75, 147

phonetic accuracy 98

phonetic confusability effect 36

phonetic cue reading 73–4

phonetic similarity effect 36

phonological awareness 54–7, 76–8; levels of 67–8, 70, structure of 78–9

phonological awareness training 180–5

phonological core deficit model 59, 207, 213

phonological deficits 6–8, 34–61, 147, 165

phonological development 54, 76–8, 124–8

phonological disorder 2, 132–6

phonological dyslexia 109, 113–18, 123, 125–8, 143–5, 199–200

phonological reading skills 141

phonological representation 8, 79, 85–9, 99–100, 121–2, 131, 155, 198, 215

phonological skills 20, 118–22, 126–32; development of 4–8

phonology, input 131

phonology, output 128–9, 133–4

planum temporale 151–2

practice, reading 208–9

precursors of dyslexia 146–9

pre-school signs 146–8

prevalence 17–19

prevention of reading failure 179–82

print exposure 122, 142–3, 191, 208–9

processing speed *see* speed of processing

production (speech) 44, 133–5

prognosis 19–20, 21–3, 213

progress *see* prognosis

RAN (rapid automatized naming) 43–4, 129–30, 147, 194–5, 207

rapid automatized naming *see* RAN

reaction-time measurements 113–14

reading-age match 31–3

reading development 4–8, 62–86; individual differences in 66–7

reading disabled, in terminology of reading difficulties 1–2

reading impaired, in terminology of reading difficulties 1–2

reading recovery 186–8

reading sub-skills 141

reciprocal influence 77–8, 95

redintegration 37–9

reference eye 159

regression 139–40

regression approach 16–19, 115–23

regularity effect 10, 84, 92–4, 109–10, 114, 130

regularization errors 109, 125, 130

rehearsal 37

remediation 177–97

repetition 44–5

repetition test *see* temporal order judgement

responsiveness to intervention 191; *see also* teaching, individual differences in response to

responsiveness to treatment 191; *see*

also teaching, individual differences in response to

retarded readers, in terminology of reading difficulties 1–2

rhyming skills 78, 129, 152–5; *see also* rime

right hemisphere 151

right-shift theory 156–7

rime 56, 69–72, 77–9, 147

risk 183

RTs *see* reaction-time measurements

semantic errors 42, 110–11

semantic skills 9, 20, 53, 65, 86, 94–5, 112, 184, 202–5

sensory processing 158–77

severity hypothesis 123, 124–37, 144–5

SLI (specific language impairment) 167–8, 205; *see also* language impairment

SM89 82–6, 203–4; *see also* connectionist models

sound linkage 186–8

spatial frequency 162–3

specific reading difficulties 1, 15–18, 21–3, 211–12

specific spelling problems 101–4

speech 99–101

speech disorders 132

speech perception 47, 54–7, 78, 119, 126, 135, 190

speech processing 157

speech production 44–5, 100–1, 132

speech rate 37

speed of processing 118–20, 144–5

speeded naming *see* RAN

spelling 5, 7, 12, 96–103, 127–8, 131, 141; development of 4–8, 62–86; in dyslexia 96–101

spoken word identification 52–3

spoonerisms 55
stage models 63–6
STM *see* memory, short-term
sub-types 106–23
surface dyslexia 109–11, 115–19, 123, 130, 143–5
sustained visual system 161–2
syllable, hierarchical structure of 70
syntactic ability *see* grammatical skills

teaching 177–97; individual differences in response to 191–5, methods 177–91
temporal lobe 149–51, 153, 155, 160, 215
temporal order judgement 168–71
testosterone 156
training studies 178–9
transient visual system 160–5
tutor training 185, 186

V5 160, 167
verbal deficit 33–5

verbal naming deficits 39–43
verbal repetition 44–8
verbal short-term memory deficit *see* memory, short-term
visual cortex 149–50, 160
visual processing impairment 158–67, 174–6
visual skills 8, 34, 63, 65, 69, 102–3, 106, 112, 118–19, 199
visual system 160
vocabulary 48, 58, 94, 146–7, 149

Wernicke's area 149–55
whole-language approach to reading 196–7
WISC (Wechsler Intelligence Scale for Children) 3, 105, 118
word finding difficulties 39–40
word frequency 10, 84
word length effect 37
word recognition 72–4
working memory 79